MONIA HEJAIEJ

BEHIND CLOSED DOORS
Women's Oral Narratives in Tunis

MONIA HEJAIEJ

BEHIND CLOSED DOORS
Women's Oral Narratives in Tunis

RUTGERS UNIVERSITY PRESS
New Brunswick, New Jersey

First published in Great Britain 1996 by Quartet Books Limited
A member of the Namara Group
27 Goodge Street, London W1P 2LD

First published in the United States 1996 by Rutgers University
Press, New Brunswick, New Jersey

Library of Congress Cataloging-in-Publication Data

Hejaiej, Monia, 1957–
    Behind closed doors : women's oral narratives in
Tunis / Monia Hejaiej.
      p. cm.
    Includes bibliographical references (p.).
    ISBN 0-8135-2376-1 (cloth : alk. paper). — ISBN 0-8135-
2377-X (pbk. : alk. paper)
      1. Tales—Tunisia—Tunis. 2. Women—Tunisia—Tunis—
Folklore. I. Title
GR353.52.T85H45   1996
398.2′09611—dc20   96-22919
                                 CIP

To the memory of my father

ACKNOWLEDGEMENTS

The study on which this book is based, has been made possible by many individuals who have contributed in ways large and small. I am grateful to them all.

My most profound debt is to the women who told me 'their stories'.

I want to thank Laura Rice for her encouragement and precious help in shaping the final text.

I am also grateful to Vicky Ben Rejeb and Dr Tony Broadbent for their assistance in the early drafts of the manuscript.

Finally I wish to extend my thanks to Ghislaine Stevenson for help in editing the English version of the tales.

CONTENTS

FOREWORD

What do we discover when we go beyond the closed doors of Monia Hejaiej's Tunis? Crossing the liminal space that divides the busy, everyday world of events and men from the reflective, ceremonial and conspiratorial space of women, we enter a world of wonder. Here, the story-teller Sa'diyya always reminds us, as she begins to spin her tales, that the 'tents are made of silk'. Hejaiej's intimate and perceptive account of the interwoven threads of the personal lives of three women story-tellers, and the shared cultural values and customs they pass on, teaches us that the tale itself is a silken space where the poetry of women's experience is performed. Just as each verse in an Arabic poem is called a *bayt* or tent, so the stories in this collection of tales are tents of words raised by women speaking to women and children about their lives.

Hejaiej opens for us a performative space where the warp and weft of tale-weaving intertwine on the cultural loom of Tunis – a city, a memory and an art. Against the weft of the collection of tales, we see Hejaiej weaving the thread of her research on the art of Beldi women narrators as they select and perform the tales. Upon the weft of Beldi traditions and cultural norms, framed most often by men, the story-tellers interlace the thread of their experience as women. Within the frame of the traditional tale passed from generation to generation, each story-teller defines her self-image, adding her individual speech, the thread of her life, to the larger pattern of the women tale-tellers who came before her.

Within each tale-telling, an intricate shuttling between the teller and the tale occurs. In the tents of silk, the protagonists are most often women through whom the tale-teller can speak things usually left unspoken – pain and desire, revolt and resignation. Here, too, is a space where narrators may become subjects in their own right as they break the thread of the narrative, splicing in their own judgements about the heroism or hypocrisy of men, the foolishness or wisdom of women, and the grace of God, before fading again into the background of the weave. The tale is an inhabited, dynamic space where characters interact with one another, the story-teller inter-acts with the tale, the performer with her audience. Each time the tent is raised anew and an old tale is retold, a space is created where criticism, approval, empathy or antipathy can be expressed. This is the space where con-tinuity and change interweave.

Hejaiej speaks as one who grew up within the magic of these tents of silk. With an ear finely attuned to the har-monies and dissonances of this performative space, she makes us aware of the nuances of the choice of words, the use of formulae. At home with these tales, she is able to see the flaws in the weave and the art and love with which they are woven. Hejaiej invites us in to the art of Beldi women's lives. Those of us who are outsiders are made welcome guests there, with all the privileges and constraints that being a guest implies. Those who are already familiar with what goes on behind closed doors, find themselves most wonderfully at home.

Laura Rice
Oregon State University

INTRODUCTION

1

THE TALE OF THE TALES

This work is rooted in my early childhood memories. I was born and brought up in the enclosed world of the medina (or old city) of Tunis, which had not yet lost its leisurely urban charm and elegance. What lives with me still of that lost universe, which seemed to me then so perfectly coherent, are traces of children's tales that lulled the dreamy nights of my childhood world. I remember, too, fragments of 'adult only' tales overheard when I ventured into the esoteric territory where women held sway.

As a new teller of these tales, I see myself as another link in the chain of story-tellers, and this commitment to narrate has enabled me to see the subversive strategies imbedded in the act of narration. I have discovered various ways in which strategies of narration undermine common perceptions of gender patterns and dynamics in Arab Muslim society, perceptions held by feminists in both West and East. The idea that Islamic society oppresses women, assigning them the status of chattel, has almost become a cliché of Western thought, however untrue it may be. In the world of the medina, by the telling of tales women have found a means of self-expression and claimed the right of reply.

Tales, within the specific context of women's lives are part of a social discourse that has hardly been explored. As a general rule, folklore studies have excluded approaches informed by female perspectives that allow space for women's oral art to be seriously considered. Many Oriental and African civilizations manifest clear distinctions between the men's and women's worlds in which roles are specific and gender-marked. In such civilizations, women generate their own aesthetics, artistic performances, privately enacted, and they leave behind products of an exclusive nature, often exquisite.

The primary intention of this book is to deal with the relationship between teller, tale and society. The focus is upon the role and importance of tale-telling in the lives of three women from the city of Tunis – all Beldi – and upon an exploration of the themes contained in their tales in the light of their personal histories.

The tales I have assembled here are a *mélange*, reflecting the times in which they were told, and the particular cultural heritage which inspired the tale-tellers. They come from the repertoire of three Beldi women, Ghaya, Sa'diyya and Kheira. In the old city of Tunis, the expression 'Beldi' is used to describe a class of élite and highly civilized city dwellers. The tales were recorded between December 1989 and April 1990. I visited the tale-tellers alone and recorded the tales in their homes in

Tunis. On one occasion Kheira was visited unexpectedly by relatives and she agreed to perform in their presence. The performer and the audience ignored the tape recorder and the spontaneity of the session and the genuine relation between artist and audience were captured on tape. Generally, however, recordings were made in separate encounters with each of the narrators alone, thus allowing me to explore their personal interpretations. I tried to tap the full depth of the narrators' repertoires and usually succeeded, except in the case of Kheira, who was only able to relate to me six stories as she fell ill in the middle of my research in Tunis.

I had three advantages in dealing with the women. First, with my parents' origin in Tunis. The women saw me as one among them. Sa'diyya has ties of kinship to my family, so I needed no introduction. The others knew my family by name. On the first occasion I was introduced to Ghaya, the question, 'Bint shkun?' ('Whose daughter are you?') was asked; her husband, a retired pensioner from the Ministry of Agriculture, asked me whether I was related to Mr So-and-So, who used to live in al-Hafeir, a quarter in the medina, and who turned out to be my late grandfather. After that it did not take me long to move beyond the façade of formality exhibited to outsiders and enter the intimate world of the tale-tellers.

The second factor was my interest in traditional Beldi culture. The tale-tellers were demonstrably pleased that I recognized the worth of traditional culture, and the idea that a researcher should wish to write about *them* stimulated them to help me to know more about the art of story-telling and its cultural background, even to the extent of elaborating their generosity by offering me special Beldi culinary delicacies! Finally the women were most willing to express their thoughts and beliefs freely to a woman. My initial conversation with Ghaya was constrained by the presence of her husband who tried to control my questions. But later I discovered that she regularly visited her son – an unmarried doctor who lived alone – and we agreed to meet there. As a result Ghaya was less guarded, more intimate, and more free in her expression in later sessions.

In almost every Beldi household, there is among the elderly women a Scheherazade, who is able to tell a good many tales from the community's repertoire. The three tellers presented here were all exceptional narrators. I chose them for the high regard in which they are held in their families and community, the extent of their repertoire and their individual skills. They all think of themselves as tale-tellers with a special ability, yet none of them was a teller by profession. They tell their tales much as their grandmothers and great-aunts did, informally in the home for the amusement of members of the immediate family, neighbours and close friends.

In my search for story-tellers in the city, Ghaya was the first find; I met her through her cousin Kalthoum, to whom I was initially introduced by others because of her own reputation as a tale-teller. But Kalthoum recommended Ghaya. ('*Lilla* Ghaya, my cousin, is the true artist;

6

she is very knowlegeable and her repertory is much more vast than mine. I am only an apprentice to her.') Kalthoum referred to Ghaya as *Lilla* Ghaya ('Lady/Mistress' Ghaya), a title used as a mark of consideration and a testimony to the prestige she enjoyed in her family.

Ghaya is a housewife aged sixty-three who lives with her husband and their daughter in La Marsa, a northern suburb of Tunis. This elderly woman is fully aware of her own traditional role in the family. During my visits to her, she was consulted on various occasions by relatives for advice. On the death of one of them, she stayed at the house of the deceased for seven days, as was the tradition. On her return, she explained to me that her presence was essential, because she knew all the funerary rules and conventions. She said: 'People no longer know how to mourn their dead.'

Ghaya was known for her talent even at an early age. Her sisters told me that she used to entertain them a great deal with 'stories she knew by heart'. 'She had an amazing memory,' one of them reported. In the first recording sessions, Ghaya's use of classical Arabic was noticeable; she then gradually shifted into the urban Tunis dialect when she became more at ease. Two factors appear to have influenced her choice of language. She is educated and lives in a society dominated by the written word and its supremacy over the spoken. She held the common view that classical Arabic, the language of written literature, was the highest form of art. She chose this language as her medium and in many cases would embellish her narration with poetry and proverbs to lend a more impressive tone to her tale and to show her literary ability.

A second factor which influenced her choice of register was my position as a researcher, which implied publication and the use of the tape recorder, which also meant that her words would be permanent. Ghaya intentionally chose classical Arabic to suit such circumstances. Later, as the project progressed and we became more intimately acquainted, she shifted to a systematic use of colloquial Arabic.

My second discovery was Sa'diyya, a distant relation. She is fifty-five and lives in a house left to her by her late husband in Rades in the southern suburbs. She enjoyed telling tales and prided herself on knowing many; her repertoire is indeed the largest. Many of her relatives testify to the fact that after the death of their uncle's wife (a very talented senior story-teller) no one among the elders except Sa'diyya was ever able to tell stories like her. She was in great demand at all family celebrations. In addition to the vividness and style with which she recounted stories, Sa'diyya was cheerful, had a great sense of humour and a fund of racy jokes. Amongst all inform-ants she was the greatest joker and the least inhibited. She considered her talent as 'a gift from God'. Her real name was Sa'diyya but she was known as *Lillahum* (Mistress of All) in testimony to the prestige she enjoyed in her family and community. Sa'diyya can neither read nor write but, for her listening to and reciting tales became a real com-pensation for her illiteracy. Her repertoire includes tales

8

from the *Thousand and One Nights* which she heard from her uncle who was a well-read teacher.

My third find was Kheira. A sixty-two-year-old single woman who lives with her brother, his wife and children in Le Bardo, to the west of Tunis. At first, I was interested in Kheira's singing ability because I was told she had a good voice and knew a large repertoire of traditional female songs. But soon I realized that tale-telling was another of her talents. However, I only had the opportunity to record three sessions with her, as she suddenly fell ill and was taken to hospital. Despite her strict religiosity, she was considered 'a first class entertainer', and was in great demand at wedding ceremonies and family celebrations. This was due to her authority in and extensive knowledge of *qwa'id* (traditional rules) and her large repertoire of stories and religious songs, many of which added a strong ethical dimension to her repertoire.

Tale-Telling in Tunis

Male story-telling was a professional art up until the late 1960s and generally occurred in public places such as coffee-houses or *makhazin* (stable yards converted into public places). The coffee-house was one of the social institutions that flourished in Tunisia after the Ottomans established their rule.

The *fdawi* or *rawi* (traditional story-teller) was a prominent figure in Tunisian folk life. He plied his trade in various ways, in market places, neighbourhood squares and in cafés, reciting to a strictly male audience. Unlike his counterpart in Egypt, the Tunisian *rawi* used no musical accompaniment. Historians document the existence of a rich male narrative tradition throughout the nineteenth century and after.[1] Describing life in Tunis at the beginning of the century, Turki, in *Tunis Naguère et Aujourd'hui*, tells of the story-teller who would sit on a high stool and punctuate his narrative with a stick.

The reciters performed, along with *Alf Layla wa Layla*, legends of the ancient Arabs: *Seerat 'Antar ibn Shaddad* and *Seerat Bani Hilal*. *Seerat 'Antar* relates the story of the pre-Islamic poet 'Antar ibn Shaddad and his love for 'Abla. *Seerat Bani Hilal*, the 'Hilali Epic', glorifies the migration undertaken by that tribe in the tenth and eleventh centuries out of famine-stricken Najd through the Levant to Egypt, the Sudan and the Maghreb. With long tales, the reciters could pace the episodes to ensure a constant audience over a long period of time.[2]

There was no specific fee, but at the end of the performance the story-teller would pass round a tray and the members of the audience would pay according to their *himma* (rank or social standing). The decline of the tradition was mainly due to government policy. After independence in 1956, the government emphasized written culture at the expense of oral, street culture. Street performances such as the travelling musicians, *al-karakuz* (traditional form of theatre) and story-tellers were officially discouraged as signs of the illiteracy that modern Tunisia was trying to eradicate. The past couple of decades, however, have witnessed a renewed interest in oral culture and serious scholarship in the discipline of folklore.[3]

The 1970s were marked by Pan-Arabism, and oral culture came to be viewed as the truest expression of Tunisia's authentic national culture. Folklore centres were set up in an effort to collect and systematically study its oral heritage. In the 1990s the *rawi* have come back on the scene during the medina festival which takes place at Ramadan. Unfortunately, this story-telling is not spontaneous, being organized by government bodies rather than the people themselves,[4] but behind closed doors, women have always managed to escape the government's restrictions and to keep the tradition alive.

In Tunis the family tale-teller is often a woman and the best artists are generally held to be old women well versed in the traditional folklore. Female story-telling always takes place in private and behind closed doors. Almost invariably one of the elders, often a grandmother or a great-aunt, will take the lead. Many men I spoke with insisted that the performance of tales is not their forte and that in any case they have left 'such childish nonsense to women', as the husband of one of my informants claimed. Story-telling on ritual occasions and as entertainment in the home, remains significantly a women's art form, developed and maintained until very recently by women.

By reason of their position in traditional Tunisian society, women rarely become public professionals. The

11

majority of women in pre-modern Tunisia were illiterate, and tale-telling was one of their central modes of self-expression. Nowadays women have begun to benefit from the spread of public education and the 1970s and 1980s saw the rise of women's magazines, short stories and poetry in print. All narrators testify that, nowadays, they perform much less frequently than they did in the past.

As a child and an adolescent I attended many sessions of story-telling. These were usually informal gatherings on winter evenings, in domestic quarters among women and children. A grandfather occasionally would join in the sessions. The long Ramadan *soirées* are especially conducive to the narration of tall tales. There is a common belief that stories can only be told at night and a taboo prohibiting tale-telling during the day: a person who tells stories during the day will give birth to bald children. All informants explained that they did not believe in such a story and that practical considerations ruled out story-telling during the day. Women are busy during the day with their household chores, and the night-time is certainly more appropriate for flights of imagination.

Exceptions to tale-telling at night are female gatherings that drift easily into tale-telling as women share special communal tasks or perform ritual duties. These may involve only the family or include the broader community. Food preparation offers an opportunity to bring women together. One occasion is during the *'awla* period, a month of preparation of the yearly provisions of *couscous*. It usually happens during August, as *couscous* dries in the sun on rooftops and in the inner courtyards. The women of the same family and neighbourhood take turns in moving from house to house, helping prepare each household's provisions of *couscous*. Men are often required to keep out of the way.

Weddings, engagements and circumcisions are solemnized with ceremonies and celebrations. They provide occasions for considerable music-making and tale-telling, with many events where women play a leading or exclusive role.

Wedding celebrations are the province of women and they are the most elaborate, prolonged and expensive ritual celebrations in Tunisian Beldi society. A traditional wedding may last up to seven days and seven nights, each packed with events. The sexes are segregated for many of these events. Women's activities usually centre on the bride's house. During the festivities, some Beldi families hire a *hennana* (an attendant) to take charge of preparing the bride, applying a herbal dye to her hands and feet and entertaining the female guests with songs and tales. But this tradition is in decline in the process of Tunisia's modernization.

Kheira notes: 'I remember no week passed without a celebration, an engagement, a circumcision, a wedding, a pilgrim returning from Mecca. Major and minor events were celebrated.' Sa'diyya relates: 'Circumcisions, engagements, weddings, religious festivals such as al-'ashura (commemoration of the death of al-Husayn, the Prophet's grandson), and al-Mawlid (anniversary of Muhammad's birth) offered great opportunities for women's gatherings and therefore for story-telling.'

The Text: Issues of Translation

The stories in this volume are grouped under their narrators' voices, in the original order of their telling in the process of my data collection. I have not tampered with selection nor with the organization, as I wanted the tales to appear according to the preference of the story-tellers who have a tendency to tell favourite stories first. In the process of the translation, foremost in my mind has been the accessibility and intelligibility of the text to readers who do not understand Arabic. Stylistically, I had to omit repetitive sections, regardless of the importance of this feature in verbal art, for their frequent occurrence in translation is neither elegant nor eloquent.

There are two features in the narrators' language that defy translation. First, the prominence of diminutives, which are not only used in names but are carried over to describe nearly all physical objects in daily life, such as spoons, cups, glasses, cabinets, etc.; and second, the repetition of religious interjections, oaths, blessings on the Prophet, invocation of God's various attributes, etc. These two features are kept to a minimum to render the text aesthetically appealing. However, I must explain what is missing in my telling, given these conscious deletions. The use of frequent diminutives is a distinctive characteristic in women's language in general and in story-telling in particular. The various forms of the diminutives convey

14

affection, endearment and empathy, but can also ridicule, degrade and belittle. Their appropriate use on specific occasions generates humour and affection, and this nuance is hardly retainable in translation. With regard to religious invocations, there are special formulae for different situations, the repetition of which exhibits the story-teller's emotional involvement with the character in the tale, as well as with me, their listener. They may cry out 'in the name God', when some disaster is about to happen, in order that I may be spared from the same. They may celebrate God's greatness in admiring the hero-ine's beauty, which is also extended to me. These religious references represent a significant religious framework for all the stories and reinforce the women's religious identity.

There is another feature in the stories, the essence of which is diluted in the translation, and that is the opening formula which prefaces each tale with a rhyme. I have retained the ones that are short and meaningful, but have deleted the long one, in Sa'diyya's case, which is arcane and needs explanation. Sa'diyya's opening for-mula, rich in imagery and metaphor is strictly a Tunisian Beldi women's verbal feature. After celebrating God's omnipresence, Sa'diyya proceeds:

Baytna hreir we baytkum kittan
Bayt al-a'da bi al-jraba' we al-firan
Hdithna 'ajeib slatna we slatkum 'al al-nabi al-habeib
Azuzet al-Stut la yirhamha nhar illi tmout
Tudkhul min 'ayn al-ibra al-misqiyya

15

Tqul maws'ik ya mulk rabbi 'aliyya

Tudkhul min zannunit al-breiq

Tqul al-dheeq la yihammilni shay la nteeq

Mshat tjeib fi al-smann

Jabit mukh al-suqi fi al-shann

Mshat tjeib fi al-'ajar mitwi jabittu yimshi

Ya sada we ya mada yidillna we yidillkum li al-khayr we al-shada

Kan ya ma Kan . . .

Our tent is made of silk and yours of linen, while the enemy's tent is full of mice and rats.

My tale is one of wonder. May our prayers and yours be offered up to our beloved Prophet.

May the old witch be damned the day she dies.

She passes through the eye of a fine needle saying: 'How large is God's kingdom.' She passes through the spout of the pitcher saying: 'I can't bear with such narrowness, may I never have to put up with it.'

She went out to get some ghee, she came back with the grocer's brain on a plate.

She went out to get a folded veil, she came back with it walking beside her.

Listeners! May we all be guided to the good and the profession of faith.

Once upon a time . . .

This formula is explicitly a meta-narrational discourse.

16

Here Sa'diyya establishes her stance towards her subject matter and the audience. She sets the scene by establishing her authority as a narrator. She demarcates herself *vis-à-vis* her audience and third parties. 'Silk', 'linen', 'mice' shows a gradation in value implying a decreasing scale of rank. This is a statement of the marvellous, fantasizing relationship and power structure. On the discursive and symbolic level, silk can also suggest the richness of the narrator and the ease which facilitates the flow of the discourse.

In the second segment, the meta-narrational function is overt and prominent. This section comments on the nature of the tale. The narrator describes her art and defines the content as marvellous, fabulous, enigmatic and strange. All is contained in the Arabic adjective *'ajeib* (*hdithna 'ajeib*, 'my tale is one of wonder'); *'ajeib*, can also stand for allegory or figurative expression, both referring to form and content. In yet another variation of the same phrase, Sa'diyya uses *bi al-tarteib*, 'well ordered'. As a rhetorical term, *tarteib* may also mean poetry, rhyme. In dealing with the marvellous, i.e. the irrational or subversive, divine protection is needed:

Slatna w slatkum 'ala al-Nabi al-habeib
May our prayers and yours be offered up to our
beloved Prophet

The third section is the most complex. It is also meta-narrational. The narrator introduces a character central to most stories, namely 'Azuzet al-Stut, 'the old witch'. We note that the old witch is other than logic would lead us to expect. The most striking image is that of narrowness and width. In the initial segment, her passage through the eye of the needle is used as a metaphor for restricted space. The conventional measures of space are inapplicable: the narrow becomes wide and the wide narrow. The old witch seems to manipulate space according to her own will. On the surface level, this clearly indicates the old witch's ability to transcend the confines of space and the natural order of things, perhaps symbolizing the breadth of her field of action. The figurative, non-linear, poetic level of deeper meaning could point to the eye of the needle as a symbolic metaphor for the vagina and by metonymy to the womb, i.e. creation/procreation, and at a wider level refers to procreation as a female prerogative just as the creation of tales, in the home, is the province of women. Conversely, the spout of the pitcher could refer to the male organ which is 'narrow' meaning sterile, non-procreative/creative. In Tunisia, men tell mainly historic legends and myths, whereas the tale is specifically a woman's art form. The metaphor could be extended to a sexual joke: the penis seems large, but is in fact small and inadequate.

The final section expresses notions of the old witch's power concealed through startling images: 'She went to get some ghee, but she got the grocer's brain on a plate;' 'She went out to get a folded veil, she came back with it walking beside her.' The veil is a symbol for the female.

The second image implies that the old witch came back with the woman herself. It was common practice, until the middle of this century, for men to use old women as mediators in gaining access to young women they were interested in and who were protected from social contact with them. A possible interpretation of both segments is that of pointing to the old witch's evil nature and infinite power over men and women.

'Azuzet al-Stut is indeed a complex and ambivalent character. The name is derived from the number *sitta*, 'six'. *Stut* is the plural, and therefore an amplification of the figure six, meaning old. In Tunisia and in the case of women, old age is commonly associated with evil, insanity and absolute freedom of action. Indeed, 'Azuzet al-Stut is an all-powerful agent of evil and a destructive force. She is a deceitful and cunning character who does not seem to be confined by the same restrictions as other people. She is an agent of disorder and disintegration; she upsets the order of things but also redresses wrongs. She changes according to the nature of her intervention and always dresses as a pious old woman; she wears a green robe, paints her stick green, carries a rosary and wraps herself in a green shawl (when connected with Islam, green symbolizes sacredness, holiness and paradise) to gain immediate respect and trust from those she intends to deceive. She sometimes appears as a long-lost aunt, or a helpless old widow, making her living from intrigues as a go-between. She sows disorder in households and stops at nothing to achieve her ends. The formula points to all this.

The formula is not easy to interpret. In an attempt to find a unifying sense comprising all the elements of the passage, one possibility is not to limit the images to their literal meaning, but to understand them as an indication of the infinite possibilities of imagination and the creative process: the narrator is saying that there is no limit to her power as a creator. She establishes herself as the creator of her own discourse. In this respect, *Kan ya ma kan* (Once upon a time) not only serves to set the scene in the distant past, removing the event of the narrative from the present, but also is part and parcel of the poetic creation and suggests a poetic departure.

Telling Words: Poetic Licence and Political Dissent

The focus of recent literature on performance as a part of verbal art has entailed the restoration of the oral product to the individual who moulds it into a personal style and injects a private worldview. The emphasis here is to view the Beldi women's tales ethnographically, in relation to their tellers, in order to discover the individual, social and cultural factors that give them meaning.[5] The tales are, no doubt, creations for enjoyment and amusement, but they are more than an aesthetic discourse. They are a part of a social discourse, well integrated into the women's lives. Idiosyncratic elements of personality transmitted through the tales are definitely linked to life experiences, and they constitute a form of personal expression.

This book is by and about women. The great majority of the stories chosen have a woman protagonist who takes the initiative in speech and action. As Sa'diyya put it, 'When we talk about women we know our ground and we have to say a lot about them because we are women ourselves.' Women devoted themselves to a form of tale-telling which is extremely attractive to other women, as, in their sphere, they are first concerned with their own gender and identity. In one sense, one always tells one's own story, thus from their story-telling the reader gains knowledge of the women's perceptions of themselves and their world and of the way they criticize and comment upon their culture. Through their recollections their young adult lives are recounted and we learn what it means socially and emotionally to be a woman in their Beldi society.

The tales reflect prevailing moral standards; and yet they display attitudes and explore relationships and practices that are sometimes in total contradiction to social norms. In telling and re-telling the stories, the women allow their identities to be determined by a cultural discourse of femininity, thus producing and reflecting historicized concepts of self and gender roles (patriarchal patterns). Nevertheless, they explore alternative subjectivities and depict alternative models through which they speak, expressing a refusal to be fixed by the gendered meanings which their society attaches to individuals. The tales explore subversive possibilities. They empower women by allowing them to transcend social conventions.

Women narrators place their female protagonists in central roles in the tales, thus allowing them to overcome the marginalization female characters suffer in patriarchal tales. Through the use of fantasy, the narrators construct identities which, while culturally sanctioned by poetic licence, enable them to subvert tangible gender limitations and allow negotiation of a more participatory social role. Armed with the freedom to say what they please, the tellers of tales reveal to us not only their ambitions and aspirations but through them a great deal about the social and emotional dynamics of their Beldi community. However these women's voices do not constitute a unified discourse, rather they reflect a range of possibilities within a larger social framework. The narrators, according to their own temperament, disposition, and degree of emancipation or adherence to tradition, have different attitudes. They entertain substantially different views of themselves, their social reality and their aspirations, aspects that are deeply influenced by their personalities. Sometimes the content of the tales is subordinate to the women's will to become mediators and interpreters of their individual and social reality. 'Poetic licence' allows social criticism to be voiced without such retribution as might follow if criticism took place outside such a context. Tale-telling gives them the space to pass judgement, condemn what they see as wrong, sanction what they approve of and express their share of power. Each judgement is 'political', in that it represents an attitude towards the existing order.

2

The Beldi and their World

Tunis has a long tradition of city life going back to ancient
times. Geographically, it is one of the world's crossroads.
The Phoenicians, Romans, Arabs, Andalusians and Turks
all entered North Africa through Tunis. Throughout con-
tinuous centuries of foreign influence, Tunis has acquired
a cosmopolitan character and has become an important
city in the Mediterranean. Arab settlement started in the
seventh century and is today the dominant culture.
Despite the presence of a strong Berber culture, the
Arabic language is firmly rooted and the majority
embraced Islam, which brought with it the accompanying
ideologies and culture. By the end of the thirteenth
century Tunis had already achieved a reputation for urban
civilization. Groups of Spanish Muslim and Jewish refugees
came to settle in Tunisia between the thirteenth and seven-
teenth centuries, and made an important contribution to
the pre-existing cultural matrix. Turkish rule lasted three
centuries. Tunisia's most recent history has been marked

by French colonization which ended with Independence in 1956.

During the early years of Ottoman rule the urban society of Tunis was already divided into a large number of Beldi family spheres of influence, dominating prestigious and lucrative branches of economic life. The achievement of considerable learning, the holding of prominent religious offices and the monopoly of certain skilled crafts were the means by which families acquired noble status. The Beys (hereditary rulers of the country) were associated with the leading Beldi families, who thus gained more prestige and power. The French Protectorate from 1881 was significant in modifying the demographic map of Tunis. The attraction of city living through the services and public utilities it offered accelerated the migration of rural population. By the end of the nineteenth century, a bourgeoisie had already emerged with a relatively higher standard of living and a sophisticated way of life. The Beldi élite retained their prestige and power under the French Protectorate which consolidated its position. They were government officials, *shaykhs* (religious leaders), skilled craftsmen and merchants monopolizing 'noble crafts'. The 'outsiders' who stayed in the city were mostly tanners, shoemakers, blacksmiths, and labourers.

The Beldi maintained a reputation for being cultured and refined, but as the population increased through rural migration, their self-esteem grew together with a sense of

24

prejudice. Scholars, merchants and craftsmen held on to their urban identity and looked down upon all outsiders.[6]

In the tales, the home is the world for women, and the public domain is for men. Women and girls hold traditional female occupations, such as housekeeping, cooking, sewing, embroidery and spinning wool within the home. Men's occupations are associated with the city. They range from *'ulama* (Muslim scholars), *qadis* (judges), *amein* (guild chiefs) and varied *tujjar* (merchants) to silkweavers and perfume makers. Among the various trades there are noble crafts and base ones; the domination of the Beldi over certain crafts is apparent. The crafts are ranked according to several criteria, the most crucial of which seems to be the type of people who practise them. In most cases prestigious occupations are those engaged in by members of families long established in the city. They consist of the manufacture of the *shashiyya* (red knitted cap) and dealings in perfume, silk and gold. The *shashiyya* and *hareir* (silk) industry, for instance, has been run by large-scale family businesses. Ghaya, the first story-teller, puts special emphasis on the Beldiness of certain crafts, and denigrates others because those involved in them are outsiders: 'the industry of silk, knitted caps, and perfumes are for the Beldi, and tanning and the like are for the *boor*', meaning the outsiders. There are references to base crafts in only two of the tales – 'The Crazy Old Woman' by Ghaya, where the central character is a mad old woman who, thinking she would help her daughter with the stained bedsheets and clothes, takes them to the tanner round the corner to be dyed, and 'The

25

Fisherman's Daughter' by Sa'diyya – and in both cases the occupations of a lower status are held by outsiders.

The internal organization of the crafts is hierarchical and this is also reflected in the tales. At the top stands an *amein al-tujjar* (chief of guild) over the master craftsmen, workers and apprentices, who are most of the time affiliated to guilds and who choose an *amein* (chief) to represent them. The economic power of the Beldi, however, is not only based on the monopoly of certain crafts, but also on property and landholdings.

Owning a house within the ramparts of the medina is an indication of one's deep-rootedness in the city. Indeed, almost without exception, every family owns a house, and a man's additional assets may consist of other property. According to Ghaya it was not unusual in Tunis for a Beldi to own land and have it cultivated by others. Indeed, in the twentieth century it is quite common for the élite among the Beldi to own fertile agricultural property within a few miles of the city and employ sharecroppers from the peasantry who then supply them with cereals, fresh dairy produce, fruit and vegetables. The separation between the Beldi and the peasants was reinforced by their living in separate districts, although linked still by economic exchanges. Landholdings at times bound the peasants to urban landlords, as the latter would go regularly to the countryside to receive supplies of wheat, meat, etc., while the peasants would come to the city to sell their produce and provide themselves with the goods of the city. The peasants were generally considered 'primitive' by

26

townspeople who considered themselves more sophisticated and 'civilized'. In the tales, the mocking of the uncouth manners of the rustic by the elegant urbanites constitutes a recurrent theme.

The social markers by which Tunisians identify themselves most readily are the family and the city of origin or 'the home town'. The distinctions provide, in most contexts, for the cleavage and opposition between *us* and *them*, characterized as '*primitive outsiders*'. The tales of the three women narrators, all from the urban community, present similar stereotyped, unsubtle and clear-cut images of the Beldi as opposed to the others.

Two terms are employed to refer to townspeople and outsiders. The people of Tunis refer to themselves and are referred to as 'the Beldi' as opposed to all outsiders lumped together as *Barraniyya*, '*Arab* used in the sense of 'outsiders'. The term 'Beldi' is highly charged. In most contexts it implies the Beldi's claim to deeply rooted origins in the city and to characterize urbane qualities in terms of social class, manners, dress, speech, cuisine and lifestyle. The Beldi identify themselves as a community, and would often proudly vaunt their excellence by referring to heritage and to their 'highly civilized culture'. The metaphor used is *Qa' al-jarra* ('the bottom of the jar'). In Tunisia jars are often used to store olive oil. The lighter oil floats and the best of the oil stays at the bottom. This Beldi metaphor reverses the common notion of the best and the purest, the 'cream of the crop', floating on the

27

top. In a society with a long history of olive culture – Carthage boasts the world's most ancient cult – olive oil is a standard means of comparison or quality. The richest and the purest in this case sinks to the very bottom of the large and deep jar, signifying at the same time profundity of character as well as long establishment in the heart of the city. Traits which have been consistently important in the Beldi's view of themselves versus the others consist of their extreme self-consciousness and their pride in qualities which are not easily acquired. Even in physical appearance, the Beldi seems to excel in their refinement.

The narrator in 'Long Live the Beldi' (see p. 189) sets the tone by portraying the man's wives, except the Beldi one, as 'dark and green with tattoos in their ethnic dress'. The Beldi woman is described as 'fair and radiant, with good smooth light skin, breeding and manners and "a touch of class" '. The image corresponds to something more general, namely the ideal beauty to which the Beldi woman aspires. In Tunis, a bedouin peasant is sometimes referred to as 'green', meaning uncouth, crude and naïve. The description shows the Beldi as fair with 'refined' features and the non-Beldi as inferior in looks, which confirms the Beldi's own view of their species as beautiful. All three women story-tellers highlight the physical exquisiteness of their heroines. In 'Long Live the Beldi' the women are asked four questions: what are their favourite dishes, dwellings and names and how would they tell night from day? All their answers reflect definite contrasts in their background, character and everyday experience. The Jerbi woman's favourite dwelling is a *housh* (traditional type of habitation with a cellar). Her favourite name is Yahyia and her favourite dish *tarfis* and *tarfous* (a mixture of ground wheat, sultanas, nuts and olive oil) both typical of the Island of Jerba. And she distinguishes night from day by 'when the cattle sleep and the cockroaches come out'.

The bedouin woman also gives answers drawn from her peasant background. Her favourite name is Salah, her preferred dish, chicken *couscous* (steamed semolina served with meat and vegetable stew) and her best habitation a *dar bla fjaj* (a straw and mud hut without a door). And she recognizes night from day when the cattle sleep and the sheep wake.

The Jerbi and bedouin women's answers are highly charged with evaluative implications. In everyday use, the names Salah and Yahyia commonly refer to an uncouth and crude *arbi*, (bedouin or peasant). From a Beldi point of view, *tarfis* and *tarfous* is peasant-like and coarse food and a proper *couscous* is cooked with lamb. As regards habitation, a *dar* (house) without a door is rustic and poor. The allusion to animals' habits further emphasizes the repliers' peasant origin.

The portrayal of the black woman has racist overtones, as her answers reflect her subservient position. Her favourite dwelling is a *kumaniyya* (a room usually reserved for black servants in Beldi houses); Her favourite name is Mabrouka which is a typical black servant's name. To the last question as to how she would tell night from day, she answers, 'When her master asks for the chamber-pot.'

29

The Beldi woman's answers to the questions reveal an urbanized taste, an eye for luxury and, most of all, an extreme piety. Her favourite dwelling is a *dar bil-'ali* (a traditional urban two-storey house with a balcony equipped with *mousharabia* which allows one to see without being seen). Her favourite dish is *ftat 'al-mri* (an expensive rich and nutty kind of pastry), which is a real Beldi delicacy. Her favourite names are Muhammad and Ali, two major Muslim prophets who have come to distinguish the two sects: Sunni and Shi'ite. And she distinguishes night from day by 'when the *muezzin* calls for prayer in Mecca, the home of the Prophet Muhammad, God bless him and give him salvation'. The times of prayer regulate her day and her language is filled with spirituality, God and the Prophet, a quality that is missing in the other women's language. By Beldi standards, the other women's answers lack finesse. The husband's decision to keep his Beldi wife and repudiate the others is his recognition of her quality. This tale clearly highlights a number of characteristics which situate the Beldi physically and culturally. The emphasis placed on religious practice, refined taste and style of life among the Beldi show that these features play an especially crucial role in the Beldi's self-view of their cultural ascendancy, as all three narrators are practising Muslims whose speech is punctuated by their religiosity in frequent invocations to the Prophet, and holy blessings upon the interlocutors. This attitude is not uncommon among the older generation in Tunis.

Beside the physical and spiritual aspects of Beldi superiority, another important trait is intelligence. Outsiders, particularly uneducated peasants, are often the butt of jokes and the fool in the stories. An ignorant and illiterate person is commonly referred to as *bagra* (a cow). In 'The Vizier's Daughter' (see p. 104) the outsiders are pejoratively referred to as 'cows', because they are unable to answer simple questions. The Beldi estimate of rural backwardness is recognizably based on stereotypes, but also partly upon perceived cultural differences.

The Beldi cult expresses itself through a way of life, a pattern of behaviour and a manner of speech. Individuals are either included or excluded from this milieu, according to their conformity to its social rules, and, as in any selective community, acceptance is restricted and membership is a social privilege. In several tales, marriage between a Beldi and an outsider fails on account of precisely the difference stipulated above, and the incapacity of the 'others' to adapt to the Beldi requirements.

The narrative tone of voice is fertile ground for observation of stereotypes and prejudices, which evolve through categorization of observed cultural differences. In its satirical and pejorative forms such as displayed in these tales, the defamatory intention of the narrators reflects their sense of superiority in every respect. The Beldi articulate their own distinctiveness in the ways Cohen stipulates.[7] Besides common ancestry, lifestyle and manners, a refined code of *savoir vivre*, a distinctive dialect, a distinctive urbane style of dress and a refined cuisine, are further markers of 'Beldiness' in Tunis.

31

Table manners, terms of address, respect for elders, etc., all form part of the refined code of *savoir vivre* which is consciously invoked and reinforced in the tales. *Lilla* (madam) and *sidi* (sir) are the polite terms of address between Beldi men and women. Husbands and wives also use them as a sign of respect.

Deference shown by the young for their elders is an important mode of interaction between the Beldi generations; examples abound. In the tale 'Ftaytma the Harridan' (see p. 126) and 'The Wicked Mother-in-Law' (see p. 301), for example, a young married man in difficulty turns to an elderly man for help to put an end to the ill-treatment of his wife by his own mother. The young bride, for her part, does not react with indignation and keeps her poise. Her reticence defines her as the daughter of a Beldi family. Breeding decrees that she does not 'show arrogance or disrespect towards her elders', as Ghaya commented (see p. 127). In her view, women's roles and their terms of address for men did not indicate inferiority, as respect was mutual. 'We never experienced it as such.' All women put a high premium on *qdar* (respect) as the basis of interaction in Beldi circles.

The Beldi are instantly recognisable by an urban accent which is quite distinctive. The narrators themselves are native speakers of this upper-class Beldi dialect. But on occasions they would imitate rural speech mannerisms. In the tale 'The Peasant' (see p. 133), the bedouin peasant is given various recommendations to facilitate his integration into the Beldi family. An important one is to drop his regional shibboleth *g* and pick up the Beldi urban *q*.

Another characteristic of the Beldi dialect is the use of diphthongs, eg. *bayt* (room) instead of *bi:t.* The diphthong is stereotypically a woman's feature but some Beldi men use it. Because of their use of the diphthong and of certain lexical terms, the Beldi men in particular are stigmatized by people from other towns and often characterized as effeminate to the extent that men nowadays try to avoid the diphthong. The pressure is such that we may be seeing a linguistic change in progress leading towards the elimination of the diphthong altogether in the speech of both males and females, especially among the new generation.[8] During my contacts with the narrators, I had the feeling that, in their speech, they place a special emphasis on the diphthong to mark their Beldi origin and show off their 'Beldiness'.

'The Peasant (see p. 133), is a tale about a bedouin peasant who wants to integrate himself into the Beldi community. One of several ways of refining him is to make him adopt proper attire. On his wedding night, he wears a traditional Beldi wedding costume which consists of a *jibba* (a kind of bat-wing, medium-length silk caftan) and a white *burnous* (a cloak). He also wears a *shashiyya stambouli* (a Turkish fez with a long tassel). Female dress is also described in the tales, ranging from the traditional outdoor floor-length silk veil to embroidered wedding and celebration costumes.

Many references are made in the tales to Beldi delicacies.

The Beldi tables described contained a large variety of regular savoury and sweet dishes as well as special treats. In the narrators' views the Beldi are 'gourmets'. They like to entertain, eat well and with style. 'Our wedding celebrations, family rejoicing and even mourning rituals are big occasions for savoury and sweet delicacies,' Ghaya comments. 'Indeed our cuisine is the legacy of several thousands of years of settlers: the Berbers, the Arabs, the Turks and most recently the French; each of these groups has added an ingredient and made it more varied.'

In the pre-colonial and colonial period, to be a Beldi was to have a prized status.[9] After Independence, being Beldi became a mixed blessing as Tunisia underwent significant changes. The growth and movement of population, the new distribution of power (the new government being in the hands of non-Beldi) and the development of modern education and new ideas all had wide social implications. The majority of the Beldi worked as craftsmen, but changing economic conditions severely undermined most of the city's traditional crafts with a flood of imported goods. The Beldi became, in a sense, *declassé*. And the idea that the status of the individual was inextricably tied to that of his group, is no longer inviolate. Today, the notion of 'Beldi' has a different significance. To many outsiders 'Beldi' means lazy, pretentious and *wild nanati* (mother's boys). But there remains a part of their identity to which the Beldi still cling in spite of the changes: their prestige is in fact more cultural than economic.

3

TALES OF FABLE AND FACT

After dinner, the son begged his mother, 'Please, mother, tell us a story.'
She said, 'What do you want me to tell you?'
'A story, anything,' he said.
She replied, 'Then I'll tell you the story of the cares of my heart.'

This is an excerpt from a story which illustrates how Ghaya, Sa'diyya and Kheira choose their tales to reveal, indirectly, circumstances which have occurred in their own lives. It also demonstrates the essence of the feminine mode of expression in the Orient, which is characterized by a style both indirect and veiled. This indirect veiled mode of expression is an example of the *kitmane* (secret), which is traditionally one of the most important social values for the Oriental woman, and one which is evident in her artistic expression. It is a part of a condition inherent in her life behind the veil, behind closed doors, where she loves and suffers in silence.

The narrators in this collection selected the stories they told from a large pool of folk tales which are meaningful to them and fit their life experiences. The act of narration is the place where imagination and reality cross. The stories begin in the imagination of the tellers, but they become interwoven with their personal histories and their views of the world. 'Poetic licence' allows social criticism to be voiced without such retribution as might follow if criticism took place outside such context. Tale-telling gives the women the space to tell accounts of their own lives and pass judgement, making the telling of tales much more than mere entertainment. At the same time the stories provide an excellent account of the social fabric of the culture and the sexual parameters of the entire society.

Ghaya: Narration as Mediation[10]

Sixty, born and brought up in Tunis, Ghaya comes from a very wealthy, educated and traditional Beldi family of hereditary social and political pre-eminence, in which learning and traditional lore are revered. 'Putting on airs' and projecting an exalted sense of self-importance, Ghaya reports: 'Our family is *'ariqa* [old and deep-rooted] in the city and is reputed to have distinguished itself by learning, piety and in government service.' She traces the origin of her family to Muslim Spain: *'Es-Sajara* [the family tree] is here to testify to it.' She proudly boasts an Andalusian ancestor who was a *qadi* and played an important role in the city's history. In fact, her unusual name, Ghayat al-Muna (the Heart's Desire), and those of her sisters,

36

'Abbasa, Burane and Umm al-'Ala, are names of Andalusian princesses, chosen by her father who was a well-read
historian. The father, a noted scholar among the religious
élite, had an ardent interest in folklore and worked for
the maintenance and the survival of Beldi tradition. He
was a teacher of Islamic law and history and travelled
extensively in the Middle East, attending Islamic confer-
ences and meeting well-known *'Ulama* (muslim scholars)
and leading personalities. In his lifetime, he collected
proverbs and wrote an impressive amount of material on
Beldi tradition and folklore.

Ghaya was among the first privileged women to go to
school at a time when girls' education was frowned upon.
In the early part of the century her father encouraged
her and his other three daughters to pursue their studies.
She did her primary education in the medina, then her
family acquired a new house in Sidi Bou Said, north of
the city, and she attended a girls' school in Carthage
until the age of seventeen. To her disappointment she
could not take a job. Only needy people would allow their
women to work. 'I wanted to get a job as a schoolmistress
or a secretary and use my knowledge, but my father, may
he rest in peace, said: "Have I failed to see to your well
being? I have always provided fine clothes and jewellery
for all of you to wear and you are well fed. You want
people to say I can't provide for my family?" ' In the Beldi
milieu, a woman worked only when her family was in
financial need, and thus her working signified a lower
economic status.

37

Her father held open house for students and colleagues. One of the visiting students saw her and asked for her hand, and so she became engaged at the age of seventeen. Ghaya fell ill with pneumonia, to the dismay of the in-laws, who eventually broke off the engagement on the grounds of her health. Ghaya was aggrieved, as she had grown fond of her fiancé. 'At that time breaking an engagement would jeopardize a young girl's reputation and diminish her chances of finding a suitable suitor.'

The Beldi disassociate themselves from the 'primitive-ness' of others in the city and of the surrounding rural people but this did not hinder them from seeking alliances with powerful rural families when it was in their interest. At the age of twenty-two her father married Ghaya off to a rich outsider. Ghaya could only acquiesce. Soon after her marriage, she moved to settle with her husband and his family in Zaghouan, forty kilometres to the south of Tunis. She had her first child the following year, and did not conceive again until sixteen years later, giving birth to a girl. Ghaya had to endure a great deal from her husband and does not recall being happy. 'It was an unhappy mar-riage, may God forgive my father; we were as different as silk and rags. Only patience and a deep belief in God helped me to overcome it. I wanted to divorce during the first years of my marriage, but on the one hand I did not want to disgrace my family and cause grief to my father in his lifetime, and on the other, I thought one victim was enough. I was ready to sacrifice my life for the sake of my child's happiness. I filled my heart with the love of God and his Prophet, peace be upon him.'

When her father died, she inherited her share under the will, bought a house in La Marsa, in the northern suburbs, and moved there with her husband; she lives there still. Ghaya is extremely pious and never misses a prayer. She has been on pilgrimage twice. When I first went to visit her, it was during the holy month of Ramadan and she was counting her beads in invocation of God's protection and oneness. She did so on each of my subsequent visits.

Ghaya learned her narrative art from both her grandmother and Hbiba Stambuliyya, a professional story-teller of Turkish origin who was commissioned by the Bey to entertain him and his court. Ghaya's mother was of noble origin and had connections with the Bey's family. After the Bey's deposition, Hbiba Stambuliyya was adopted by Ghaya's grandfather to entertain his only daughter, Sayyda Bent Muhammad Shadli, Ghaya's mother. Ghaya's grandmother was also a talented tale-teller, who learned her art from her aunt and greatly benefited from the presence of Hbiba Stambuliyya to extend her repertoire. Ghaya's father kept a personal library, and she read a lot as a girl. Her repertory is varied and also includes stories and anecdotes from written Arabic literature.

In Ghaya's life story two points stand out: her great pride in her Beldi background, which may have caused the failure of her marriage to an outsider, and her sense of wasted education. Ghaya regrets her marriage as well

39

as the fact that she was educated and yet confined to the house and forbidden to take a job.

In 'Sabra' (see p. 97), Ghaya relates the story of a young girl who was married off to a rich man who was able to satisfy her father's greed for money with three loads of gold as her bride price. Resigned and patient, Sabra suffers the worst indignities from her husband, but endures and never complains or rebels. In fact her very name – Sabra, meaning 'patient' in Arabic – echoes throughout the tale. She represents the essence of the feminine spirit. Ghaya elevates suffering and resignation into a female career and reinforces the traditional value system requiring that women be patient and resigned. She identifies renunciation and patience with womanhood: 'She is a woman; such is her lot, to endure with patience,' Ghaya comments, 'She who endures with patience will build a happy home; all sacrifice is good.' Renunciation and patience are quintessential female virtues.

One can imagine the immediacy of Ghaya's identification with the heroine. The parallel between the life story of Ghaya and the tale of Sabra is remarkable. Such a coincidence of story pattern with life experience makes for a highly charged symbolic shaping of reality. The tale offers a creative depiction of Ghaya's suffering, it becomes a cathartic ritual dramatization of her own life in literal and figurative terms. Likewise, 'Ftaytma', which relates also the sufferings of a young bride who was bullied and badly treated by her mother and sister in-law, is also Ghaya's story – the story of a woman who finds it hard to live up to the life of sacrifice demanded of her, yet perseveres, becoming a model of female piety. For Ghaya, rebelling is inappropriate in the sense that even if the rebel won on one front, i.e. escaping the rural suitor or getting a job, she would lose on another level: loneliness, loss of her father's esteem, no possibility of motherhood. In short, between Ghaya's legitimate desires and her father's earned respect there is a dissonance that cannot be harmonized, a gap that cannot be bridged. It is not a case of Ghaya versus her father but rather a situation in which there is Ghaya's desire to please herself and her wish to please her father on the one hand, and on the other her father's wish to educate his daughter and his wish to protect his daughter via traditional practices. The various discordant desires are orchestrated and partially harmonized in the telling of the tale which allows room for the expression of 'conflicting yet not opposed' sentiments.

Three tales, 'Rdah Umm Zayed', 'The Peasant' and 'Long Live the Beldi', also exhibit topics and concerns that are important to the narrator and of immediate relevance to her own situation. In her own voice Ghaya celebrates the Beldi identity, through their way of life, food, language and rituals. The tales portray the Beldi as religious, sophisticated and refined; and the Barraniyya (outsiders) as uncivilized and crude. Marriage contracted between the two parties is bound to fail.

'The Peasant' is the story of the daughter of a Beldi family who marries an outsider and cannot cope with it, and the marriage is eventually broken off. 'Rdah' relates

41

the story of the aristocratic and delicate Beldi girl who dies of grief for having chosen Hmid al-Hilali, the bedouin who had disregarded her rank and had left her to die in the hands of boorish peasants. She died saying: 'A bird of the land cannot live over the sea, and silk and cotton are for the nobility and merchants. I am soft and he is rough. We are poles apart. That is my real grief.' The narrator concludes: 'It is hopeless, silk and rags don't mix; that is why I am so worried about Layth, he will not be happy with her.'

Layth is Ghaya's son. At the time I was conducting my fieldwork, he became engaged to a provincial girl. On that occasion, Ghaya disclosed her personal troubles and apprehension that history would repeat itself. The oral nature of the discourse allows this openness: Ghaya is in a good position to move in and out of the tale safely and easily. Here again, in the telling she harmonizes disparate points of view without needing to choose between them or make them agree.

'Aysha, in 'The Vizier's Daughter', is Ghaya's educated, intelligent and self-assertive woman who engages in overt confrontation and competition with a man. A prince challenges his vizier with intrigues. The vizier solves them with the help of his intelligent, learned daughter, 'Aysha. Defeated and seeing the intelligence of the girl, the prince takes her as a bride to suppress her and avenge himself. 'Aysha is shut up in a cave and subjected to a routine ritual questioning, but, to the prince's dismay, she always has an answer and stands up to him. The prince eventually acknowledges her merit and she resumes her rightful place in his household and rules with him.

Ghaya is educated and knowledgeable but she sees that her knowledge and abilities have been wasted. She wanted to take a job, but she was forced into marriage and confined to a traditional female role. Women's education and status is of interest to her: 'We have brains just like them and we can use them. Why waste them?' The issue of women's identity is addressed here. Her narrative is a powerful vehicle of resistance against silence and absence. In her discussion, Ghaya comments on the painful dispute between the ingrained popular stereotype of a woman and her proper place in that society. She addresses women's loss of self which results from their alienation in a world whose order is structured around their non-being: lack of voice, lack of value, lack of power. Her heroines fight for recognition of female abilities and seek power and a valued position in both the family and society.

'Aysha is a woman who speaks and makes her voice heard. Power is inextricable from the use of voice. Ghaya presents the longings for fulfilment of an intelligent young woman in conservative Tunisian society, and advocates indirectly a re-thinking of sexual roles within a conservative framework. She is less preoccupied with sexuality than with self-assertion and independence in marriage. Both are explored within *halal*, legitimate marriage. Couples engage in sexual relations only after completing the marriage contract. The only instance of illicit sex in her stories is justified on the grounds of a large gap in age between the partners: 'Baba Turki was married to a very young and pretty woman. He could have been her father, so she took a lover.' Ghaya did not utter a single word of condemnation. She was, however, slightly inhibited. The first time she told me the story, she used the colloquial word *sahib* (lover or boyfriend). But when I wanted to record it, she shifted to classical Arabic *khalil* (close friend) to overcome her shyness and inhibition, on the one hand, and in deference to the tape recorder, on the other. Through her language and tales, Ghaya unveils truths about herself and her own life which become blended with the narrative reality in a process of cross-influence, expressed in her views about marriage and women's status.[11]

Sa'diyya: Love and Words

Fifty-five, Sa'diyya was born and brought up in Tunis in a fairly wealthy Beldi family. She also traced her roots in the city into the distant past and claimed descent from the Prophet. 'Our family enjoyed a special status because they were *shurafa* [descendants of the Prophet]. We have *sajarat al-shurafa* [the genealogy chart of nobles]. Their ancestor migrated to Kairouan from the Arab Peninsula. He was a *shareif* who lived a pious and virtuous life. He made water jugs for a living. Local tradition claims that one day the *shaykh* took out his jugs to dry in the sun, but suddenly clouds gathered. The *shaykh* prayed to God to spare his water jugs. It poured with rain but not a single drop fell on the jugs. When the *shaykh* died, a tomb was built in Kairouan and it became a popular shrine, Sidi al-qallal, drawing till the present date hundreds of pilgrims at religious festivals.

Sa'diyya's parents died when she was young. At the age of ten she was adopted and brought up by her uncle. She did not go to school as it was considered at that time disgraceful to send girls to school where they were taught by male foreigners. 'My uncle was too narrow-minded; many of our peers went to school but he wouldn't allow us to pursue any studies, so now I can't read or write. It is so painful I will never forgive him. There was an incident of a young Beldi girl who eloped with a French teacher. All the parents were scared that this might happen to their own daughters.' Sa'diyya was very clever and was particularly meticulous and tidy. She soon became her uncle's favourite and took pride of place in his household. She had the key to the provisions room. Her cousins were spoiled and never helped her with the domestic chores. In the early fifties, the family moved from the medina to settle in Rades, the second core residential area of the Beldi. Her cousins eventually married and moved out to settle with their husbands' families. At the age of sixteen, Sa'diyya fell in love with a schoolmaster, a distant relative who returned her love. But her cousin wanted to arrange a marriage between the schoolmaster and her own daughter, so she used all possible means to impede the marriage. Sa'diyya used to meet her lover in secret. When the romance was discovered she was forbidden to see him, and for four years the young lovers managed to meet occasionally in secret. 'It was tragic; I cried my eyes out.'

One day her beloved kinsman went to his father and announced that he wanted to marry Sa'diyya, but the father objected on the grounds that Sa'diyya was frivolous. The young man left the country.

Sa'diyya felt abandoned and betrayed and vowed never to marry. She turned down all the suitors and devoted herself to taking care of her uncle and his wife, hoping the man she loved would come back. Suddenly her uncle died. His wife followed forty days later. Sa'diyya continued to live in the same house with her cousin and his young bride. She took a job at a shoe factory which hired girls in the neighbourhood. Nobody objected. When the young couple moved to their new house a few kilometres away, Sa'diyya had to move with them and give up her job. She was treated so badly by the young bride that when a seventy-year-old widower proposed, she accepted and moved out to live with him. He died three years later leaving her the house and his pension to live on.

Sa'diyya learnt her art from her uncle's wife, who was a very talented story-teller, and her own uncle, an educated man who used to read them *The Thousand and One Nights*. Sa'diyya's talent manifested itself very early. 'It has been some years now since, as a little girl, I used to listen to tales from my uncle's wife and from *Alf Layla wa Layla*.' For her, listening to tales is a kind of compensation for her illiteracy: 'It was on long winter nights that I waited impatiently for my uncle's wife to tell me and my cousins tall tales. I can't remember going through an apprenticeship. At the age of ten I was able to repeat stories I had

46

heard the night before without omitting a single episode. My uncle used to say: "She possesses a verbal facility, a captivating story-telling manner, which reveal an extraordinary gift. If this girl had been to school she would have achieved wonders." I think it was a gift from God.'

Like Ghaya, she has a repertoire which exhibits concerns of immediate relevance to her life. The tales she likes to tell are laden with themes inspired by personal experience. Sa'diyya's account of her life suggests an analogy between herself and her art. Two points stand out: the loss of both her parents at an early age and subsequent adoption by her uncle, and her painful love story. In her favourite tales, sometimes hidden behind various characters and sometimes explicitly, Sa'diyya enacts her own tragedy: her painful experience as an orphan but, more so, her resentment and frustration at the injustice suffered through being thwarted in love. She will draw inspiration from her own personal memories and past experiences to make her heroines evolve in a familiar universe. In a sense, most stories arise not only from the combination and recombination of motifs, upon which the story-teller is free to build,[12] but also from their resonance with the teller's social and personal experience.

'Aysha the fisherman's daughter is an orphan mistreated and starved by her stepmother and relegated to the status of a maid. During the telling Sa'diyya intervenes, speaking in her own voice: 'From early morning till nightfall, 'Aysha would sweep the floor, do the washing and cooking. Who cares? Her loving mother is in the grave.

47

She would cry her eyes out remembering her dead mother' (see p. 247). Much of the story is idiosyncratic and has meaning for Sa'diyya in terms of her own story. Her personal experiences are clearly evident through the consciousness of 'Aysha. Her own life was a replica of her heroine's; cleaning, sweeping and cooking. In a strongly felt aside, she tells how she did all this without any recognition – 'We were neither thanked nor praised.' The hinge between the tale and reality is seen in Sa'diyya's use of the dual pronoun 'we', including both the heroine and the 'self'.

In this tale, animals speak to reward 'Aysha for allowing them to quench their thirst; pearls stream from her mouth and flowers spread all around her. Despite the fantastic nature of the narrative, the heroine nevertheless takes on a real human dimension, perhaps because of the real Sa'diyya's identification with the imaginary 'Aysha.

While Ghaya tends to use stories to express competing feelings, among which she cannot or will not choose, Sa'diyya tends to use stories to give artistic shape to a painful life. Many tales feature great loves, separations and reunions, and display passions and yearnings, and overt sexuality and eroticism. 'The Salt Pedlar' (see p. 291) relates the story of a young loving couple separated by the young man's parents. During the telling, Sa'diyya puts forward her own experience and views on men and the world. 'They lived happily together until one day he went to his father and announced that he wanted to marry her. His father objected, on the grounds that he was promised to his cousin.' Sa'diyya intervenes: 'This is like my story, they separated us; damn the bastards.' The lovers were disappointed and decided to elope. They travelled overland until they were exhausted. They decided to stop for a while. She laid her head in his lap and fell sound asleep. When she awoke, she found a stone under her head for a pillow, and the prince was nowhere to be seen. 'You see, one can never trust men. They are mere puppets in their father's hands.' Sa'diyya comments. 'Maybe we will have some justice in the world to come, but even there God seems to favour men. He promised them *houris* (beautiful angels) but there is no mention of male *houris* for women,' she adds jokingly.

In her view the world is a man's world. Her bitterness at having been abandoned and betrayed and her anger and protest against social pressure very often filter through the stories as she comments casually in the course of her first tale: 'Men and time are not to be trusted.' She speaks from personal experience.

In 'Fate' (see p. 309) Sa'diyya also endorses the role of her heroine, who like herself was abandoned by her lover, and expresses her own resentment and frustration: 'Hussayna sat down on a bench and started to cry and cry. She remembered her dead father and cried; she remembered her unhappy days and cried. She cried over her bad luck, her self-sacrifice, her lost husband – I am the one who has loved you so dearly, I am the one who cried over you, I am the one who has sacrificed her life, I am the one you should have married – but to no avail.' Hussayna was to cry until

49

she filled seven drinking cups and seven jars with her tears, thus breaking the spell on her husband-to-be who would wake up and marry her. She hired a serving girl to help her fill in the last jar and fell into a sound sleep. But when her destined husband awoke he thought the slave girl had broken the spell and married her as a reward. The intensity of Sa'diyya's description of the wailing and lament of Hussayna and the manifestation of her emotional involvement left little doubt that her heroine's anguish echoed her own, thus providing catharis.

The tales quite simply allowed Sa'diyya to express emotions which had been denied expression in her interaction with others in ordinary discourse – because, if communicated in everyday discourse, these emotions would violate the canons of female modesty.[13] Modesty required that romantic love should not be expressed, but the tales afford a certain amount of protection to allow Sa'diyya to do so.

Love and sexuality outside the boundaries of social conventions are explored in the tales. In the performance, Sa'diyya is uninhibited and speaks freely about love, desire and passion. Of all the informants, she is the only one who tells explicit sexual jokes without any hesitation. This could be partly due to her recognition of the hypocrisy about love and romance she has seen in the persona of her jealous cousins. She depicts heroines who seek sexual fulfilment, who break social barriers and surrender to impulsive passions, such as Rdah, al-Hajja Mkada in 'Hmid

50

al-Mitjawwil', the *qadi*'s mother in 'Overpowering Desire', the king's wife in 'Lulsha', as well as even the conservative who would preserve her family's honour in 'The Bird that Flew'. Her heroines are on the whole passionate, rebellious and hungry for love.

In Sa'diyya's second tale, Rdah falls in love with Hmid al-Hilali and receives him in her apartment and spends three nights with him. A strain of intense female sexual fantasy and eroticism runs through the descriptions of Rdah and al-Hajja Mkada. The setting for both is a chamber with voluptuous decor: 'Rdah, the fine lady, walked about her apartment furnished with silk curtains, wearing a fine see-through nightgown, letting her hair hang loose down her back' (see p. 212) and 'Al-Hajja Mkada took a quick musk bath and put on a fine silk nightgown. As she walked about her apartment, the perfume of musk wafted all over the place. She sent Dadah downstairs to invite the man to join her in her sleeping chamber' (see p. 221).

Her heroines express female sexual energy, and they initiate encounters. Sexual adventure is a response to an ebullient, rousing desire. Sa'diyya speaks freely about it and enjoys her own fantasies; her tales talk of women's desires and women taking the initiative in making advances. In reality the situation in Tunisian society is one in which sexual initiative and power are essentially the masculine prerogative.[14]

51

Kheira: Narration as Consolation

Sixty-two, born and brought up in Tunis, Kheira comes
from a large family which enjoyed a position of respect in
the city. Until the age of twelve she went to a girls' school,
from which she graduated with a Certificat d'Etudes Prim-
aires. Each day when she left for school, she went out
wearing *al-Khama al-rihiyya* (a short black, head-shawl),
which was customary at the time for girls, and
accompanied by Ali, their black servant. Protected by the
shawl and the servant, Kheira was allowed to go to school
until she reached puberty. She wanted to pursue further
studies but her father objected on the grounds that she
was now grown-up and should learn domestic tasks: 'Out
of concern for the family's honour,' Kheira explained,
'parents confine their daughters to the house as soon as
they reach puberty.'

At the age of nineteen, she became engaged to her first
cousin, but three years later the two families split over the
question of inheritance, and the engagement was eventually broken off. Her sisters and one of her brothers got
married and moved out of the house, but she turned
down all suitors because she did not feel they were appropriate. 'I preferred spinsterhood to accepting marriage to
the firstcomer; I suppose God willed it so for me.'

Kheira developed a close friendship with a girl of her
own age, living next door. 'We were like sisters, we went
to school together, then on to *dar al-m'allma* [traditional
institution where girls were sent to learn sewing, embroidery and the like]. I was her confidante throughout a mis-

52

fortune which I suppose was ordained by God. She was seduced and abandoned by her brother-in-law. But God sent her an angel who married her and saved her honour. Where can one find such loyalty nowadays?'

Kheira lived with her parents and younger brother in their ancestral house. Her brother eventually got married and his bride came to live with him. When both her parents died, her brothers decided to sell the house and give each one his share of the inheritance. Her younger brother bought a house in Le Bardo, to the west of Tunis, and she moved to live there with him and his family, where she still is today.

She went on her first pilgrimage when she was thirty-five and on her return, to the dismay of her brothers and sisters, she decided to give up the idea of marriage, lead a pious life and devote her life to God and his Prophet. She has been on pilgrimage to Mecca four times and hopes to live to complete the cycle of seven pilgrimages aspired to by pious Muslims 'if God wills'. When I first met Kheira she was wearing the Muslim head scarf which she wore when she first went on pilgrimage. She gave me the following explanation: '*Al-Hajj* [pilgrimage] is not a game; we are supposed to give up all life's pleasures and lead a strict and pious life.' Kheira is indeed strict, and is reputed to be extremely religious.

Kheira learnt her narrative art from her grandmother and from her grandfather who, after an elementary education, devoted himself to studying the Qur'an. In addition to his thorough religious knowledge he had an

53

intimate acquaintance with the whole range of *Hadith* (the Prophet's oral traditions) and the Arabic historic legends, *Antar, al-Amira dhat al-Himma* and *Sayf Ibn dhi Yazan.* He used to attend sessions for men only. In her early childhood, they used to be visited by her great-aunt who was a very talented story-teller. At the age of thirteen, she reported 'I started telling stories to my cousins and insisted on being paid out of their pocket money. Later, when my gift was acknowledged, I was in great demand to tell stories at all family gatherings and rejoicings; I knew all the *twashi* (formulae) and recited a lot of poetry from memory in my narration. I even invented a closing formula: *Hkayitna hakka hakka, we al-'am al-jay nimshiuw li bayt Makka* (our story has come to an end, may we go to Mecca next year). Kheira's stories, like everything else in her life, revolve around religion.

In her own life, two emotions predominate: a reverence for religion, particularly the Muslim idea of fate, and a deep nostalgia for 'the good old days', expressed as a regret for the changes that Tunisian society has undergone: the deterioration in human relations under the banner of individualism and the change in women's position in the name of modernism. For Kheira, narration is a form of consolation. She told me six stories altogether, all of which exhibit the same concerns. The idea that all things large and small are subject to fate and God's will is fundamental to her stories. Four stories out of six deal with fate in human lives and the futility of any attempt to escape it. As a religious person, Kheira is primarily a fatalist who seeks explanation from the perspective of providence. She believes that whatever good fortune or misfortune life contains, its major and minor events are always foreseen. Just like her characters, she submits to God's will in her own way.

Her heroines are portrayed as loyal, affectionate and keenly aware of injustice, even to the extent that they will fight to right it. Kheira's favourite tale is 'Al-'ishra', 'Companionship' in which the heroine suffers a misfortune that is overcome with the help of a young girl. In the details, she draws inspiration from her own past, particularly her relationship with her neighbour. The story is interspersed with nostalgic comments on the 'good old days' and the regrettable changes in human relations. Central to this tale is the bond between the two girls, al-'ishra, a companionship based on affection, devotion and loyalty.

The word derives from the root 'ashara, meaning 'to live with'; the term is used to express the bond of kinship and applies to shared lives, such as in neighbours and 'ashira, 'community'. The story was elicited during a conversation about how sentiment and loyalty could sometimes bring people closer together than flesh and blood. In a strongly felt aside, Kheira makes the following comment: 'In my generation the relationship that existed between neighbours was similar to that which related brothers and sisters, maternal and paternal cousins. Our neighbours used to visit us, and help us in sickness, during weddings and during mournings; we shared *ma wa milh* [water and salt – meaning food for sustenance]. Nowadays neither the one nor the other matters any more. No one cares about anyone else except his *nfayyistu* [little self].' Kheira regrets that the links that united individuals in a cohesive social structure are broken. According to her, 'The Beldi composed one family; flesh, blood and *al-'ishra* united us. Islam recommends that Muslims should value blood relationship and Muhammad, peace be upon him, recommends that Muslims should love neighbours and treat them as kin.'

She idealizes a past when the tenets and practices of Islam appear to have provided absolute harmony in the lives and affairs of women: 'Girls used to be modest, decent and considerate of their elders; their voices were not to be heard; unlike girls nowadays who are arrogant and callous.' The cultural horizons have changed. 'Modernity has altered the traditional roles. Young girls are now influenced by alternative cultural ideals and practices,' she adds. In Kheira's traditional view, 'a woman's dignity is enshrined in her marriage, her home and the veil which shields her from the disrespectful gaze of men'. In the West the veil is often taken as a symbol of oppression for women, but Kheira considers it as protection for a woman's dignity. 'The veiling of women in Islam is intended to protect them and enhance their dignity and not to imprison them as they say in the West. The Prophet said modesty leads to solemnity.' At the time I was doing fieldwork in 1990, there was a government decree banning the wearing of the scarf in public offices. When I brought up the issue with her, she was outraged: 'Instead of reinforcing traditional practices and reviving Islam, the government wants us to turn into heathens.'

Even though she refused to marry, she still regards marriage as a means of protection and sexual fulfilment for women. On the occasion of the marriage of one of her heroines, she makes the following comment: 'A husband is for a woman what a lid is for a cooking pot.' The expression is common in Tunis and more specifically among women to emphasize the complementarity of the couple and the importance of marriage in their lives. All her heroines are happy in marriage, and loyalty figures strongly in their universe.

In her first story, 'You Who Rebel Against Fate' (see p. 337), Kheira celebrates the love and loyalty which bind the couple. The heroine, upon hearing about her pre-destined misfortune which consists of becoming a beggar, a singer and a prostitute each for a year, takes her own life: 'I would rather die than disgrace my beloved husband.' In 'The Clever Peasant Girl' (see p. 355), an unjustly divorced wife is given three days to leave the house and take with her 'whatever she values most'. The woman gives the husband a sleeping potion and carries him in a wooden case to her father's home in the country. Upon waking he asked, 'What brought me here?' She replied, 'You told me to leave and take with me whatever I valued most. I thought, gold and silk are earthly possessions. What else do I have dearer than you? So I brought you with me.'

Considered in retrospect, the attitudes and comments

of Ghaya, Sa'diyya and Kheira, through their stories, are disparate and yet complementary. They sketch the framework of women's lives, both then and now. While Sa'diyya's view of sexual mores and women's status is liberal, Kheira's is more traditional in that she sees men and women's roles as strictly differentiated to secure the stability of family, and in that she believes women of her generation were more respected and had a better position than the young women of today. For her part Ghaya joins traditional values with modern thoughts; while believing in virtues such as sexual modesty and patience, she also promotes the notion that women should be able to exercise their intellect outside the home. Their views are representative of modern Tunisia, where often a justified and unavoidable desire for change fulfils itself at the expense of the loss of cherished traditions; this double bind is visible in the society at large.

Telling tales is not so much recounting past events, as a reflection of present cultural values.[15] In the act of narration, memories are brought back to life. The narrators Ghaya, Sa'diyya and Kheira also recreate the past for present purposes. Their tales provide them with a platform to shift from the imaginative to the actual and to express their personal traumas and divergent attitudes. In so doing, they also comment upon and criticize their culture, adding a political dimension to the practice of tale-telling.

In Greek tradition, women's weaving is a metaphor for

narrating the truth. The Greek myth of Philomela is one of several which connects the speech of women with weaving, and it may serve as a paradigm for the narrative power of the female. Philomela was not only raped by her brother-in-law Tereus, but had her tongue cut out to prevent her from revealing his assault. Tereus proclaimed her dead, and only by sending her sister Procne a woven tapestry depicting her fate could she pursue her revenge.

The importance of the paradigmatic myth of Philomela lies in two essential acts: first, the forced silencing; and second, the representation of truth through an alternative method: the art of weaving. Equally the multiple threads of the stories and warp and weft of past and present inherent in the act of narration may serve to communicate, like Philomela's tapestry, the painful experiences of the narrators, and to express the unspeakable. The semantic link between tale-telling and yarn-spinning is established in the classical myth. In Tunisian colloquial Arabic the verb *haka* means to tell tales, to fantasize, and in its extended meaning, to spin, weave. The context reinforces the association. Sa'diyya reports that domestic crafts, i.e. lace-making and embroidery, were sometimes accompanied by the spinning of tales.

The narrators grew up in a conservative Tunisian milieu where women were silent as part of their basic identity. The tales that the narrators like to tell are thresholds through which certain truths about genuine social experience are admitted into discourse; as Sa'diyya explained, 'The chagrins of life would prey too severely if we did not entertain ourselves with tales.' The tales offer a more subjective, ambivalent kind of drama. Reality is depicted as harsh and wearying for most women; fantasy is common in their stories as a compensation and an escape from the unbearable. Women are confined; but not in their imagination. In addition to their moral function, the tales serve as a vehicle for personal aspirations and can, therefore, be seen as a search for a resolution of personal problems.

Overall a picture emerges of women who experienced both economic and intellectual subordination. Barred from access to public spheres, they were confined to the house to fulfil traditional roles, and excluded from any public discourse. The limitations that circumscribed women's lives were nowhere more apparent than in the area of speech. Men monopolized the official public discourse. Women could 'speak' through stories, but compared to the male genres, their stories are dismissed as *khraf* (nonsense) or *hikayat 'ajayiz* (old women's tales).

Men, while quite happy to tell me historical events which were believed to have actually taken place, like the Hilali epic, always referred me to women for fictional tales. The fabulous element in folk tales lends them an air of improbability and unreality. Men's legends describe events that are thought to have happened, and so are supposedly more serious in content. In a society where women were marginalized, their ignored voices were naturally carried over into their tales and narration becomes an exercise in power of sorts.[16]

4

CODES DECODED:
READING THE CULTURE OF CORRECTNESS

Social Correctness

A Beldi family's *sharaf* (honour) is gauged by the sexual comportment of its women, so the maintenance of family honour requires patriarchal control. Many tales portray women as sharing this code of honour and promoting it, whereas in others, the narrators present alternative images of women which conflict with the established model. They express a divergent consciousness which in many ways rejects male control of their persons, proposing instead a model of women's management of their own lives. *Al-hishma* (modesty) is expressed in a variety of ways and particularly through the behaviour of women. In the tales, it has three modes of manifestation: first in physical appearance, as in the customary covering for various parts of the body; then in prescribed personal traits, such as humility, reservation and modesty; and most distinctly, in the social requirement of seclusion; which is intended to ensure chastity and fidelity.

Young married women did not generally come face to face with their male in-laws; and if they did, they were supposed to cover their heads. The practice was necessary, especially when a woman encountered unrelated male guests. In general, women were required to keep out of public places and not to leave their home unless veiled from head to toe. In many tales they are described as 'wrapping themselves in their *sifsari* [white silk veil] and putting on *al-khama* [a black face-veil]. By means of the veil, a woman maintains a symbolic distance between herself and male outsiders to maintain her respectability. Girls of marriageable age, for their part, never cut their hair or uncover it because hair is of the utmost importance to a woman's sexual attractiveness in Arab culture. The idea of the 'eternal feminine' is always associated with a woman whose splendour culminates in her long hair. Uncovering the head and showing the hair loose before marriage is a violation of the modesty code because it suggests a manifestation of sexuality. An example is found in 'The Sparkling Maiden' (see p. 281) where the narrator Sa'diyya comments on the ceremonial ritual of *qassan al-dlal,* (the putting to an end of a girl's spoiling by her parents): 'Her hair had never been seen before, as tradition had it that a girl of marriageable age should bind her hair in an *'oksa* and never show it to her male kinsmen or keep it loose . . .' As soon as they are capable of provoking men's desire, girls' hair is hidden. At puberty, in a ritual led by an elderly woman, a girl's long hair is tied and 'bandaged' in an '*oksa* and she will never show it loose or cut it until her marriage.

Likewise showing parts of the body is, as examplified in the tale 'The Frivolous' (see p. 298), a sign of disrespect and a violation of this social code. 'The two girls undressed and started playing around. The father-in-law came back from work and was shocked. He retired hurriedly to his room shouting: "If you do not feel ashamed you can do what you want, there is no more modesty and respect in this house." ' The girls' husbands were then summoned to discipline their wives. A woman's body is taboo and should be concealed from the gaze of men; thus a modest woman is usually referred to as *mastura* (covered). The traditional garment was often taken as a symbol of the Islamic ethos regarding sexual modesty which is instilled into girls at an early age, and 'proper attire' is the predominant image of feminine respectability in society.

The second aspect of modesty refers to various feminine traits summed up in the Arabic expression: *hishma wa ja'ra wa ras wati* (modesty, shyness and lowered head, or downcast eyes). Most of the girls described in the tales received from their mothers a strict, if informal, training in comportment, so that they learned the graces and the ideals of feminine propriety and discretion associated with speech in public.

A good example is found in 'The Sparkling Maiden' (see p. 281), who is described as her teacher's 'favourite one because, unlike her cousin Za'frana, she is modest

63

and shy, and never speaks loudly'. The *m'allma* was the 'mistress' in the *dar al-m'allma* where girls were sent to learn feminine virtues in addition to sewing, embroidery and lace-making. These older women had the reputation of being extremely strict in relation to the girls' upbringing, and were always likely to succeed where mothers failed. Silence was valued very strongly and was considered an indication of modesty and good upbringing. In 'Sabra' (see p. 97), a man marries a woman and kills their children one by one, but she 'never uttered a word of complaint'. He praises her saying: 'You were well-mannered, you never raised your voice, you never complained, may the womb that bore you be blessed.' Therefore keeping silence becomes an element of proper behaviour for women. Likewise, Kheira recalls nostalgically the strict education, *tarbiyya*, of olden days which considered it shameful for a girl to raise her voice: 'In olden times, girls were modest, their voices were not to be heard, let alone their complaints and grievances.' *Naghma*, 'soft melody', is a descriptive term for a feminine voice, considered a fine quality. Loudness and arrogance can be grounds for divorce. In 'The Frivolous', a young bride who is loud and arrogant is sent back in shame to her father's house, for her inability to behave properly. It is obvious throughout the tales that the girls are always described in terms of their appeal to men, and their suitability as wives. Silence and modesty are particularly recommended in a woman to secure a stable marriage. Hence these desirable qualities are essential for stabilizing and preserving the family, in the view of my informants, who attribute the growing rate of divorce in modern Tunisia to the disappearance of these traditional virtues.

The last and the most crucial aspect of the code of modesty is that which limits a woman's freedom of movement and prescribes correct sexual behaviour. This means that young women should keep out of public places so as not to jeopardize their reputation, compromise their honour and bring *al-'ar* (shame) on their family. A man's house appears throughout the tales as a sanctuary in which the integrity of women is protected. The wives and daughters of kings and rich merchants spend their lives confined in order to defend the family's honour.

In the tales the division of the internal space in the house serves to seclude women, particularly the unmarried ones, effectively cutting them off physically from the public world. Female space is often identified with the house, as opposed to male space which is the outside. *Hurma* is 'the inside', 'the feminine territory which is the enclosed world of secrets, forbidden to men, as much as the open world is reserved for men.' It follows that *haram* (namely, taboo in the exact sense) should be linked with the inside. In accordance with the Islamic concept of *hurma*, women fall into the category of persons and places which are inviolable and worthy of protection. Women are seen as an extension of men's violable physical and social space which it is their duty to protect.

The norm of seclusion is adhered to faithfully in the stories and remains a strong and explicit form of behaviour. All women, with a few exceptions, are described as having never set foot outside home. Such isolation from all men except relatives, clearly ensured that young girls would not jeopardize their reputation. Traditionally the family safeguarded morality by imposing seclusion on women. If a woman violated the rule, she sullied her husband's honour and deserved the pejorative stigma of *hamla* (promiscuous/whore). In the tale 'Women of the Moon' (see p. 164), four old divorcées met to discuss the 'good old days and the story of their marriages'. One of them related that her husband called her a *hamla* and sent her back in shame to her father's home, after discovering that she had spent the whole day out. The use of space reflects and delimits definitions of gender. A woman loses respect when she usurps the masculine space, thus a man's honourable position is in part defined by women. Men are only honourable when their wives are respectable and respectful. To reclaim honour, the husband must assert his moral superiority by condemning her disrespect for the social system and those who represent it.

In her book *Sex, Islam and Ideology*, Mernissi (1983) points out that in North African Muslim society, honour is an emotionally charged concept which relates men's prestige to the sexual behaviour of the women under their authority, be they wives, sisters or mothers. Staying at home means maintaining the integrity of the household, as the respect of the home depends on that of the women in it. Women seen in public are not decent: going out constitutes a threat to their respectability and that of their male kin. The men's place is in the public domain which calls for their visibility, whereas women are to be at home and remain invisible to the public. A deviation from this traditional division would reflect badly on the woman and her family/husband, and might challenge the very structure of patriarchal society.

In the tales, men's honour and dignity are directly linked with their women's respectability and integrity. Thus, women's modesty and seclusion become prerequisites for both men and women if they are to be sanctioned as socially correct. Their roles are intricately linked, as well as stringently defined, and each has his or her restrictive space in which to function. Transgression of each other's space is extremely negative behaviour. Women in the street were seen as promiscuous and shady; as the narrator Ghaya observes: 'Only prostitutes wandered freely.' The necessities that justify a woman's appearing in the street or entering the public sphere are occasional visits to the baths or to relatives' houses or when she is required to perform duties in the absence of a male head. In many stories, the status of women as widows or divorcées enables them to go out and make a living for themselves and their families, mainly through traditional female trades such as spinning wool. There are instances in the tales when men's mismanagement of public affairs legitimize women's transgressing their roles, even dressing like them, thus obtaining the powers, and coming out of the home to redress wrong and set things straight.

Men are not expected to be present in the forbidden

areas which are women's sanctuaries except when eating or sleeping. They have to earn their living outside the home and have little right to enter interior spaces. Though the roles and spaces are well divided, the situation is still asymmetrical; men cross between the private and public areas more freely, the roles being much more diverse and their power more extended, whereas women are confined to limited space and can only share the power exercised in the home.

Containing Sexuality

Islamic doctrine associates women with *fitna* (chaos) and orders men to avoid them in order to preserve social order. Mernissi (1985) has argued that there is a transhistorical view of women's sexuality as dangerous and destructive in its power. Sexuality outside legitimate channels is a challenge to the system, and order in the society can only be maintained when the gender roles are well defined. The structure of society can be disrupted by deliberate transgression, thus the social codes of correctness are laws required by both men and women to preserve harmony and stability. In a discussion with Ghaya and Sa'diyya, it became clear that they believe that women and men cannot meet without the presence of Satan. They are bound to give in to their *shahawat* (sexual drive). One of them added: '*Al-nar we al-barud ma yitqablush*' ('Fire and gunpowder shouldn't get close'), indicating that the meeting of men and women outside the prescribed conditions would cause an explosion – in other words, would inevitably lead to disruption of social order and security. Both women in this instance are interpreting social practices as if they were natural essences. A society that perceives unbridled sexuality as the defining essence of men and women may act to contain it with such intensity that the least gesture becomes a sign of this hidden and forbidden desire – the accidental meeting, the scent of jasmine. When sexuality is seen as the only realm of interaction between the sexes, then other possible forms of interaction are pushed to the margins, or are seen as merely preludes to sexual involvement, and no action such as going to the baths or visiting relatives is innocent.

In the prevailing social system of the tales, the family is an instrument of socialization and control. Girls are under the absolute control of their mothers and the old women in *dar al-m'allma* and are taught from an early age to obey and respect the men of the family. They soon learn the ethics of pre-marital chastity, the reverent fear of men and that preserving *sharaf* (honour) and avoiding *al-'ar* (shame) mean being housebound and morally beyond reproach, for the honour of a girl and her family depends on her chastity and virginity. In several stories, the virginity of the heroine is the concern as well as the guarantee of the family honour. In reality many girls did adhere to these ideals of feminity, observed the rules strictly and refrained from any deviant behaviour which would destroy the honour of the family.

'In 'The Virtuous' (see p. 118), the behaviour and attitudes of the female protagonist are powerfully shaped by the cultural ideals of honour and modesty which have been fostered in her since an early age. The ethics of pre-marital chastity and her respect for the family honour prevent her from abusing her liberty when an occasion arises. 'I am my mother's daughter, I have not been brought up to disgrace my family's *sharaf*,' concludes the heroine, after explaining to her brother that the merchant's story of sullying her honour was slander.

Before leaving, the brother bequeaths a substitute in the person of the bird, explicitly designed to watch over and guard the sister. When she is invited to go out, the bird does not fail to fulfil its role and to remind her of the prohibition of the master: 'If you go out you will regret it;' in other words, 'You will compromise your virginity.' The closed door symbolizes the girl's virginity. The fervour publicly demonstrated by the brother in guarding his sister's honour is intense. His concern for maintaining the family honour takes the form of an obsession with the sexual conduct of his sister: 'She has never stepped across the threshold, no man has ever seen her toe,' he says proudly. It is the woman's personal behaviour which threatens to undermine his prestige. The chastity of the girl is a matter almost of greater importance to her younger brother than to herself, and he finds himself disgraced when her supposed violation of the code becomes public knowledge. This brother is dishonoured, loses 'his manliness', social standing and respect and becomes a slave to the merchant.

Al-'ar is the Arabic word for shame. Actions of *al-'ar* in this context fall on the shoulders of not only the girl herself but on her brother, who stands in a unique position in relation to her, especially where her sexual life is concerned.[17] In another version of the same story, 'The Birthmark' (see p. 224), it is the husband's honour which is sullied by his wife's infidelity. He also loses the respect of his fellow merchants and has to sign over his fortune. In opposition to *al-hishma* which reflects only on an individual, *al-'ar* is a collective attribute; its actions fall on the family.

The loss of virginity is the cause of the most terrible shame, *'ar*, and in one story it casts 'an entire family, seven brothers and their father, into total humiliation'.[18] One means devised to protect a girl's virginity is to seclude her from the outside world, ensuring that she has no opportunity to transgress sexual mores. In 'The Virtuous', the mother is very reluctant to allow her daughter to go out: 'Her father and brothers will kill me if they know,' she said to the old lady. She is protective of the girl's virginity and afraid of the males' reactions. Virginity is the capital the merchant's daughter represents. The family's honour, safeguarded by the eight *shashiyyas*, referring to the male heads, depends on it. In Tunisia the *shashiyya* (red knitted cap) is commonly said to symbolize family honour. It is said to be *m'angra* (straight) if a bride is proved to be a virgin on her wedding night. On seeing her daughter coming back in a nightgown, the mother fears the worst, meaning the loss of her virginity, but her daughter reassures her in a subtle way that the

71

family's honour was 'thanks to God, safe': her continence saved it.

Indeed it is a most humiliating and destructive blow to the honour of a lineage if a girl is discovered to have yielded to her sexual impulses outside marriage. Cleansing with blood is common in villages as 'The Chief of the Tribe's Daughter' (see p. 273) illustrates. On hearing about his unmarried sister's pregnancy, a brother takes his sister under a scorching sun to a distant deserted land and leaves her to die of hunger and thirst.

Within Beldi circles, however, it is usually dealt with among the close relatives. 'God forbid!,' Sa'diyya exclaimed, in a discussion of virginity following the tale. 'Among the Beldi it is not something to talk about, only bedouins publicize it: *shuha*! [it's a shame].' She remembers this happening only once in real life. Among Beldi families, 'if a girl is proved not to be a virgin on her wedding night, she is sent back home on the same night in a white sheet', meaning she loses all her belongings, jewellery, trousseau and so on. The incident is kept secret among close relatives. Men had the right to repudiate their brides on the very first night of their wedding if they did not appeal to them. This tradition was often used to cover up a more serious reason. The paramount importance of virginity for women is a well-known phenomenon in traditional Tunisian society.

Pre-marital sexual relations are the most condemned and shameful act in the case of women. For men, on the other hand, violating the code does not diminish their own honour, but is tacitly tolerated. The two men involved in 'The Virtuous' and 'The Birthmark', the prince and the merchant, are not subjected to any reproach. Their actions are not seen as shameful and do not raise any indignation or disapproval from their fellow merchants. 'Different standards of conduct are demanded from men and women', Raya explains, women have little choice but to accommodate their husbands' promiscuity. Social pressure will be exerted on them to accept it for the sake of the children. 'I was ready to sacrifice my life for the sake of my child's happiness.' If the marriage is in trouble, the woman's sacrifice and tolerance for the husband are deemed essential in preserving the family: 'We must be tolerant and forgiving, for the sake of the family.'

The concept of virginity still figures importantly in the universe of my informants. In a discussion following the tale, Ghaya said: 'It is intrinsically valuable, to be given only to its proper owner, the husband.' Young men and women engage in a certain amount of mild flirtation which is tolerated, but '*Al-busa tsheih we al-qarsa treih we al-fayda kan fi al-saheih* [the kiss will dry, the bite will fade, but your virginity is most important],' Sa'diyya, on that occasion, commented.

At the time I was doing my fieldwork, instances of dead babies found in dustbins, wells or fields were reported in the local press.* I brought up the topic with Ghaya, who

* 19 May 1990.

73

lives in the area where the infanticides were reported. Abortion is legal in Tunisia and is carried out in hospitals. But fear of being punished by the immediate family for sullying its honour seems to be the major reason for infanticide. Ghaya dismissed it as happening not in her neighbourhood – a Beldi upper-class area – but rather among outsiders in the poorer quarters around the fringes of La Marsa. The evil exists, but not in her own group, so it does not damage its honour.

The concept of honour and modesty as it is presented in the tales is related mainly to the correct conduct of the women of the family (voluntarily observed). Modesty, discretion and sexual continence are necessary for the good functioning and preservation of a traditional and closed society.

Embracing Sexuality

The containment of feminine sexuality is the prevailing but not the only ethic in the tales. Some tales offer an opposing image, that of the sexually active and assertive woman who disregards gender segregation and rules of modesty.

'Rdah' (see p. 208), is a story of resistance and has several remarkable features. It celebrates the desire of individuals against the demands of the system, as codified in curbing women's sexual freedom and in the cousin's right to marry his cousin. The merchant's daughter, in 'The Bird without Wings' (see p. 251), seeks to enforce the system, but Rdah refuses to accept it. Rdah, a girl who

74

is not supposed to show an active sexuality, asks her father to bring her musk oil to perfume her hair. This outrages her father who takes it as a manifestation of her sexuality and slaps her. Musk oil, considered as an aphrodisiac by Arab tradition, could be smelt for miles around. Hmid al-Hilali falls in love with Rdah on hearing her description, and he travels to win her love; his passion grows when he smells the perfume of her hair. Rdah is described walking about her apartment, 'dressed in a fine transparent silk petticoat, letting her long hair hang loose, perfumed with musk oil'. This is a manifestation of her femininity and sexual awareness which sets her apart from Sharqat, in 'The Sparkling Maiden' (see p. 281), who covers her hair and keeps it tied back until marriage.

Rdah also escapes her father's control by choosing her marriage partner and disregards the tradition which confers on the parents the right of arbitration in marriage. She is promised to her cousin, but she falls in love with Hmid al-Hilali and receives him in her private apartment in spite of the strict surveillance set by her father. She spends three days and three nights with him in marital bliss, then gives him her necklace as a token of her love. She not only dresses in such a way as to draw attention to her beauty, but she goes as far as to break the rule of seclusion, allowing a lover into her private apartment, which is the most audacious violation of the modesty code. The language of the tales is very 'sexualized'. Dada describes H'mid al-Hilali on his horse as follows:

75

shabb m'ankar zeinu m'zankar
tahta 'uda tibri fagra
ghzarli ghazra
ma dagni sabra

A proud young man
Whose beauty is unique
Mounting a horse/stick
which would cure the heart's desire
He cast a fatal glance at me
and I was lost/could not resist

The word for horse is the same as stick in Bedouin Arabic and is commonly associated in Tunisia with the male organ. When I asked Sa'diyya what was meant by the stick, she made an obscene gesture showing her forearm.

Al-Hajja Mkada (see p. 221) also falls in love with Hmid al-Mitjawwil as soon as she sets eyes on him. She takes a bath perfumed with musk, puts on a fine silk nightgown and invites him into her private apartment and 'they spend three days and nights together'. The images are again very 'sexualized'; in an episode where the hero is offered sweets, he says: '*Sallim 'ala lillak we qullha ma hajti bi qruss bil-'asal hajti bi al-sheykh Hmuda!* [Give my greetings to your mistress and tell her I don't want your pastries; it's a different sort of honey-cake I want!]'

In traditional sweet pastries, the shape of the honey-cake is round with a hole in the middle. It is remarkable that sexual metaphors are extremely explicit in this piece.

When recounting this episode, Saʻdiyya actually imitated love making sounds by humming: 'hun . . . hun'. For her the pleasure of voicing eroticism is obviously a substitute for the physical pleasure that is denied her.[19] In 'The Silk Merchant and His Neighbour' (see p. 258), a married woman engages in a clear campaign of temptation by using all the aphrodisiac resources of seduction known to the Arab tradition to seduce her handsome neighbour.

A step beyond simple manifestation of sexuality and desire is the actual engagement in illicit sex (extra-marital). In 'Baba Turki' (see p. 131), a married woman is involved in illicit relations with the help of her own sister. Women are here markedly seen in a conspiracy against men in authority. The tale points to the tactics of women in support of each other and in co-operation to subvert the stringent code of sexual modesty. The woman expresses the revolt against male control of her body in a form that is legitimate in the women's world. A free union allows a free choice of partner, whereas an arranged union does not. Taking a lover, in this context, is a reaction to the denial of legitimate choice of sexual partner, and a form of release of the frustrations wrought by such a marriage.

In yet another tale, 'Overpowering Desire' (see p. 322), a woman becomes aware of her chaotic sexual response, which cannot be tempered by any social code. She justifies her infidelity by the fact that she couldn't overcome her *nafs* ('self' or 'inner lifeforce'). 'He was tall and hand-some, and as soon as I set eyes on him I was seized with burning passion and desire to lie with him, I have sinned, may God forgive me, *nafsi khanitni,* I could not resist my *nafs.*'

Women's sexuality and their emotional needs are affirmed. In 'Lulsha' (see p. 195), as soon as the sultan's wife sets eyes on the handsome scribe she is seized with passion and desire and presses him to accompany her to her sleeping chamber: 'She sent him her maid saying: "Could you return the passion of one who burns for you." '

In this example we observe a reversal of the situation more usually present in Arab society, where sexual initiative is a masculine prerogative. Sex is explored beyond the boundaries of social conventions. Women's transgressions are glossed over or indirectly justified, nature being 'blamed' for their violations of social codes. Their immoral actions are inexcusable, but the outcome of these tales shows that for women the standards of the cultural models are ignored. The language and the conduct of Ftaytma in 'Ftaytma the Harridan' (see p. 126) are the antithesis of the dominant cultural norms of virtuous modest womanhood. The protagonist is abusive, arrogant, extremely shameless and breaks all taboos. Her licence and non-conformity with the rules of 'normal' behaviour for women earn her the stigma of 'insanity', i.e. lack of judgement, wisdom and responsibility. Her revolt against the in-laws and her self-assertiveness incur disapproval, but she is none the less the agent through whom order is restored in the family, though she must disappear once the objective is achieved. The moral of this story is the undesirability of excess as an escape from the control of the patriarchal order, and Ftaytma is the personification of excess, hence her disappearance at the end.

The fact that Ftaytma has chosen to cut out her father-in-law's tongue is very significant. She attempts to usurp speech and power by cutting out the tongue of the patriarchal tyrant. In her enterprise she is helped by her young husband whose complicity is essential. Out of love and concern for his first bride, he sets out to defy the traditional attitude of his mother and takes an active role in redressing the wrong, changing the status quo and reversing the traditional role. He decides to choose his new bride and robs his own mother of her power and respectability as mother-in-law. Ftaytma is a widespread and popular stereotype in Tunis, and her name is currently used to describe a woman who is frivolous and lacks self-control.

The mad heroine is a new element in the dynamic of resistance, a role which is politically subversive. The narrator Ghaya thoroughly enjoyed the telling of this story. She took delight in expressing Ftaytma's plan of revenge. She created a 'monster heroine', a parody of the angel, and also a mirror of the enraged self that many women suppress. Choosing a woman on the margin of normality makes her suitable for Ghaya's political agenda. Madness appears as the point at which the narrator decides to voice her suppressed desires, her truth. In her extreme actions, Ftaytma avenges not only herself and the young woman who preceded her, but, for Ghaya, she avenges as well all the Tunisian women who were bullied and ill-treated by their female in-laws. Through her, the narrator manages to break with the Beldi propriety which places the wife completely under the control of the mother-in-law, a negative memory in her own life. The excess in the story is vicariously experienced by Ghaya, whose freedom is regained in the imaginary time and space provided by the tale.

Women's folk tales are a powerful conditioning agent; they promote continuity in the culture. Yet they can, at the same time, bring great comfort to women's lives. In the act of story-telling, the women narrators transcend their Beldi identity and social norms to express their own personalities. They express their sexuality and inner desires artfully and wilfully without reservation, thus subverting the strict demands of social decorum.

Sexuality as Performance

Racy jokes among women is another form of irreverent subversive discourse. They portray an example of humour that ridicules mainstream cultural beliefs and targets men and manhood as butts of the joke. The pattern of a female protagonist and a male victim is recurrent in the humorous tales in the present collection. Racy tales are told to make fun of men and manhood as well as to challenge the foundation upon which the entire system of gendered beliefs and behaviours have been elaborated. The ironic distance between ideals represented by these cultural codes about gender, and the reality of these codes in practice, makes us laugh.[20]

'The Innocent Virgin' (see p. 262) provides a good example. The beginning of the story could have been the framework of a conventional story except for the language which indicates that it is not. But the twist at the end subverts the initial framework. The tale, however, does not posit that there are no women virgins; rather it takes a mainstream cultural belief and subverts it. It allows sexual freedom that is socially taboo for women. In this example, the mainstream cultural notion that promiscuity is a male prerogative and that girls should be chaste is reversed: the 'chaste' young bride is not only the opposite, but questions the man's sexual adequacy. It is a common thing that women, to ridicule men, talk about their sexual inadequacy.

The husband in the tale is doubly or triply duped by 'the innocent young bride' who knows more than he expects, and she literally humiliates him. His preference for innocent women turns against him and reveals his own inadequacy and ignorance. On a larger scale, men's underestimation of women's knowledge is often a manifestation of their own lack of it. We see also in the story that men have obtained their power not by merit, but by biology. The 'phallus', the symbol of patriarchal power that not only denotes but justifies at every level the domination of men, is conflated with the biological; the penis is symbol of the petty power men wield over women because they happen to be born men in a male-dominated

81

society. Social coding, then, becomes funny when we see it not as a logical construction based on merit or wisdom in reality, but instead as performance that society demands. It is especially funny when the 'powerful' are foolishly egostistical, like this character, and self-right-eously reveal their ignorance while presuming to instruct others. The story makes us laugh because the male protag-onist, in his arrogance and smugness, reduces male power (the phallus) to its common denominator – the penis – which all men have, whatever the content of their charac-ter or the wisdom of their spirits. All the rights and responsibilities that should be part and parcel of male power are lost on this fellow; he is an exhibitionist, who also lays bare the hypocritical foundation upon which essential concepts of gender are based. By the same token, the crude realism of the third female protagonist's response redefines the whole idea of female innocence. For however crude she may be, she is not hypocritical: a penis is not a phallus.

How do the tellers and listeners react to this tale? On the one hand, the improper behaviour of both the chief male and female protagonists makes us laugh and realize that proper gendered behaviour must have more positive content; it must uphold the spirit of the gender codes, not just the biology. On the other hand, by showing that all men enjoy privilege, although only some earn it, and by showing that all females can be accused of feminine sexual weakness, despite their obedience to the sexual code of modesty (i.e. the first two 'ignorant' female protagonists), this tale raises the spectre of gendered sexuality as performance rather than an essence. We are born with a sex but we become gendered. The difficulty of reading sexuality as performance is that it does not replace a false code with a true one, rather it challenges the believability of all codes. Nevertheless, society cannot operate without codes.

Women here are not merely laughing off oppression, rather they are laughing at improper behaviours. The narrators find it easier to translate the laughable distance between codes and their practice into a call for more responsible, appropriate behaviours than into a call for the subversion of all codes. What gives the story its power to make us laugh is the dynamic and ironic distance between the ideal and the real. This distance may make us adjust the real to come closer to the ideal; or alternatively, it may suggest the need to adjust the ideal to fit the real. Neither the ideal nor the real are static categories, rather they exist in dynamic relation to one another, and can give rise to repression on the one hand (forcing the ideal) and to revolution on the other hand (exposing a distortion of the real, a distortion based on an individual or a group's desire for power). The narrators, Ghaya, Sa'diyya and Kheira, can then still support 'proper behaviour' in gender divided spheres while ridiculing the hypocrisy that this division can give rise to.

These humorous stories provide a vision of a laughing sub-culture. Female humour in this context is largely anti-male pretension and induces women to laugh together at the expense of men, and to recognize their own strength and intelligence.[21] In this sub-culture, serious matters of unbearable weight on mind and body are seemingly laughed off by womenfolk.

5

CONCLUSION

One of the main characteristics of oral literature is its
verbal flexibility and openness, which allow the perpetual
creation of new features. Orality allows a teller poetic
licence and leaves a place for women story-tellers to pass
on a form of tradition that is not rigid. Ghaya, Sa'diyya
and Kheira manipulate this flexibility to expand,
embroider and suit their inspiration. Past and present
background information and personal experience make
up the material from which they draw the originality of
their inspiration, enriching of the text and making living
tradition of it, continually composing rather than
imposing. Some folklorists have placed emphasis on performance as an act of creation. The narrators are not only
tradition bearers, but they are also creators in their own
right and their choice of narratives and narrative choices
reflect their personalities.

The tales are old stories but retold to bring past into
present and to understand the present through the past.
In telling and retelling the stories the women allow their

cultural identities to be shaped, explore alternative consciousness and interpret their individual and social reality; the oral nature of the discourse affords them a medium to do so. Tale-telling gives the women the space to probe certain issues, pass on values, condemn what they see as wrong, sanction what they approve of as being valuable and want to keep. Sometimes their choices support patriarchal patterns because they are meaningful to the narrators and validate a code that matters, in short, express their share of power.

Tales are told at communal times, to share and pass on the secret lore concerning love, marriage and destiny, a kind of ritualization of social values. The narrators are obviously in complete agreement in terms of the value system that should be kept. They are representative of a generation sharing the same geographical and cultural space. By looking at what they leave behind, what they struggle with and what they insist upon keeping, we see the tales as the living traditions they are.

Notes

1. Interest in Tunisian oral literature started with the work of French missionaries, in particular André Louis, who compiled an ethnographic bibliography of Tunisia. Some isolated attempts to collect tales were made at the beginning of the century among local intellectuals and published in the *Revue Tunisienne* and the *Revue de l'Institut des Belles Lettres Arabes* (IBLA). There was no attempt to collect the tales systematically. These reviews contained about thirty tales but no commentary relating the texts to any background. The resulting texts are often little more than abstracts or summaries which were clearly inadequate for any analysis in depth. The early collections (Labonne 1920, Bou-

quero 1922, Ben Attar 1923, Aslan 1933, Rivals 1947, Mzali 1949) were frequently intended for primary education. Most editors did not even include the names of those who told the stories, and there exists no information on where and when the stories were told.

2. Connelly noted: 'In case of some narratives, such as 'Antar or Hilali tales, a skilled story-teller well versed in his tradition could stretch the episodes out over a year, while maintaining an interested and paying audience.' (1986: 7)

3. In the later collections in Arabic and French (Guiga, T. 1968, Laroui 1978, Houri-Pasotti 1980), a few editors have commented upon the texts themselves, in terms of form and style, but have given only the most basic information regarding the narrators and the context of narration.

The existing published literature suggests that little attention has been paid to the importance of women's expressive behaviour. During the 1940s and the early 1950s researchers were interested in women's expressive behaviour only as mani-fested in charms, quaint customs and beliefs and home remedies, but tale-telling was neglected, in particular in women's folklore. This trend continued throughout the 1960s and into the 1970s. André Louis's investigation of tales and their tellers, while pri-marily concerned with men and tale-telling as a cultural activity, discusses women story-tellers only very briefly. Bouhdiba's collec-tion and study of ten children's tales is mainly concerned with the sociological function of tale-telling and refers only in passing to the roles of women in this activity. Baklouti (1988) has col-lected and published tales from both men and women, but does not relate the tales to their tellers or undertake any work of comparison.

A man who for many years has been a major force in the co-ordination of the collection of folk literature throughout Tunisia on behalf of the Ministry of Culture is Muhammad al-Marzouki. He has edited and published a great number of folktales and poetry (al-Marzouki 1967, 1968, 1971, 1976), and incorporated folklore into plays and the media through radio and television. Another contemporary Tunisian who has been active in this undertaking is Tahar Guiga, who published the texts of some of the Hilali tales collected by his father in both Arabic and French (Guiga, T. 1968). In-depth studies of the literary and social significance of tales and tale-telling in Tunisia are generally lack-ing. Some efforts have been made by various researchers at the

87

Institut National d'Archeologie et d'Arts, but the emphasis in the works published in their quarterly *Cahiers d'Archeologie· et d'Arts* tends to be restricted to the form of the tale as written, without commentary on the oral text.

4. A collection of tales by Laroui (1989) has been published recently. Laroui, who died a few years ago, was not a traditional story-teller, but a professional media programmer who adapted women's tales for radio and television. Moreover, women's tales when told by a male broadcaster lose their authenticity and this recontextualization renders them unsuitable as primary sources.

5. Previous folklore studies in Tunisia have been mainly rooted in formalist tale-type analysis or structuralist approaches to literature, and have been carried out by men clearly unaware of the body of women's folklore that is given voice only in the exclusive presence of women. As a result, earlier studies of folklore have generally focused only on male art forms. In traditional Tunisian society, as I noted above, men's activities usually take place in the public arena, and women's in a private setting. As Ardener (1972) has pointed out, surface structure expresses the male view of the world, obscuring the existence at a deeper level of an autonomous female worldview. Influential studies of the tale as a genre have often considered the tale as an independent entity and have therefore isolated the content from the narrator and the social and historical context. The tale as a product has been studied for its structures, with a focus on commonly occurring components, e.g., in the manner of Propp (1970), and symbolic representations, in the manner of Levi-Strauss (1958, 1963). Scholars using comparative techniques, e.g., the historico-geographic method, have looked at the tale in terms of its distribution, its place of origin and the history of its dissemination. The oral formulaic school concentrated upon the procedures whereby tales are generated, an approach pioneered by Parry (1971) and Lord (1960). In many cases, the anonymous collectivity has been the focus of folkloric attention.

The past couple of decades, however, have witnessed a shift in perspective in the disciplinary conception of folklore that has begun to change the research emphasis. Recent performance-centred perspectives (Dégh 1972, Ben-Amos and Goldstein 1975, Pentikainen 1978, Bauman 1986) have focused on a growing awareness of the role of the individual narrator in oral narration, the performance context and the meaning of folklore for its users. Folktale narration as a social phenomenon has been most thoroughly studied by Dégh in her attempt to chart the teaching situation, the context of presentation, and the personality of individual folktale narrators in the southern Hungarian village of Kaskad.

Recent approaches to the analysis of folk tales (Ben-Amos 1975, Pentikainen 1978, Dégh 1979, Bauman 1986, Kaivola-Bregenhoj 1989) reveal what the individual story-teller brings to the performance. Through the actual story-telling process, the audience gains insight into the narrator's worldview. In my fieldwork, I asked the narrators about their lives, their sources and the occasions of story-telling. In the present collection, the narrators Sa'diyya, Ghaya, and Kheira occasionally interrupt their narratives to inject personal remarks, making tale-telling much more than mere entertainment; it becomes a process of creativity and a means of addressing cultural issues.

The repertoires seen in relation to the narrators and their own lives, become important biographical sources leading to a more complete understanding of these cultural products. It is interesting to note that the narrators have different attitudes *vis-à-vis* their worlds. Analysing the prevalent themes in their repertoires on the one hand, and considering the socio-cultural views and values expressed in asides containing personal opinions on the other, can reveal much about their worlds and their perspectives on it. In fact, the tales the narrators like to tell fit their life experiences and are rich in features that are not only individual to the narrators, but also reflect the world of their female audiences.

Başgoz (1987), using data from Turkey, demonstrates that the digression (individual remark of the narrator) can express the ideology, values and worldview of the performer. During the performance, the plot line is sometimes temporarily suspended, and the teller comes to the foreground to speak in a personal voice: 'He speaks about his own troubles ... He renders his judgement about the attributes and behavior of the story characters. He discloses his opinions, ideas, and values ... He criticizes like a social commentator.' (Başgoz 1987: 7)

6. In his book *Catégories de la société tunisoise dans la deuxième moitié du XIXème siècle*, Ben Achour (1989) explains that the Beldi's sense of worth and their disdain for outsiders were derived from the city being a prestigious economic, religious and cultural centre. (Achour 1989: 137)

7. In *Two-Dimensional Man* (1974) Cohen focuses on the

89

processes whereby interested groups manipulate different types of symbolic patterns of action in order to articulate a number of organizational functions when they cannot organize themselves along formal lines. He defines symbols as, 'objects, acts, relationships or linguistic formations occurring in patterns of activity, ritual, ceremonial, gift exchange, acts of etiquette, eating and drinking, and various cultural traits that constitute the style of life of a group.' (Cohen 1974: 32)

8. In her thesis on the language of women of Tunis, Trabelsi explains that the decrease in the use of diphthongs among women is due to geographic mobility and mixing. (1988: 253)

9. Harris sums up the idea of an urban ethos succinctly: 'An urban ethos may be said to exist when a people, consciously or unconsciously, abstractly or concretely, values, endorses and seeks to perpetuate the various urban traits of its culture.' (Harris 1956: 279)

10. The following information about the narrators and their sources is based on material gathered during fieldwork in Tunisia from December 1989 to April 1990.

11. Abu-Lughod in her book *Veiled Sentiments* (1986) came to the same conclusions. She studied *ghinnawas*, the poetry of sentiment in a bedouin society, and concluded that poetry was used in certain contexts as a medium of expressing and commenting on personal life and experience: '*Ghinnawas* can be considered poetry of personal life: individuals recite such poetry in a specific context, for the most part private, articulating in it sentiments about their personal situations and closest relationships.' (Abu Lughod 1986: 31)

Abu Lughod pointed out that this poetry was collective; it was either the changes wrought on the expected lines or the circumstances of the poet that gave these standard forms their human dimension. In a similar way, the Beldi stories, especially as they seem to be passed from woman to woman, from generation to generation, are generic to a great degree, but reveal their personal and cultural specificity in relation to the narrators' artistic innovations and personal circumstances.

12. In her study, Finnegan concluded that most stories arise from the combination and recombination of motifs, upon which the individual is free to build. (Finnegan 1970: 387)

13. Different studies of tales have postulated various sorts of psychological functions that the tales serve. According to Fischer, one of them would be to express emotions which cannot be

expressed directly. The folk tale is 'a vehicle for the expression of existing emotions which have for one or another reason been denied expression.' (Fischer 1963: 257) Abu-Lughod in *Veiled Sentiments* noted a discrepancy between the sentiments generally expressed in the poetry of the intimate world of the bedouin tribe of Awlad 'Ali and those expressed about the same situations in ordinary social interaction and discourse. She studied closely the poetry of Fayga, a young bedouin woman whose verses reflected her reactions to her arranged marriage to a cousin, and described it as 'a medium in which she could voice responses not culturally appropriate for a young bedouin'. As a bedouin girl from a 'good family', who is expected to comply with the rules of modesty and propriety, 'she should not resist a marriage arranged by her brother'. (Abu-Lughod 1986: 221) But her poems suggested a deeply frustrated self that her ordinary behaviour and discourse disguised.

14. The tales reveal a direct reversal of social roles, similar to the reversals in the context of festive behaviour in early modern France. See *Women on Top* (Davis 1979: 210)

15. In his research on the Hilali tradition in Libya and Jordan, Ayoub (1984) reported two instances of this phenomenon. He shows how the Libyan and Palestinian story-teller re-tells the Hilali Epic in terms of present culture and how each uses the past to protest against the present through his 'double articulation of the message'.

16. Ghazoul (1980) examines narration as power, in terms of gender opposition. She looks at the position of women as narrators and considers Scherazade's art as an appropriation and inversion of power; the discourse of the night involves an inversion which is the only solution for the *conteuse* to gain power and save her neck. The power of the word, in an intimate situation, compensates for women's powerlessness in public life and becomes a substitute for the real power they are denied.

17. In an analysis of the concept of honour in an Andalusian village, J. Pitt-Rivers came to the same conclusion: 'Honour is a collective attribute shared by the nuclear family. Individual honour derives from individual conduct but produces consequences for others who share collective honour with the individual.' (1977: 24)

18. Abou Zeid discusses honour and shame among the Bedouins of the western desert of Egypt. He draws a distinction between *sharaf* and *'Irdh*, two terms translated into English as 'honour'.

'Irdh, the term for honour in the second tale, is not an exact translation, for, as Abou Zeid explains, it is 'used only in connection with female chastity'. (Abou Zeid 1965: 256)

19. Foucault's 'discourse/intercourse'. (Foucault 1979: 199)

20. Women seem all too glad when men fail to live up to the ideals of manhood, the ideals on which their superiority is based, especially when lapses occur through desiring women. See *The Romance of Resistance: Tracing Transformations of Power Through Bedouin Women.*

21. The political use of humour, especially as a mechanism for social change and for cultural expression, is commonplace. Clinton (1982) stresses that feminist humour exposes the sources of imbalance and attempts to eradicate them. According to Clinton, because feminist humour sheds light on women's oppression and points out the need for its elimination, it functions as a source for cultural and political change.

Select Bibliography

Abou Zeid, Ahmed, 'Honour and Shame among the Bedouins of Egypt', *Honour and Shame: The Values of Mediterranean Society*, Peristiany, J. G. (ed.) (London, Weidenfeld and Nicolson, 1965)

Abu-Lughod, Lila, *Veiled Sentiments: Honour and Poetry in a Bedouin Society* (Berkeley and Los Angeles, University of California Press, 1986)

Ardener, 'Belief and the Problem of Women', *The Interpretation of Ritual*, Jean La Fontaine (ed.) (London, Tavistock Publications, 1972)

Aslan, M., *Scènes de la vie du bled* (Tunis, 1933)

Ayoub, A., 'The Hilali Epic: Material and Memory,' *Revue d'Histoire Maghrebine* 35/36 (1984)

Baklouti, Naceur, *Contes populaires de Tunisie* (Tunis, Institut National d'Archeologie et d'Arts, Maison Tunisienne d'Editions, 1988)

Başgoz, Ilhan, 'Digression in Oral Narrative: A Case Study of Individual Remarks by Turkish Tellers', *Journal of American Folklore* 99 (1987)

Bauman, R., *Story, Performance and Event* (Cambridge, Cambridge University Press, 1986)

Ben Achour, Mohammed al-Aziz, *Catégories de la Société Tunisoise dans la deuxième moitié du XIXème siècle* (Tunis, Institut National d'Archeologie et d'Arts, 1989)

Ben-Amos, Dan and Goldstein, K., *Folklore, Performance and Communication* (The Hague, Mouton, University of Pennsylvania Press, 1975)
Ben Attar, S. *Le Bled en lumières: Folklore Tunisien* (Paris, 1923)
Bouhdiba, A., *L'Imaginaire Maghrebin: étude de dix contes pour enfants* (Tunis, Maison Tunisienne d'Editions, 1977)
Bouquero de Voligny, R., 'A Tunis derrière les murs', *Contes et legendes*, Geunard and Franchi (eds.) (Tunis, 1923)
Clinton, K., 'Making Light: Another Dimension – Some Notes on Feminist Humour', *Trivia* 1 (1982)
Cohen, Abner, *Two-Dimensional Man: An Essay on the Anthropology of Power and Symbolism in Complex Society* (London, Routledge and Kegan Paul, 1974)
Connelly, Bridget, *Arab Folk Epic and Identity* (Berkeley and Los Angeles, University of California Press, 1986)
Davis, Nathalie, *Les Cultures du Peuple* (Paris, Editions Aubier-Montaigne, 1979)
Dégh, Linda, *Folktales and Society: Story-Telling in a Hungarian Peasant Community* (Bloomington: Indiana University Press, 1972)
Finnegan, Ruth, *Oral Literature in Africa* (Oxford, Oxford University Press, 1970)
Fischer, J. L., 'The Sociopsychological Analysis of Folktales', *Current Anthropology* 41 (1963)
Foucault, Michel, *The History of Sexuality, Vol 1, An Introduction* (London, Penguin Books, 1979)
Ghazoul, Ferial, *The Arabian Nights: A Structural Study* (Cairo, Cairo Associated Institution for the Study and Presentation of Arab Cultural Values, 1980)
Guiga, Tahar, *La Geste Hilalienne* (Tunis, Maison Tunisienne d'Editions, 1968)
Harris, M., *Town and Country in Brazil* (New York, Columbia University Press, 1956)
Houri-Pasotti, M., *Contes de Ghezala* (Paris, Editions Aubier-Montaigne, 1980)
Kaivola-Bregenhoj, Annikki, 'Folklore Narrators', *Studia Fennica* 33 (Helsinki, Suomalaisen Kirjallisunden Seura, 1989)
Laroui, Abdelaziz, *Vieux Contes de Tunisie* (Tunis, Maison Tunisienne d'Editions, 1978)
— *Hikayat Laroui* (Tunis, Maison Tunisienne d'Editions, 1989)
Labonne, A., *Le Pervier d'or: Contes et legendes de la régence de Tunis* (Lyon, Editions du Fleuve, 1920)

Levi-Strauss, C., 'The Structural Study of Myth', *Myth: A Symposium,* T. A. Sebeok (ed.) (Bloomington, Indiana University Press, 1958)

— *Structural Anthropology* (New York, Basic Books, 1963)

Lord, Albert, *The Singer of Tales* (Cambridge, Harvard University Press, 1960)

Louis, André, *Bibliographie Ethno-Sociologique de la Tunisie,* Institut des Belles Lettres Arabes, Centre National de Recherche Scientifique (Tunis, Imprimerie N. Bascone, 1977)

al-Marzouki, Mohammad, *Al-Adab al-Sha'bi fi Tunis* (Tunis, Maison Tunisienne d'Editions, 1967)

— *Abd al-Smad Qal Kilmat* (Tunis, Maison Tunisienne d'Editions, 1968)

— *Al-Jaziya al-Hilaliyya* (Tunis, Maison Tunisienne d'Editions, 1971)

— *Hassuna al-Lili* (Tunis, Maison Tunisienne d'Editions, 1976)

Mernissi, Fatima, *Beyond the Veil: Male-Female Dynamics in a Modern Muslim Society* (London, Saqi Books, 1985)

Mzali, H., *Contes de Tunisie,* Receuillies par Ecoles de Tunis (Tunis, Maison Tunisienne d'Editions, 1949)

Parry, Milman, *The Making of Homeric Verse* (Oxford, Clarendon Press, 1971)

Pentikainen, Juha, 'Oral Repertoire and Worldview' *Folklore Fellows Communications* XCIII (Helsinki, Suomalaisen Kirjallisunden Seura, 1978)

Pitt-Rivers, Julian, 'Honour and Social Status in an Andalusia Village', *The Fate of Schechem or The Politics of Sex: Essays in the Anthropology of the Mediterranean,* Goody, Jack (ed.) (Cambridge, Cambridge University Press, 1977)

Propp, V., *Morphologie du conte* (Paris, Le Seuil, 1970)

Rivals, L., *Contes de la gazelle en pays d'Islam* (Paris, 1947)

Trabelsi, Chadia, *Usages linguistiques des femmes de Tunis* (Thèse de 3ème Cycle, Paris III, Departement des Langues et Civilisations de l'Inde, de l'Orient et de l'Afrique du Nord, 1988)

Turki, Zouheir, *Tunis Naguère et Aujourd'hui* (Tunis, Maison Tunisienne d'Editions, 1978)

THE TALES

GHAYA

I
Sabra

God is omnipresent.

Once upon a time there was a king who had a daughter called Sabra who was of exceptional beauty, exceptional wisdom and exceptional patience and modesty. When she was of an age to get married, he put up a sign on the door of his palace which read: 'I would marry Sabra to whoever gave three loads of gold as a bride-price. One for her beauty, one for her wisdom and one for her patience.' This put off many suitors. One day, the king was sitting on the verandah of his palace when he saw the sea fill up with ships. The vizier said to him, 'If they are warriors coming in peace, we have no provisions for them, and if they have come to fight, we have no means of fighting back.' The king told him, 'Go and see what they want and come back.' So the vizier went to see the captain of the ship and asked him if they came in peace or war. The captain answered, 'We haven't come to fight, we have come seeking kinship with his honour the king.' The vizier asked, 'Do you know the conditions?' The captain said, 'We do, and we have brought everything we need in the ships.' The vizier asked, 'Who do you want her for?' He said, 'For Prince So-and-So.' They went to see the king and asked for his daughter's hand in marriage. The order was given to celebrate the wedding.

Seven days and seven nights of festivities ensued. Then the prince invited them to be his guests for three days and three nights as was the tradition. Eventually the marriage was concluded and on the last day of the visit, a new day is born and he who prays for the Prophet will be blessed, the prince instructed the bride that she was not to take anyone with her except her black maid, Dadah. So he took his new wife and Dadah and they boarded the ship heading for his father's land. When they landed, a carriage took them to a far-away palace. The palace was magnificent; the courtyard was paved with marble with a fountain in the middle, the rooms were vaulted with inner chambers and bed alcoves with upholstered divans, but there wasn't a soul there. He showed her the kitchen and the provisions and everything she needed. Dadah cooked the dinner, they ate and went to bed. The next day, Sabra got up and saw to the housework herself, as if she had never been a princess.

Time passed, and Sabra conceived a child. When Sabra

was eight months' pregnant, it was announced that war had broken out, and that the prince was to lead the troops. Before he left he told her: 'Your child is due next month; may God be with you. I have asked an old lady who lives round the corner to come and keep you company until you have the baby. I have provided linen, cotton and silk for you to prepare the baby's layette.' With that he left.

The old lady came to keep her company every night. One night, God willed it, her hour came and Sabra went into labour and gave birth to a bouncing baby boy. *Praise to God who created him with such beauty.* The baby crawled and toddled, held to the wall and walked. In real life a child grows in a year or two, but just in a couple of words in a tale. When the prince returned victorious from the war, his son was three years old. Dadah suggested she would take him to meet his father and the mother agreed. She bathed and dressed the child up and put on his royal golden bracelet. The maid took him to the ship. The streets were decorated and music was playing to celebrate the victory. Everybody came to congratulate the prince: the viziers, the courtiers. When the prince saw the child he asked Dadah: 'Is this my son?' She replied: 'Yes, master.' He kissed him, then took him and threw him into the depths of the sea. Dadah lost her senses and went back home, wailing. She found Sabra dressed up in her best clothes, perfumed and made up, waiting for her husband. She asked what was going on and the maid related to her what had happened. Sabra answered: 'Don't say a word. The master has been away for three years and we shouldn't cause him any trouble or discomfort. It was his son and he was free to do as he pleased with him.' So the maid kept quiet. Sabra had the great virtues of humility and modesty, *she is a woman, such is her lot.* So when the prince arrived at the palace she welcomed him with great joy and made no mention of her son and showed no sign of grief.

Five years passed and Sabra conceived again. She was seven months' pregnant when the prince had to go and lead the troops into battle again. The same old lady living round the corner came to keep her company until she gave birth to a second bouncing baby as beautiful as the moon, *praise to God who created him with such a beauty.* The baby crawled, toddled, held to the wall and walked. In real life a child grows in a year or two, but just in a couple of words in a tale. When he was two years old, the prince came back victorious and Dadah suggested she should take his second son to meet him, hoping that this time he would have learnt the importance of a child and wouldn't treat him as he had treated the first. But when the prince saw his son he took him and threw him into the sea. Again, Dadah went back home wailing, and the mistress of the house asked her to keep quiet and not discomfort the master.

After five or six years Sabra conceived again and the prince had to lead the troops into war. She gave birth to a girl as beautiful as the moon, *praise to God who created her with such a beauty.* The baby girl crawled, toddled, held to the wall and walked. The prince came back after two years, victorious and Dadah suggested that she would take the

100

baby girl to meet her father, hoping that he wouldn't do the same with her as with her brothers, because she was a girl. The girl was bathed and dressed, and taken to meet her father. But when he saw her, he kissed her and threw her into the sea. Sabra showed no sign of grief and uttered no word of discontent.

Sabra lived with the prince for fifteen years. She was now forty. The prince addressed her one day saying: 'You are old now, and you can't conceive any more, and I love children. I would like you to find a bride for me. I have provided a carriage to take you and Dadah to look for her. I have one condition.' She asked, 'What is it?' He answered, 'I want a girl as beautiful as you are, but eighteen years younger.'

She wrapped herself in her white silk veil and began her search from house to house. When she was asked whom she wanted the girl for, and answered that it was for her husband, all the women insulted her: 'Shame on you! How could you be such a fool looking for a bride for your own husband.' Sabra was subjected to every humiliation. For a whole year she had to go out every day and come back late in the afternoon with sore feet and dizzy head. She said to him one day: 'No luck. I've seen them all – short, tall, beautiful – but I haven't been able to find anyone exactly like me.' He told her: 'I understand the old lady who lives at the end of the street has a beautiful daughter. Go and ask for her hand and accept any bride-price she asks.'

She knocked on the old lady's door and asked to go in

and see the daughter. She stood marvelling at the girl's beauty and asked for her hand for her husband. When she said it was for her husband, the old lady exclaimed, 'What? Are you serious?' But Sabra begged her to accept and explained she would give her a basket of pearls, a basket of diamonds and a basket of rubies as her bride-price. The old woman agreed and Sabra heaved a sigh of relief.

The prince brought in builders to transform the palace and build on four identical rooms. He had them decorated and furnished in exactly the same way. He had Sabra prepare the cake for the wedding celebrations and asked her to help him dress in preparation for the ceremony. She did so. He then told her to go and bring the bride. When she came back with the girl, he asked her to give him away by placing her hand on his head and taking him to the bridal chamber as was the tradition. This she did, and then offered them the traditional sweet drink. As she did so, the end of her scarf brushed the candle flame and caught fire. She quickly took it in her hand and put it out, saying: 'You killed my children and burned my flesh and blood. Now I have a rival, my patience is exhausted and my wisdom has run out.' He stood up and kissed her on the forehead, saying: 'You were good-mannered, you never raised your voice, may the womb that bore you be blessed. Come with me to the hallway. *The woman who is patient will build a happy home. All sacrifice is good.* She went with him to find three handsome young men. He told her: 'Here are your own children, and the third is your son-in-law. The bride is your daughter. I want you to go and take the carriage and bring your daughters-in-law.'

The order was given to celebrate the three weddings. Seven days and seven nights of festivities. Later he told her: 'We are going to start our marriage anew. Don't think that I have emptied my father's treasury for nothing. I saw your beauty from the start, but how could I test your patience and resignation?' There is no resignation with a rival, and no patience until the loss of a child. And they lived safely and procreated until death did them part.

II

The Vizier's Daughter

God is omnipresent.

Once upon a time there lived a king, *there is no real king but Allah*, who had a vizier who was so close to him that he had the final say in everything. His privileged position made him many enemies and as 'whoever is fortunate is envied' (Arabic proverb) they went to set the king's mind against him, saying that he was corrupt and had become rich by taking bribes. 'His house is better than yours,' etc. Eventually the king was turned against him and decided to find a way to get rid of him. One day, he decided to take him as usual for a drive. They got into the carriage and set off. They went on until they reached Mornag or Al-Muhamadiyya. They found the locals lounging around making tea, as usual. The teapot was bubbling on the brazier. The king addressed the vizier, saying: 'What is

104

the water saying?' The vizier answered: 'Does the water really speak?' The king answered: 'Yes, it does.' The vizier went on: 'How come?' The king said: 'You tell me why.' He granted him three days to give him the answer, otherwise he would be beheaded.

The vizier went home, sad and heavy-hearted. His daughter 'Aysha who was dear to him and he to her, noticed his mood and enquired: 'Father, what's wrong? May God protect you. I am ready to die for you.' He answered: 'What can I say? I think my hour is drawing near.' She replied: 'May God protect you! Lifespans are in God's hands.' He continued: 'The king has been set against me,' and he told her what had happened. She answered: 'Is that all?' He answered: 'What else? Does water really speak?' She answered: 'Yes, it does.' He asked: 'How come?' She answered: 'Laugh your morose ideas away and in three days I will give you the answer.'

For two days he was happy and jolly, eating and having a good time. *A new day is born and he who prays for the Prophet will be blessed.* On the third day she gave him the answer: 'I am water pouring from the heavens, making the earth smooth and giving life to the plants that give you warmth in the cold.' He went to see the king and gave him the answer. The king said, 'Fine, you have saved your skin.'

Time passed, but the king's mind was still turned against the vizier. He asked him to go for a stroll with him. They walked and walked until they came to a pile of marble stones. They found one piece more beautiful than any

105

they had seen before. The colour was white and pink and grey. The king asked the vizier to pick it up and make out of it forty uniforms for his guards within three days, otherwise he would be beheaded. The vizier went back home, sad and heavy-hearted. He said to his daughter: 'You found the answer for me last time but I don't think you can this time. He has asked me to make out of this marble forty uniforms for the guards.' She said: 'Is that all? Don't you worry. Laugh your morose ideas away. In three days' time I will give you the answer.' On the following day she asked her father to let her have the carriage to go for a drive. She got in and set off for Kelibia, where the beach is wide and the sand shines like silver. She filled her embroidered kerchief and went back home. She said to her father: 'Go and see the king and say, "The uniforms are ready. I have tried all the haberdashers, Jews and Muslims, in all the souks of the medina, but I couldn't find anyone who could have the trimmings ready in three days. Since you have the authority as king, call them and ask them to supply the trimmings."' *A new day is born and he who prays for the Prophet will be blessed.* The vizier took the kerchief filled with sand and told him: 'The uniforms are ready but we are running late because of the trimmings. Call the haberdashers and ask them to supply them.' He called them all, Jews and Muslims. They said: 'Can we make trimmings from sand?' The vizier asked: 'And can we make uniforms out of marble?' They all went out. The king addressed the vizier, saying: 'Again you have saved your skin.'

106

Time passed and again the king was still not satisfied. One evening, as they were sitting on their balcony, he told him: 'I grant you three days to bring over food that has never been cooked by fire, borne on a tray on four cows without spilling it.' Again the vizier went back home, sad and heavy-hearted, and related his anxiety to his daughter. Again, 'Aysha quelled his fears, saying: 'Laugh your morose ideas away and tomorrow God will fulfil our wishes. I will accomplish it within three days.' She asked him to let her have the carriage and the maid to go to their country estate. *A new day is born and he who prays for the Prophet will be blessed.* She set off. When she arrived, she waited for the sheep to come back from grazing and chose the youngest lambs. She had them slaughtered and asked for three bags of lime and a bag of stones to build a hearth. On the third day she cut the meat and prepared it for different dishes. She put it in clay pots, covered them, placed them on the hearth and poured water on the lime beneath them. In a couple of minutes the meat was ready. She served it in a Louis-Quinze dinner service.

Her father asked her: 'Now that the meal is ready, who is going to carry it?' She answered: 'That's very easy; go up to the corner and stop four "peasants". They will be dirty, raggedly dressed with no hats or shoes. Ask them the following questions: their age, which day they were born, what is today's date, month and year. Whoever is unable to answer, bring him over. He is a cow.' He said: 'Fine.' He went up to the corner and waited for the first bedouin passer-by and asked: 'What's your name?'

The man answered, 'Abdallah [Slave of God].'

'Come on, we're all slaves of God. Tell me your real name.'

'Muhammad.'

'Peace be on him. How old are you?'

'God knows. I'm as old as I am.'

'When were you born?'

'God knows.'

'Which day of the week is it?'

'How should I know? I'm not a wage-earner waiting for pay-day.'

'Which year is it?'

'God knows.'

Before long the vizier had found four people. He took them to his daughter and said: 'Here are the four cows you want.'

She put the tray of food on their heads and covered it with an embroidered silk cloth, and asked him to take the whole thing to the king. The king asked the vizier: 'What do you take me for? Are these cows?' The vizier answered: 'Ask them their age – they can't tell you. What year it is – they can't tell you. Which day of the week – they can't tell you. Which month it is – they can't tell you. Wouldn't you call them cows?' The king said: 'Indeed they are. Good for you.'

He tried the food and found it the best he had ever tasted. He ate his fill, then asked the vizier: 'Now, tell me who is helping you? Otherwise you will be beheaded. This isn't all your own work.' The vizier answered: 'You are right. If one can get by with telling lies, one does better by telling the truth. It's my daughter who always saves me.' The king asked: 'Would you give her to me in marriage?' 'I would give her to you to be your slave, but I need to consult her.' He went back home and told his daughter that the king had asked for her hand. She answered: 'I don't think he really wants to marry me. I can see what he's up to. He wants to take his revenge.' 'Are you sure?' queried her father. She said: 'Yes, I saved you from death, and now he wants to kill me.' He said: 'May God protect you. I won't give you to him.' She answered: 'No, I will marry him. I know how to deal with him.' He answered proudly: 'I knew you would.' She continued: 'On one condition. You must build me a secret tunnel between our house and the palace.'

Work on the tunnel started as soon as she got engaged to the king. By the time the wedding approached, it was ready. She had two keys for the tunnel door. The order was given to celebrate the wedding. Seven days and seven nights of festivities. On the wedding day 'Aysha was bathed and dressed and taken to the bridal chamber, as all brides are. When the king arrived, he took her to a small empty cell with just a chair and a window. She sat on the chair all night. The king came to see her the next day and passed her a loaf of bread through the window, calling: "Aysha!"

She answered: 'Yes, master.'

He asked: 'What makes a room beautiful?'

She answered: 'The curtains.'

109

'What makes a table beautiful?'

'Little spoons.'

'What makes a woman beautiful?'

She answered: 'Her children.'

'May you never have the joy of any of the three.' With that, he left.

Her cell was bare, she had only a loaf of bread to eat, and her marriage was unconsummated, so how could she have children?

As soon as he left, she opened the door to the tunnel which led to her parents' house. She ate, laughed with her sisters and enjoyed herself. Shortly before the king was due, she went back to her cell and sat waiting for him. He brought her the same food and asked the same questions. Several months went by in this way – the king would bring her the same food and ask her the same ritual questions, and 'Aysha would answer in the same way. One day he came and told her he was going on a pleasure trip to Sfax, and asked her if she needed anything from there. She answered: 'May you come back safely. I have a sister there who is very like me. Give her my love.' The king was to travel the following day. 'Aysha went back home that evening through the tunnel and asked her father to organize a travelling-party for her: guards, tents and provisions. She dressed herself as a man, and started her trip to Sfax, travelling night and day, crossing country after country. She arrived two days before the king and set up camp. The day the king arrived, she dressed herself in her best clothes, made herself up with care, perfumed herself and sat in the middle of her tent within sight of

110

the king who, seeing her beauty, *as men can never resist women,* asked his vizier to go and ask her to grant him her favours. The vizier went to see her and said: 'Our master the king greets you and asks if you would like to spend the night with him.' She answered: 'I would be honoured, but on condition that he wears a peasant's costume and sells salted beans to my guards, barefoot and bareheaded. When he has finished, he is welcome to join me.'

Outraged, the vizier went to see the king and related what had happened. The king said: 'The bitch! How dare she ask a king of my status to walk barefoot and bare-headed selling salted beans!' The vizier answered: 'You are in the middle of nowhere. Nobody knows you here. What of it if you did it and then had a good time?' The king answered: 'It wouldn't do any harm. Get me a plate of salted beans and let me go and sell them.' He dressed himself as a peasant and went out to sell the beans to the guards, who made fun of him. When he had finished, he went back to his tent, bathed and dressed and went to sleep with the woman. *After all, she was legally his wife.* She said to him: 'Give me something as proof that you have spent the night with me.' He gave her his royal armband with his seal engraved on it. After a week, the king informed her that he was leaving the following day. She left early before sunrise, and reached her parents' house, ate, laughed with her sisters and went back to her cell before the king was due.

The king arrived, gave her her 'sister's' greetings, passed

her the loaf of bread through the window and asked her the same ritual questions.

'Aysha conceived. Nine months later, she gave birth in her parents' home to a child as beautiful as the moon whom she named Tur. The baby crawled, toddled, held to the wall and walked. In real life a child grows in a year or two, but just in a couple of words in a tale. The child was put in the care of a wet-nurse, then a tutor who was entrusted with his religious education and general knowledge.

Time passed. One day the king came and told 'Aysha he was going on a pleasure trip to Bizert and asked her if she needed anything from there. She answered: 'May you come back safely. I have a sister there who is very like me. Give her my love.' The king was to travel the following day. 'Aysha went back home that evening through the tunnel and asked her father to organize a travelling-party for her: guards, tents and provisions. She dressed herself as a man and started her trip to Bizert, travelling night and day. She arrived two days before the king and set up camp. The day the king arrived, she dressed herself in her best clothes, made herself up with care, perfumed herself and sat in the middle of her tent within sight of the king who, seeing her beauty, asked his vizier to go and ask her to grant him her favours. The vizier went to see her and said: 'Our master the king greets you and asks if you would like to spend the night with him.' She answered: 'I would be honoured, but on condition that he wears a peasant's costume and sells chickpeas to my guards, bare-

foot and bareheaded. When he has finished, he is welcome
to join me.'

Outraged, the vizier went to see the king and related
what had happened. The king said: 'The bitch! How dare
she ask a king of my status to walk barefoot and bare-
headed selling chickpeas.' The vizier answered: 'You are
in the middle of nowhere. Nobody knows you here. What
of it if you did it and then had a good time?' The king
answered: 'It wouldn't do any harm. Get me a plate of
chickpeas and let me go and sell them.' He dressed himself as a peasant and went out to sell the chickpeas to the
guards, who made fun of him. When he had finished, he
went back to his tent, bathed and dressed and went to
spend the night with the woman. She said to him: 'Give
me something as proof that you have spent the night
with me.' He gave her his royal chain of office with his
seal engraved on it. After a week, the king informed her
that he was leaving the following day. She left early before
sunrise, and reached her parents' house, ate, laughed with
her sisters and went back to her cell before the king was
due.

The king arrived, gave her her 'sister's' greetings, passed
her the loaf of bread through the window and asked her
the same ritual questions.

'Aysha conceived. Nine months later, she gave birth in
her parents' home to a child as beautiful as the moon
which she named Sur. The baby crawled, toddled, held to
the wall and walked. In real life a child grows in a year or
two, but just in a couple of words in a tale. The child

was put in the care of a wet-nurse, then a tutor who was entrusted with his religious education and general knowledge.

One day he came and told her he was going on a pleasure trip to Kairouan, and asked her if she needed anything from there. She answered: 'May you come back safely. I have a sister there who is very like me. Give her my love.' The king was to travel the following day. 'Aysha went back home that evening through the tunnel and asked her father to organize a travelling-party for her: guards, tents and provisions. She dressed herself as a man and started her trip to Kairouan, travelling night and day. She arrived two days before the king and set up camp. The day the king arrived, she dressed herself in her best clothes, made herself up with care, perfumed herself and sat in the middle of her tent within sight of the king who, seeing her beauty, asked his vizier to go and ask her to grant him her favours. The vizier went to see her and said: 'Our master the king greets you and asks if you would like to spend the night with him.' She answered: 'I would be honoured, but on condition that he wears a peasant's costume and sells doughnuts to my guards, barefoot and bareheaded. When he has finished, he is welcome to join me.'

Outraged, the vizier went to see the king and related what had happened. The king said: 'The bitch! How dare she ask a king of my status to walk barefoot and bare-headed selling doughnuts!' The vizier answered: 'You are in the middle of nowhere. Nobody knows you here. What of it if you did it and then had a good time?' The king answered: 'It wouldn't do any harm. Get me a tray of doughnuts and let me go and sell them.' He dressed himself as a peasant and went out to sell the doughnuts to the guards, who made fun of him. When he had finished, he went back to his tent, bathed and dressed and went to spend the night with the woman. She said to him: 'Give me something as proof that you have spent the night with me.' He gave her his royal ring with his seal engraved on it. After a week, the king informed her that he was leaving the following day. She left early before sunrise, and reached her parents' house, ate, laughed with her sisters and went back to her cell before the king was due. The king arrived, gave her her 'sister's' greetings, passed her the loaf of bread through the window and asked her the same ritual questions.

'What makes a room beautiful?'

She answered: 'The curtains.'

'What makes a table beautiful?'

'Little spoons.'

'What makes a woman beautiful?'

She answered: 'Her children.'

'May you never have the joy of any of the three.' With that, he left.

'Aysha conceived. Nine months later, she gave birth in her parents' home to a child as beautiful as the moon which she named Bint Frukh al-Rum. The baby crawled, toddled, held to the wall and walked. In real life a child grows in a year or two, but just in a couple of words in a tale. The child was put in the care of a wet-nurse, then a tutor who was entrusted with his religious education and general knowledge.

One day, news reached 'Aysha that the king was going to marry his cousin. She asked when the bride's trousseau ceremony was to be held. They told her Thursday. She bathed her children and dressed them and had each one wear one of the king's royal insignia. She asked Dadah, her maid, to take them to the king's palace. She instructed her children to mess things up in the palace and if they were reprimanded they should answer that it was their father's house and they had every right to do as they pleased. The bride's trousseau was brought. *New plates and glasses, Louis-Quinze dinner service, the fifty-piece set of crystal glasses, the fifty pieces of copper kitchen ware, couscous steamer, pots and pans, embroidered bedsheets (cross stitch, Nabel stitch, appliqué, fleur-de-lys decorated with pink ribbons), silk curtains and cushions . . .* Anyway, the children did as instructed, broke the bride's new plates and glasses, and used the embroidered silk cushions as horses, and whenever anyone reprimanded them they answered: 'It is our father's house and we have every right to do as we please.' The bride's mother was horrified and asked for the bridegroom to come and see for himself what was going on. When he came and saw them, he recognized his ring, armband and chain of office, and it dawned on him that that was one of 'Aysha's ruses. He quickly went to see 'Aysha and told her: 'You've taken me in again.' She said: 'Of course I have. Don't you see that I saved my father, so

116

how could I not save my own self?' He asked her: 'What about my wedding tonight?' She answered: 'Go and see your uncle and tell him that you have a chest and that you have lost its golden key. You asked to have a new silver one made, but in the meantime you found the one you had lost. Ask him what you should do.' He went to see his future father-in-law and related the story to him. He answered: 'I can't see why you should have a new key since you have found the old one.' The king said: 'Keep your daughter; I have found my wife.'

That night's celebration became 'Aysha's postponed wedding. Seven days and seven nights of festivities, and 'Aysha was finally united with her husband and children.

And they all lived safely and procreated until death did them part.

III

The Virtuous

God is omnipresent.

Once upon a time there was a merchant who had a boy and a girl. The girl was a few years older than the boy. One day he fell ill and sensed that his hour had come. So he called his daughter and told her: "Aysha, I think my hour has come. I want to ask you to look after your younger brother. I'm leaving you my shop; there is hidden in the store-room a big jar full of gold coins. Don't mention it to him until he comes of age.' She said: 'Don't talk like that; you'll live a long time yet.' But he died the following day and was buried. She was left with her younger brother to look after and bring up. Three or four years passed . . . She asked him one day: 'If I borrowed a hundred dinars from our neighbour, what would you do with it?' He said:

118

'I would buy a spinning top, a balloon and toys.' She said to herself: 'He's still young.'

Her brother was now fourteen. She asked him again one day: 'If I gave you one hundred dinars, what would you do?' He said: 'I would buy a bike.' He was now eighteen. She asked him the same ritual question: 'If I gave you a hundred dinars, what would you do with it?' He answered: 'I would open my father's shop again, get rid of the old stock and start with what is saleable. I would also contact father's old fellow-merchants to learn the trade from them.' She said to herself: 'Now my brother is grown-up.' She told him: 'I will borrow some money from our neighbour Auntie Fatma and when you begin to make a profit you can pay her back.'

After he left she went to the store-room and took a hundred dinars from the jar, which she sealed up again. When he came back she gave him the money. The following day he went to the souk and opened the shop. He threw out what was damaged, lawn and taffeta and silk, shook out and aired what could be saved and displayed the rest for sale. He went to see one of his father's fellow-merchants and asked him to teach him the trade. The man was delighted with his initiative and praised him for not letting his father's trade die out. Time passed and he soon became a master merchant in the souk, employing many apprentices. After a while, he paid the money back to his sister.

One day, as he was working in his shop, a man passed by selling a bird which could sing and tell stories. He said to himself: 'Why not buy it for my sister to keep her company?' He bought it, and bought for it a golden cage and two bowls, one gold and one silver, and took it home to his sister. He filled one bowl with rose water and the other with bird-seed. Of course, the bird could talk. Each and every day the sister would get up in the morning, see to her household chores and then sit and listen to the bird entertaining her with stories. She grew very fond of the bird.

One day, a group of fellow-merchants decided to go on a business trip. *In olden times, merchants would be away for a whole year.* He was asked to join them. He went home and informed his sister about the trip. She said to him: 'How can you think of leaving me alone, a helpless woman?' He answered: 'Such is life ... I have to make a living. After all, you've got your bird to keep you company.' She said: 'May God protect you.' She prepared a year's provisions for him. *A new day is born and he who prays for the Prophet will be blessed.* He bade her farewell and left.

The expedition reached Baghdad. They would buy and sell during the day and gather at night to play cards, dominoes and chess, and to chat. One evening the topic of women's fickleness was raised. One of them said: 'No one could even dream of seeing my wife's fingernail.' Another added: 'It would be easier to reach heaven than to catch a glimpse of my sister.' The brother intervened, saying: 'No matter what you say, there will never be a woman as virtuous as my sister. She has never stepped across the threshold and no man has ever seen her toe.'

One of them answered: 'Who do you take her for! Let us bet on it.' The brother said: 'Done! Let us play a game of cards.' They played, and the other man won. He said to him: 'Does she have any distinguishing mark on her body?' The brother answered: 'Yes, she has.' The other merchant asked: 'What if I discovered it?' The brother answered: 'Then you may do as you please.'

The merchant took ship and sought out an old witch, told her the story and asked her to help him reach the woman, otherwise he would lose all his fortune and become a slave to the brother. They came to an agreement, and he directed her to the woman's house.

The old witch dressed herself in a green robe, covered her head with a green shawl and painted her stick green and went to see the woman. She knocked on the door and posed as her aunt, but the woman was surprised to hear that she had an aunt. The old witch explained: 'Your father, God rest his soul, cut me off from my sister, so we weren't able to see each other. Now he is in God's care, and I have forgiven him.' She started to cry and sob. The woman was taken in by her sweet words and let her in. She entertained her to tea, and then she left. The old witch would come and visit her every day. One day, she came and invited her to attend her supposed daughter's henna ceremony, which would be incomplete without her presence, now that they had been reunited, thank God. The woman answered: 'You know my brother is away and I cannot go out in his absence.' The witch replied: 'How can you disappoint your cousin like that? Don't you want her to be happy?' She eventually talked her into it. The woman put on her finery, took out her silk and silver veil and was about to go out when the bird intervened: 'Mistress, put your silken veil away in the chest and your gold in your jewel-box, and let me tell you the story of Kasim and Kuwasim.' The old witch said: 'Is this the time for telling stories? Damn the bird!' The woman answered: 'I must listen to my bird's story.' The old witch left in a rage. The bird started his story. 'Once upon a time there was a maker of oriental shoes who was famous in the souk. One day the king came to see him and asked him to prepare a hundred pairs of slippers for the following morning. The shoemaker closed his shop and sat inside, weeping. Around midnight he was still weeping. Suddenly, the wall parted and there appeared a maiden as beautiful as the moon. She greeted him. He asked her: 'Are you human or a genie?' She said: 'A genie.' He asked: 'What do you want?' 'Give me your food and get a good night's sleep. Tomorrow you will find all the slippers ready.' He replied: 'Help yourself and welcome.'

A new day is born and he who prays for the Prophet will be blessed. As he got up he was delighted to find all the slippers ready. Each and every day he would buy a doughnut and offer it to the genie who was making the slippers for him and leaving him a gold coin every night. Soon the days smiled to him and he made his fortune. He moved into a grand new house, married off all his daughters and placed all his sons in jobs. One day, one of his fellow shoemakers enquired about his sudden wealth. The

122

GHAYA

shoemaker related the story to him. The man said to him:
'How can you give away your own food to a genie? Next,
she'll be wanting your soul.' The following morning he
got the doughnut ready but when the genie appeared and
reached out for it, he slapped her hand. She said to him:
'You will regret it,' and she went back in closing the wall
behind her. He waited for her for a month, but she never
appeared again. He took two stones and started to beat
himself on the temples until he died of remorse saying:
'Time has turned against me.' The bird concluded: 'Destiny struck the man cruelly and he became poor again.
Mistress, if you leave your house you will regret it too.'
She folded her veil, placed it in the chest and declined
the invitation.

The old witch left in a rage. She went to see the man
who was waiting to carry the woman off on his horse, and
related what had happened, saying: 'It's an impossible
task. Did her brother mention anything distinctive about
her?' He answered: 'Yes, she has a birthmark.' She replied:
'Don't you worry. I will tell you what it is.'

She came to visit her on a scorching hot afternoon and
suggested they should take a refreshing shower, explaining: 'I can see your hair is dirty. Let me give you a good
wash, scrub your back and pour the water over you, just
like your mother would have done, God rest her soul.'
And she started to cry. The woman heated some water
and they went into the kitchen. As she was taking off her
clothes, the old witch noticed her birthmark: a slice of
watermelon, green on the outside and red in the middle,

with black pips visible on her thigh. As soon as she saw it, she took to her heels to find the man. Immediately he heard, he went back to find the brother and tell him that he had had his sister, proving it by describing the mark on her thigh. 'From now on I claim your fortune and you become my slave as agreed.' The brother opened a doughnut shop to survive, dressed in rags and fried doughnuts, barefoot.

The woman was surprised at the old witch's disappearance but the bird told her: 'You are so naïve.' Time passed until one day he told her: 'Do you know that my master is now in Baghdad, a slave to a fellow-merchant, making doughnuts for a living?' She immediately disguised herself in men's clothes, prepared provisions for herself for a full year and asked her bird if he wanted anything from there. He told her: 'After you save our master, and on your way back across the Red Sea, call out three times for Morjan, my cousin, and tell him: "Yakut greets you and asks you how he can escape from his cage and leave this foreign land." '

A new day is born and he who prays for the Prophet will be blessed. She gathered together provisions and took ship. When she reached Baghdad she sought out her brother and enquired what had happened. He related the whole story to her. She told him: 'I am my mother's daughter, I have not been brought up to disgrace my family,' and told him all about the old witch. She redeemed her brother and they sailed away together. When they came to the Red Sea, she called out: 'Morjan, Morjan! Yakut greets you and asks you how to escape and leave this foreign land.' Morjan replied: 'Why don't you just bang your head against the wall?' *Obviously the woman couldn't understand the message.* When they arrived back home the bird was delighted to see them. After they had had a meal and drunk tea, the bird enquired: 'Did you talk to my cousin?' She answered: 'Of course I did.' He asked: 'What did he say?' She replied: 'Bang your head against the wall.' They had a good night's sleep. The following morning she got up to find the bird dead in its cage. She wailed and cried and mourned him. 'My poor bird. He was my only companion and adviser.' The brother intervened: 'All this for a bird!' *As you know, men can't bear misery.* 'I will buy you another one.' He reached out for the bird and threw it on the rubbish heap. The bird flew off and settled on the edge of the terrace, and said: 'Mistress, here I am.' She said: 'My little bird, come back to me.' He replied: 'I finally got what I wanted: my own freedom. I can't come back to you. I was hurt to hear your brother say he would buy you another bird,' and he flew away.

There we left them and we have never seen them since.

IV

Ftaytma the Harridan

God is omnipresent.

Once upon a time there was a merchant who married a girl chosen by his mother. *In olden times, in-laws were respected, and girls were expected to behave modestly in front of them. Mothers-in-law particularly were very powerful, and took control of the whole household.* His mother had two daughters who were spoilt and hard to please. The father-in-law was rich and every day he would send to the house two baskets full of provisions. The mother-in-law and her daughters took charge of the kitchen, thereby ensuring the best of the food for themselves. The newlywed daughter-in-law was given the dirtiest tasks to do. At dinnertime (*women used to eat separately from the men*) they would look for any excuse to send her on pointless errands ('Bring some water,' 'You forgot the olives'), while they ate their fill.

126

When asked she would say: 'Oh yes, I've had quite enough to eat, *al-hamdullah*,' despite her hunger.

The young bride grew thinner and more listless every day, but she was a girl of great modesty who never complained to her husband as she was the daughter of a respectable Beldi family which considers it most important for a girl not to show arrogance or disrespect towards her elders. Her husband saw that she was pale and subdued and always went to bed early. He reported it to an old fellow master merchant, who explained: 'She can't be getting enough to eat.' Surprised, the husband exclaimed: 'How come? There's plenty of food prepared every day.' The old man said: 'Put her to the test. Take a cock, pluck it completely except for one feather, and throw it into the courtyard. If she isn't really hungry, she will come out of her room and laugh at this marvel. If she is, she will stay in her room and ignore the whole thing.' The young merchant did as he was told. His mother and sisters rushed laughing out of their rooms to see what had fallen from the sky. The young bride, however, did not move. The husband concluded she must be hungry.

He went back to the old man and recounted what had happened. The old man enquired if she had ever complained. The husband replied: 'Never.' The old man told him: 'Go and buy some cakes from the souk and smuggle them into the house. Make sure she eats them. When she does, she will remember the cock and laugh.' The young merchant brought the cakes to his wife and fed her. After eating, she started to laugh, remembering the cock. The husband recalling the old man's words: 'She is hungry', asked her: 'Now tell me what's happening. You're not eating properly, are you?' She said: 'It's your mother and sisters . . . I can never manage to eat as they always find things for me to do at mealtimes.' The husband told her: 'Then we must do something about it. We'll pretend to have an argument and I will repudiate you. You can go home to your parents and I will teach my family a lesson.'

The following morning, they started to argue, and the raised voices brought the rest of the family running. He pretended to be furious and pronounced: 'You are divorced.' The young bride took her belongings and went back to her home, explaining the subterfuge to her father.

A week later, his mother suggested she should find him another wife. The young merchant said that this time, he would make the choice himself. Now, there was a young tomboy of a girl called Ftaytma living nearby. He went to see her and asked her to help him take revenge on his family, and he would pay her. They would pretend he had chosen her. To their surprise, his mother and sisters were sent to go and ask for her hand. Her own mother was away, so she received them herself. They asked: 'Where is your mother?' She answered: 'She went to deliver the soul from the soul.' 'Where is your father?' She answered: 'He's gone to accompany a soul who will never return.' 'Where is your brother?' 'He's gone to fight with one who never fights back.' The women were nonplussed and uneasy. When Ftaytma broke wind, it was the last straw, and the women left, affronted.

They rushed back to the house and cried: 'What kind of a wild woman are you marrying? When we asked about her mother, she said she was out delivering a new soul; when we asked about her father she said he was accompanying a soul who would never return; and when we asked about her brother she said he was out fighting one who never fought back. As if that wasn't enough, she farted!' The son laughed to himself and explained: 'Her mother is a midwife, her father an undertaker and her brother a hunter. I have chosen her and we must lose no time in writing the marriage contract.'

The first day Ftaytma came to their house, she took charge of the kitchen. She would pick out the best of the provisions and eat while the others watched. When they sat down to eat, she found any excuse to send her mother- and sisters-in-law in turn to run errands.

Tired of being treated like this, her mother-in-law complained to her son and asked him to repudiate this wild woman and take back his meek first wife. The son said: 'I can't do that any more,' thinking to himself, 'I must make sure you learn your lesson.'

One day, the women decided to go to the Turkish baths and asked the daughter-in-law to prepare some nice thick *mhammas* soup for their return. After they left, Ftaytma took a big jar of grain, emptied it into a huge cauldron, added tomatoes and water and put it on the fire. When the women came back from the baths, they were outraged to discover she had used the whole year's provision of

129

mhammas. They complained to her husband again, but he told them he was not ready to divorce her.

On another day, the women went to the baths again and asked her to look after her sick father-in-law while they were out. Ftaytma asked two notaries to come to the house, promising them each a purse of gold if they would draw up her father-in-law's will in which he left her his fortune. As her father-in-law took the first mouthful of his dinner, she said to him: 'Be careful! I think there's a hair in your mouth.' He stuck out his tongue; as he did so she swiftly cut it off. When the notaries came to write the will, he was unable to object. The women came back from the baths and discovered the tragedy. Shocked, they begged the young man: 'Repudiate the horrible Ftaytma and take back your former wife, and we will gladly serve her.' So his former wife was brought back and regained her rightful position.

V

Baba Turki

God is omnipresent.

Once upon a time there was a middle-aged man who was married to a beautiful young wife. The wife had a lover. When Baba* Turki was out at work, his wife would entertain her lover. This went on for some time. One day, Baba Turki came back unexpectedly to fetch his umbrella as it was raining. What was she to do? Her sister was visiting at the time, so together they decided to hide him in the *maqsura†*. Baba Turki came in and sat on the seat in the living-room between the two women. The wife's sister said: 'Why don't you tell Baba Turki?' The wife asked: 'What about?' 'The neighbour,' said her sister. 'Well,' addressing Baba Turki, 'the neighbour's wife entertained

* term of respect used to elderly men
† inner room

131

her lover while her husband was out at work.' Baba Turki said: 'Damn her! I would have killed her if she were my wife. What happened?' His wife answered: 'Her husband came back unexpectedly one day. Taken aback, she and her sister hid him in the *maqsura*, then they each took hold of one edge of a sheet and made a passage for him to pass through, saying, "Come out, come out, wherever you are!" '

As they demonstrated to Baba Turki how it happened, the lover made his escape. Baba Turki rose to his feet, cursing: 'Damn her husband for being a cuckold! If it had been me, I wouldn't have been taken in. I would have killed both of them and drunk a glass of their blood!'

VI

The Peasant

God is omnipresent.

Once upon a time there was a bedouin chief who had a son, but he was lazy and feckless. One day, fate caught up with his father and he died. On the fortieth day, a group of thieves came to rob the tribe, knowing that this time they would be powerless to resist. Hearing voices, the chief's widow tried to scare them off by calling out. The son shrank from tackling them, and so the thieves took what they could carry and left. The following day, the widow scolded her son, but he answered: 'What did you expect me to do? God allotted their share to them.'

One day, a wedding was going to be celebrated. In his lifetime his father, as a good horseman, would participate in the *fantasia*. The mother asked her son to put on his father's costume, mount his horse and honour his father's name. He was supposed to take seven women singers with him: 'Aysha his cousin, 'Aysha his next-door neighbour, 'Aysha his neighbour round the corner, 'Aysha his maternal cousin, 'Aysha his father's sister's daughter, 'Aysha his mother's brother's daughter and 'Aysha his wife.

When he arrived, 'Aysha his next-door neighbour was kidnapped. He said: 'I don't care about her, but woe betide you if you touch 'Aysha my neighbour round the corner.' She too was kidnapped. The young bedouin said: 'I don't care about her, but woe betide you if you touch 'Aysha my cousin.' She in turn was kidnapped. One by one, all the 'Ayshas were kidnapped, including his wife. So he threw away his sword, cast off the costume and went back home, bare-headed and barefoot.

His mother received him wailing and saying: 'You have dishonoured our tribe. There is no place for you here any more.' She gave him his share in the inheritance and he left. 'I'll go to Tunis and have a good time,' he said to himself.

On arriving in Tunis, he didn't know where to go. Then he had an idea. 'I should go and see the go-between,' he thought. He approached the first passer-by he met, and it was the *qadi*, a Beldi from the bottom of the jar, wearing a silk *jibba* of extreme elegance. 'Can you tell me where to find the go-between?' he enquired. 'God forbid!' exclaimed the *qadi*, invoking God the Merciful. The young bedouin approached a tattooed man and asked: 'Can you tell me where to find Ummi* 'Aysha the go-between?' he asked. The other bedouin answered: 'Indeed I know her.' And he pointed to a house further up the street.

Ummi 'Aysha welcomed him and gave him some water to wash his feet. 'Meanwhile, I shall prepare you some food from your provisions,' she said. She opened his bag. To her surprise, it was full of gold, not wheat. She gaped and went back to him saying: 'You must go and wash in the baths.' 'What baths?' he asked. 'Well, the public baths where anyone can go for a wash and massage,' she answered. 'But wait here.' She went to the old city and bought him a fine cloak and *jibba*. She tied them up in a cloth, added a silver box containing jasmine-scented *tfal* [washing-clay] and gave him two gold Louis from his own money. One was for the bath and one for the barber, she instructed. The young bedouin went to the bath. At first he was received coolly, but when he showed the gold coins, the attendants rushed to serve him.

Ummi 'Aysha the go-between took good care of the young bedouin for seven days and seven nights, feeding him and looking after his needs and teaching him Beldi manners. One day, she said to him: 'I must find you a fine bride.' He said: 'That's a good idea.' She went on: 'Take this apple. Go and find a girl you fancy, throw your apple at her, and I will go and ask for her hand for you.'

The young bedouin went to the old town. It was summertime, and the barrow-boys were selling beautiful melons. 'Why don't I buy one of those instead of the

* a term of respect used for elderly women

apple?' he thought. So he bought one, and went and stood in front of the Turkish baths. All kinds of girls came and went; short and tall, dark and fair, but not one appealed to him. The *qadi*'s pregnant wife, a Beldi from the bottom of the jar, came out of the bath wrapped in her silk veil. He immediately took a shine to her, and threw the melon, which hit her on the belly. This sent her into labour and she gave birth on the spot. The bedouin was arrested. Ummi 'Aysha took three gold coins, filled two bags with fruit and provisions and went to see the *qadi.* 'Your honour is of a higher rank than he is. Forgive him.' And she gave him the gold coins and the bags. So he set him free. The young bedouin went home with Ummi 'Aysha.

A week later, Ummi 'Aysha suggested that this time she would choose him a bride. So she went to ask for the hand of a daughter of a modest Beldi family. She had a large marble courtyard in the middle of her house and this she cleaned with spirit of salts. Now it looked like a blue sea. She built him a nice extension and furnished it with silk curtains and fine carpets. Meanwhile, she instructed the young bedouin how to behave in Beldi circles; first to drop his regional G and pick up the Q, to use a knife and fork, to wait to be served, to start a meal with *bismillah* and to show deference to the in-laws.

On the wedding day, the bridegroom, wearing his *jibba barnus* [cloak] and *shashiyya stambuli* [Turkish fez], went to the bride's house and sat down to eat with his guests. It was the tradition to have *bazeine* [a rich, nutty cream] on that day. Ummi 'Aysha instructed him not to use his fingers while among the guests. She saved him a small portion, saying: 'After your guests leave, you can eat with your hands – and feet, if you want! Use the bathroom to relieve yourself instead of going outside.' Ummi 'Aysha tried to think of every way in which he might disgrace himself and teach him to avoid it. But the young bedouin, to everyone's disgust, used his fingers to eat the *bazeine*.

The bride was brought and sat in the place of honour with her guests. The young bedouin came with his party. He stood at the door, and mistook the newly cleaned courtyard for the open sea. He said: 'The deep blue sea lies between us. I can't reach you.' From behind, Ummi 'Aysha gave him a shove. 'Go on, it's not the sea.' After some hesitation, he went in and joined his bride in the bridal chamber.

The bridal bed was decorated with silk curtains and cushions. The peasant gazed in wonder and marvelled at the drapes and curtains decorating the walls and the cushions. He mistook them for the donkey's panniers and played with them. Then his attention was drawn to the pearl necklace the bride was wearing. Mistaking it for his donkey's leading chain, he pulled it, singing: 'Jingle, jingle, goes my donkey's chain!' The beads fell to the floor. He apologized and asked for a needle and cotton to rethread them for her. The young bride realized she was married to a boor. She gave him the thread and a needle and sat crying. The bridegroom's party were bang-ing on the door, as was the tradition, to drag him out. 'I'm still struggling to put it in the hole!' he exclaimed.

Confused, the groom's friends pushed open the door. They were shocked at what they saw. He was sitting on the floor, threading the pearls. They dragged him out and all sat down to the wedding dinner. Ummi 'Aysha stood watching from a corner. When the dessert was served, the bedouin first used just one finger, then gestured to Ummi 'Aysha to ask if he could use the others as well. Ummi 'Aysha scratched her cheek in protest, but the bedouin went ahead anyway, with both hands, with the result that the *bazeine* went all over his *jibba*. A little while later, he needed to relieve himself. He had never seen an indoor lavatory. Ummi 'Aysha was once again on hand to instruct him to use the bathroom.

The bride's mother and close relatives stayed with her as was the tradition until the seventh day. The mother, bitterly disappointed by the match – her daughter, a fine Beldi girl, married to a boorish bedouin – fell ill and took to her bed. Ummi 'Aysha told the bedouin: 'I think you should pay a call to your ailing mother-in-law.' He answered: 'I was thinking of it myself.' Ummi 'Aysha replied: 'Make sure you take her something nice, and most of all, weigh your words carefully.'

The bride, finding her groom utterly repugnant, seized on her mother's illness as a reason to go back and stay with her. The bedouin went to visit his mother-in-law. She was lying in her bed, seriously ill, with the curtains drawn and no one daring to disturb her. As soon as he came in, he said: 'Is she dead yet?' The visitors were all shocked. Ummi 'Aysha dragged him out, scolding him for his tact-lessness.

The following day Ummi 'Aysha was summoned. They said to her: 'As we met in a spirit of goodwill, so must we part. Oil and water don't mix. We are not compatible; the marriage must be ended.' Ummi 'Aysha replied: 'I do apologise. They are ill-suited in every way.' Then she went back home and told the bedouin to send the divorce papers, which he did straightaway.

Our story has come to an end, may we have a fine crop next year.

VII

Rdah Umm Zayed

God is omnipresent.

Once upon a time there lived in Tunis a childless king who had always yearned for a child to fill his house with joy. He prayed day and night to God to grant him a child. One night an angel came to him in a dream, asking him: 'Do you want a daughter with a misfortune but who survives, or a son with a misfortune who dies?' He turned on his side and exclaimed, 'God forbid!' But the angel appeared again, explaining: 'I am a messenger sent from God to fulfil your wishes.' His wife the queen noticed his agitation and enquired what was the matter. He recounted what he had seen and she advised him: 'You are king; you have authority and can overcome any misfortune.' So when the angel returned, the king asked him for a daugh-

140

ter, and in due course his wife conceived. The baby's layette was prepared.

Nine months later the queen went into labour and gave birth to a bouncing baby girl as beautiful as the moon. Praise to God, who created her with such a beauty. For forty days, mother and baby were pampered and spoilt. The baby crawled, toddled, held to the wall and walked. In real life a child grows in a year or two, but just in a couple of words in a tale. 'What name shall we give her?' the king enquired. 'Rdah,' said the queen. Out of concern to have her secluded, the king built a glass palace for her private use and to prevent any misfortune from befalling her. But whatever is written shall be.

Thus the girl grew up knowing nothing and no one but her mother and father and the maid. One day the princess tapped on the floor, which broke open, being glass, and through the hole she saw for the first time ever the outside world and people going to and fro. 'So there are other people besides my parents!' she exclaimed. As she marvelled at the sight, she heard a bedouin woman chanting beautifully some *dhikr* [liturgical singing]. She invited her to her palace and the woman was allowed to come. When she saw the princess's long flowing hair, she praised Allah and said: 'Glory to Allah the exalted creator! What beautiful hair you have! The only thing missing is musk oil to perfume it.' 'Where can one get it?' the princess asked. 'Your father is the king and could get you anything.' With that, the woman left.

The following week, Rdah's face turned as pale as straw

and she fell ill. Her father was summoned urgently to visit her. When he came and enquired about the cause of her illness, she answered petulantly: 'I want some musk oil.' No sooner had she uttered this than the king slapped her on the face angrily, saying: 'Who put that idea into your head?' She didn't answer, fearing to tell him about the woman coming to visit her. Her father came back to the palace, angry and full of foreboding. The queen met him, enquiring about her daughter's health. He answered: 'There is nothing wrong with her health, but I fear this is the beginning of her *mihna* [misfortune].' 'Tell me what has happened.' He answered: 'Your daughter is now asking for musk oil to be brought to her. You know how its perfume can be smelt for miles around and it is bound to attract attention to her.' 'Have you gone mad?' The queen exclaimed. 'How could she know about it?' asked the king. The queen answered: 'Our daughter is well read. She must have read about it in her books. You shouldn't have hit her. Get it for her and apologize.' So the king sent his vizier to get it and took it with him when he next went to visit her.

Hmid al-Hilali, a member of the Beni Hilal tribe, was already married to a girl from the same tribe. One day, he heard the rumours about a woman of exceptional beauty living in Tunis. He said: 'I will find her.' He was a handsome bedouin Arab. He put on his *barnus* and head-cloth, picked up his rifle and set off. He travelled and travelled and travelled, crossing country after country, until he came to a group of bedouins. A woman among

them asked: 'Have you come for us, O handsome young
man, or are you visiting other lands?' 'I have neither come
for you nor am I visiting other lands. Tell me about Rdah,
who has driven suitors mad with her beauty.' She
answered: 'An evil fate must have driven you all the way.
If you seek Paradise it is close at hand; but Hell lies at the
end of the path you have chosen.' He answered: 'Had I
wanted wheat I would have eaten it at home.' He turned
his horse and rode off. He travelled and travelled and
travelled, crossing country after country, until he came to
another gathering of bedouins. An old woman, seeing his
beauty and thinking of him as suitable suitor for her young
daughter, enquired: 'O handsome young Arab knight,
have you come for us, or are you heading for other lands?'
He answered: 'I have neither come for you nor am I
heading for other lands. Tell me about Rdah who has
driven men mad.' She said with a wink: 'Paradise is close
at hand; but Hell lies at the end of your path.' He said:
'Had I wanted wheat I would have eaten it at home.' And
he rode off.

As he drew closer to Tunis, the perfume of musk oil now
wafted stronger and stronger and Hmid's heart throbbed
more wildly. He arrived at Bab Bhar, in the centre of the
city. He approached an old woman and enquired: 'What
is this perfume?' She answered:

'It is the perfume of Rdah, Mother of Beauty.
Her breasts are like two golden apples,
Her locks, dressed in sixty-six plaits,

Are perfumed with musk oil.

Her lips are coral-red and her teeth white as pearls.

Her cheeks are like pomegranates.

She is not as tall as a palm tree nor too short to be seen.

Her skin is neither as white as milk nor brown as a berry.'

On hearing her description Hmid's heart pounded with love and tenderness. He asked where he could find her. The woman answered: 'Just there,' pointing to the glass palace. Hmid turned his horse and headed for the palace. When he came to the palace, he found a horse-trough and a bench. He tied up his horse and lay down to rest on the bench, reading a book.

That day, Rdah had decided to bathe, so she sent Dadah to fetch some water and heat it for her. When Dadah reached the spring outside the palace she was amazed to find a handsome young man mounted on a horse. She stood marvelling at his beauty and forgot about the water. When she came to her senses, she hastened to draw the water and return to the palace. Rdah scolded her, asking: 'What kept you?' Dadah replied: 'A handsome young knight, mounted on a fine horse, who fixed me with piercing eyes until I could bear his gaze no longer.' Rdah told her: 'Go and ask him where he comes from.' So Dadah went and asked him: 'Who are you and where do you come from?' He replied: 'Give my greetings to your mistress and tell her I am Hmid al-Hilali of the Beni Hilal

144

tribe, whose prowess in battle is legendary.' Dadah went back and reported what she had heard. Rdah covered herself in her wrap and went down to look. Their eyes met. He told her: 'I was destined to come all this way to woo you, despite warnings. My heart will always beat for you, even if I should repent.' She replied: 'Your folly is boundless. How dare you ask for a treasure you can never aspire to, a mighty tree you could never climb.' On hearing this, he turned his horse to leave, but she said: 'Are you angry or running away? Anger is unworthy of noble people.' He replied: 'I am neither angry nor running away and, indeed, anger is unworthy of noble people. It's of no consequence; only Destiny can decide. If Destiny delivers you into my hands, even if you resist, you are bound to give in.' She invited him to follow her, and they spent three days and nights together . . . On the third day she gave him her necklace as a token of her troth and sent him to see her father.

Hmid took the necklace and travelled with it to his own land. He went straight to see his cousin and related to her what had happened. She told him: 'Bring her to me so I can rejoice at your marriage.' He gave her the necklace and told her: 'I have to go and settle some tribal matters. Give this to 'Ammar and Khaleifa and send them to ask the king for her hand on my behalf.'

Hmid went back to see his wife, who had heard of his plans, and asked her to prepare some *mesfuf* [sweet semolina and milk] quickly before he set off. She got it ready and served it to him. Usually she prepared it with butter, sugar, nuts and milk, but this time she served it plain and he remarked on it. 'Nothing is better than sweet *mesfuf* to give strength to face the day, but yours today is bitter.' She replied: 'No one can either bear or want a cup of bitterness. You are taking another woman in my place; we must go our separate ways.'

His cousin took charge of the painting and decoration of the house in readiness for the wedding. She summoned 'Ammar and Khaleifa and gave them the necklace and asked them to go and visit the king in person. They put on their best clothes and set off. They arrived in the city and headed for the palace, asking for an audience. 'Have you come to make a complaint?' They replied: 'Certainly not. We have come on a private matter.' So the king was informed that two bedouin peasants wanted to see him. He told the footman to show them in after he had finished with the legal affairs of the kingdom. As soon as they were shown in, 'Ammar and Khaleifa greeted the king and threw the necklace before him. The king was taken aback. *Tradition had it that whenever a daughter gave away her necklace, it meant that she accepted the suitor.* Beside himself with rage, the king summoned the vizier and told him to throw Rdah out in rags, like a dog.

Now Dadah came to see her mistress, scolding her for her ingratitude, saying: 'My lord has spoilt and pampered you in a glass palace, away from prying eyes and you pay him back by choosing an uncouth Bedouin peasant.' When Rdah saw the two men, she understood. She found herself outside, dispossessed and stripped of all her belongings. Rdah, being the king's daughter, had always lived a sheltered and leisurely life. The two men took her and on the way tried to molest her. She resisted, but they took turns in abusing her. She was of the city and not used to the scorching sun. She got sunstroke, and by the time they reached the village she was almost dying. His cousin immediately took care of her and nursed her. Hmid al-Hilali sent a messenger to announce his return. By now Rdah was dying. 'Ammar and Khaleifa came to visit her. She threatened them, saying: 'You won't get away with this. Hmid al-Hilali will avenge me.' They said: 'What arrogance! Let her die.' When they went out, she called Hmid's cousin and told her: 'I have a secret; I want to confide it to you.' The cousin said: 'Tell me, I promise to keep it forever.' She said to her: 'A bird of the land cannot live over the sea, and silk and cotton are for the nobility and merchants. I am the softness and you are the dagger. We are poles apart. That is my real grief. I feel sick from no illness and he is finished without being killed.' And she sighed her last. *It is hopeless; silk and rags don't mix.*

Hmid's cousin grieved and wailed over her death. She buried her in an inner room and decided to find him a new bride. She had many slave girls, all of extreme beauty and different talents: singing, dancing, poetry reciting. She chose the most beautiful and the wittiest and got her ready for the wedding and carried on with the preparations for the planned celebration.

On his return, Hmid al-Hilali went straight to his cousin

147

and asked if Rdah was there. She answered: 'Indeed, she is to be your bride, just as you wanted.' So she showed him the bridal chamber but when he lifted the bride's veil he turned to his cousin. 'This isn't Rdah! Tell me where she is!' She replied: 'I can't lie to you any more. Rdah died, and I had her buried in there.' Hmid went to see the tomb, saying: 'A thousand fair maidens and a thousand dusky ones would not make me forget Rdah. After Rdah no woman would content me.' And he sighed a deep sigh and died.

There we left them, and we have never seen them since.

VIII
The Enchanted Maiden

God is omnipresent.

Once upon a time there was a man who lived happily with his wife. Years and years passed, but they had no children. They prayed day and night for a child to fill their house with joy. One day, as the wife was preparing a meal a man went past the house selling apples. 'Apples to help you conceive!' he was crying. The woman rushed out, saying: 'Why not try it? I must buy one.' So she bought one. Her husband came back from work hungry. He found the apple and ate it. *In olden times, women were shy and wouldn't dare speak of such a thing.* The wife didn't ask him about the apple.

The man's knee grew bigger and bigger until the skin was so taut that it shone. 'Shame on me!' he thought. He took some rags and went into the forest. He sat under a

149

palm tree and cut his knee open. Lo and behold, a baby girl emerged! She was as beautiful as the moon. He wrapped her up in the rags and left her. There was a peahen watching from the tree, so when the man left she came and picked the baby up, and put her with her own young. She fed her and looked after her. She gave her fresh food and water whenever she brought it to the nest. Thus the girl grew up and reached her fifteenth year. She had beautiful long hair which covered her nakedness. Now the girl would climb down to find food for herself and return to the nest. One day, the prince went out on a hunting expedition and saw her in the forest. 'Praise be to God, the Creator of such beauty!' When she saw him, the girl ran away. He followed her until he saw her climb up the tree.

He went back home, his face as pale as straw, and he took to his bed in a fit of melancholy. As he was the king's only son, all the physicians of the kingdom were called to try and cure him. Every one of them diagnosed that he was suffering from depression. An old witch was called to entertain him. She said: 'What's wrong, my Lord? No one will deny you any wish. Even your enemy's head would come rolling to your feet. What can I do for you?' He replied: 'This is a difficult task.' She answered: 'Tell me all about it.' He began: 'I went out to hunt as usual. I saw this beautiful girl and ran after her, but she disappeared into the middle of a tree.' She replied: 'Is that all? Give me a pottery dish and some barley. I will go to the tree.

150

When I win her trust and you see her come to me, throw your cloak around her.'

The old witch went to the forest, lit a fire under the palm tree and sat down to toast the barley, using the pottery dish turned upside down. The girl was watching from the top of the tree. 'Turn the dish over! You're doing it wrong!' 'How else can I do it? Come down and help me, then.' The young girl slid down from the tree and turned the dish over. As she did so, the prince appeared, threw his cloak around her and flung her on to his horse. He took her home and asked his mother to prepare for his wedding the next Friday. He had three wives already. She was young and extremely beautiful and the others were very jealous. The prince was thrilled with his new bride and neglected the others.

One day, he came to his mother and informed her that he was going on a journey. He asked her to keep an eye on 'Aysha, the new bride. He asked his other wives to behave and live in harmony in one house until he came back. All the wives lived in the same house as they were instructed. One day, as the first wife sat massaging 'Aysha's head, she pulled out a hair and put a pin in its place. These pins were magic. When the last pin was inserted, 'Aysha changed into a bird and flew off. All the wives sighed with relief. 'What shall we say to the prince?' One of them suggested: 'Say she died.' So they built a tomb for her in her own chamber.

Now the prince was fond of his gardens, which were planted with roses, jasmine and other scented plants. He had a gardener who took good care of it, watering and pruning every day. One day, the bird came and asked the gardener: 'Gardener, gardener, has your master come back?' 'Not yet,' he answered. She said: 'May you be turned upside down with your eyes popping and wetting yourself.' As soon as she uttered that, the gardener found himself upside down, his eyes popping and wetting himself. The bird then attacked the plants and tore them up before flying off. The following day the same thing happened again.

Time passed. The prince came back. His wives informed him that his new bride had died. They claimed she had pined away with grief at his absence. All the physicians had been called, to no avail. The prince sat every day beside the tomb, weeping and wailing. The vizier warned him one day: 'My lord, you are neglecting your kingdom and your people, crying over a stone. You must see to your kingdom and to the needs of your people.' The prince replied: 'Life is meaningless without her.' The vizier suggested: 'Let's go out into the garden for a change of scene.' So they went out together. The prince was saddened by what he saw. The garden was parched and the plants dying. He called the gardener. 'What happened to the garden?' The gardener replied: 'Don't ask me. But I would like you and the vizier to come in the afternoon and you will witness yourselves what is happening.'

In the afternoon, the prince and the vizier settled themselves on a bench in the garden and waited. Soon the bird came and asked the gardener: 'Has your master come back?' He answered: 'He hasn't yet.' She said: 'May you be turned upside down with your eyes popping and wetting yourself.' As soon as she uttered that, the gardener found himself upside down, his eyes popping and wetting himself. The bird shouted: 'My mother craved me but my father bore me. A peahen raised me in the top of a palm tree. May the old witch be damned for leading me astray.' Then she attacked the plants and tore them up before flying off. The prince sat every day to watch the same spectacle. 'I must unravel this mystery.' He advised the gardener to answer always that his master was still away, if asked.

One day, when the bird came back, the prince got hold of her. He caressed her head, but felt the pins, so he plucked them out, one by one, until the last one was gone. As he did so, the spell was broken and a beautiful girl burst forth from the bird. She sneezed, saying: 'May whoever brought me back to life, live and whoever killed me, die.' Then she related to him what had happened in his absence. 'They tortured and tormented me.' 'Who did?' he asked. 'Your wives, my lord,' she replied. He answered: 'They shall be sent away, and you will remain my only wife.' So he repudiated the three wives and lived safely with 'Aysha until death did them part.

IX
Baba Dahdah

God is omnipresent.

Once upon a time there was a childless couple, who always yearned for a child to fill their life with joy. One day a diviner passed by, shouting: 'Water for the barren! Water for the barren!' The woman heard this and rushed out to speak to the man. 'I am barren. Sell me some water, God bless you!' He answered: 'This water cannot be bought with money, only with a condition: if you conceive a baby boy, it is yours; if it is a girl then it is mine.' The woman had never known the joy of a child, so she accepted. 'Agreed!' she said. 'Give me the water.'

She drank, and conceived. Nine months later she gave birth to a bouncing baby, *Praise to God, the creator, who created her with such a beauty.* The baby crawled, toddled, then held to the wall and walked. In real life a child grows

154

in a year or two, but just in a couple of words in a tale. Time went on until the girl was six or seven. One day, as she was playing in the alley, the diviner passed by again: 'Greet your mother from me, and remind her of her vow.' The little girl went on playing until it was time to go in, then went home, had supper and remembered the old man. 'By the way,' she said, 'I have got something to tell you.' 'Something good, I hope,' said her mother. The girl went on, 'An old man with a white turban approached me and asked me to remind you of the vow between you.' On hearing this, the mother felt her heart sink and started to cry. She cried and lamented, then gave in to God's command. She said to her: 'Next time he approaches you, say to him: "Take me with you." ' On the next occasion the old diviner came, the little girl did as her mother had told her. He told her: 'Put your hand in mine and your feet on mine.' As soon as she did so, she found herself flying through the air. They flew on and on until they came to No Man's Land. They landed near a sumptuous palace. They went through a first door, a second, a third, and so on until they had passed through seven doors. Baba Dahdah, the old man, gave her some food and soothed her tears with different toys and presents. Now 'Aysha grew up surrounded by every luxury. One day, Baba Dahdah informed her that he was to travel to a distant land and gave her seven keys to seven rooms. She was to open all of them except the seventh. 'These are the keys for the seven rooms, but you must not open the seventh one during my absence.' With that, he left.

'Aysha after a few days felt bored, and started opening the first room. It was full of rubies. She made necklaces and bracelets, and when the sun set she closed the room and went away. The following day she opened the second room, which was full of emeralds. She made more necklaces and bracelets, closed the room at sunset and went away. Each room had different jewels and 'Aysha spent her time exploring and enjoying them.

When she came to the seventh room, she said to herself: 'By God, I will open it, I can't resist. What else could there be inside? More rubies and emeralds, pearls and sapphires, I suppose.' 'Aysha opened the room and to her surprise it was empty, except for a little window overlooking a garden. She looked out. The gardener saw her and said: "Aysha, Baba Dahdah will feed you up, Baba Dahdah will fatten you, then he will turn on you and eat you.' 'Aysha closed the window and sat crying. Baba Dahdah came back from his travels and found her face by turns as yellow as saffron and as green as grass. 'She must have opened the room,' he thought to himself. 'So you opened the seventh room?' 'Yes, I did,' she answered sadly. She continued: 'I opened the window and the gardener asked me: "Whose daughter are you?" I told him, "Baba Dahdah's daughter." He replied, "Baba Dahdah will feed you up, Baba Dahdah will fatten you and then turn on you and eat you." ' Baba Dahdah told her: 'Next time he tells you that, tell him this:

Baba Dahdah will feed me up,

Baba Dahdah will fatten me,

To the Sultan's son he will marry me.

I will kill you on my wedding day,

Use your head for a stool and your skin for a bed.

Your eyes will be my mirror, in which I shall see my

face and the back of my head.'

The following day, 'Aysha opened the room and went straight to the window. On seeing her, the gardener said: 'Whose daughter are you?' She answered: 'I am 'Aysha, Baba Dahdah's daughter.' The gardener went on: 'Aysha, Baba Dahdah will feed you up, Baba Dahdah will fatten you, then he will turn on you and eat you.' She answered confidently:

'Baba Dahdah will feed me up,

Baba Dahdah will fatten me,

To the Sultan's son he will marry me.

I will kill you on my wedding day,

Use your head for a stool and your skin for a bed.

Your eyes will be my mirror, in which I shall see my

face and the back of my head.'

The gardener was shocked and surprised at her answer. He became sad and began to neglect the garden. Now the prince was very fond of the garden and always delighted in strolling around it. One day he went out for a stroll as usual, and was dismayed to find that the garden was in disarray. He enquired angrily: 'What's happening to the garden?' The gardener answered: 'My lord, it's a mystery. For some time now, a beautiful girl has appeared at Baba Dahdah's window every afternoon. I tell her: '"Aysha, Baba Dahdah will feed you up, Baba Dahdah will fatten you, then he will turn on you and eat you." She answers:

Baba Dahdah will feed me up,
Baba Dahdah will fatten me,
To the Sultan's son he will marry me.
I will kill you on my wedding day,
Use your head for a stool and your skin for a bed.
Your eyes will be my mirror, in which I shall see my
    face and the back of my head.'

Now, the gardener was really a sheep who had taken on the form of a man, and when no one was looking, he browsed around the garden grazing on the plants. The prince was surprised by the news of the girl and decided to put the gardener's words to the test. In the afternoon he sat on a bench and waited. Soon the window opened and a beautiful young maiden appeared. The gardener said: 'Whose daughter are you?' She answered: 'I am 'Aysha, Baba Dahdah's daughter.' He went on: "Aysha, Baba Dahdah will feed you up, Baba Dahdah will fatten you, then he will turn on you and eat you.' She answered confidently:

'Baba Dahdah will feed me up,
Baba Dahdah will fatten me

To the Sultan's son he will marry me.
I will kill you on my wedding day,
Use your head for a stool and your skin for a bed,
Your eyes will be my mirror, in which I shall see my
    face and the back of my head.'

With that, she disappeared.

The prince was surprised and exclaimed at her beauty.
'Praise to God, who created such beauty. I must make her
my bride.' He turned to the vizier: 'I grant you three days
to bring me Baba Dahdah's daughter, otherwise your head
will roll.' The vizier answered: 'Your wish is my command.'
The following day the vizier went without delay to ask for
the hand of Baba Dahdah's daughter. Baba Dahdah said:
'I will be honoured to give her to the prince, but on
certain conditions. I want as the bride-price seven sets of
jewellery: one in gold, one in pearls, one in diamonds,
one in rubies, one in sapphires, one in emeralds and one
in marcasite.' The vizier said: 'Agreed!' The order was
given to celebrate the marriage. Seven days and seven
nights when no fire was lit and no food was prepared
except in the Sultan's palace. As 'Aysha was leaving Baba
Dahdah's house for her new home, Baba Dahdah said to
her: 'Do not speak to the prince unless he begs you for
my sake.' 'Aysha promised.

Now the prince had three other wives, and 'Aysha was
the fourth. She was young and beautiful, and he immersed
himself in her loving company and neglected the others.
One day his first wife said to him: 'My lord, I want to visit

your new bride.' The prince answered: 'What business is it of yours? Are you in love with her?' She answered: 'I want to see her. I have heard how beautiful she is.' The prince informed his youngest bride, who welcomed the idea. She gave orders to the servants to prepare a special meal; meat and fish and all good things. The first wife arrived, and they embraced with feigned warmth. They sat down to eat. The table was set with all kind of sweet and savoury dishes; meat and fish dishes; *briks*, stuffed peppers, varied tajins, *Ragout sucre* and *baqlawa*. 'Aysha called the servants and asked for the primus stove, a frying pan and some oil. In those days there were no gas cookers. The first wife asked, surprised: 'What's that for?' 'Aysha answered: 'There is no sausage on the menu. I must prepare *merguez* for my dear sister.' The first wife protested: 'It doesn't matter.' 'Aysha answered: 'But it does. I must prepare *merguez* for you.' The oil was now smoking. 'Aysha dipped her fingers in the boiling oil and drew out fried *merguez*, and put it in the serving dish, again and again. They ate, and chatted. Just before she left, the first wife invited 'Aysha to repay the call.

The following Thursday 'Aysha arrived and was received with the same feigned welcome. They sat down to eat. The first wife asked the servant to bring the primus stove, a frying pan and oil. 'Aysha asked: 'What's all this for?' 'There is no sausage on the menu,' replied the first wife. The oil was smoking, and she dipped her fingers in. But her hand stuck to the pan and burned, and she died instantly. 'Aysha breathed a sigh of relief to be free of her.

In turn, the second wife asked the prince if she could visit his new young bride. The prince answered: 'Didn't you see what happened to my first wife?' 'She deserved it; after all, she didn't really love her,' answered the second wife. The prince went to see 'Aysha and informed her of the visit. 'Aysha welcomed the idea. She gave orders for the servants to prepare a special meal with lots of sweet and savoury dishes. The second wife arrived and was welcomed just like the first, with feigned warmth. They sat down to eat. 'Aysha called the servants and asked for the primus stove, a pan and some oil. The second wife enquired: 'What's that for?' 'Aysha replied: 'There is no fish on the menu. We must have fish.' By now the oil was smoking. 'Aysha dipped her fingers in the boiling oil and drew out a huge whole fried fish, which she placed on a big serving dish. The other wife gaped in amazement. They ate and chatted and, just before leaving, the second wife invited her to return the visit.

The following Thursday, 'Aysha arrived and was received with the same feigned welcome. They sat down to eat. The second wife asked the servant to bring the primus stove, a frying pan and oil. 'Aysha asked. 'What's all this for?' 'There is no fish on the menu,' replied the second wife. The oil was smoking, and she dipped her fingers in. But her hand stuck to the pan and burned, and she died instantly. 'Aysha breathed a sigh of relief to be free of her.

In her turn, the third wife asked the prince if she could visit his new young bride. The prince answered: 'Didn't you see what happened to my first and second wives?'

'They deserved it; after all, they didn't really love her,' answered the third wife. The prince went to see 'Aysha and informed her of the visit. 'Aysha welcomed the idea. She gave orders to the servants to prepare a special meal with lots of sweet and savoury dishes. The third wife arrived and was welcomed just like the other two, with feigned warmth. They sat down to eat. After lunch 'Aysha said it was the day for the *hammam*, and invited her guest to accompany her. The third wife said: 'What for?' 'Just for fun,' replied 'Aysha. She called the servants and asked them to bring jasmine-scented *tfal* [washing clay], towels, an incense-burner, silver pattens and a bucket. When everything was assembled, she asked everyone to clap their hands and jump into the well. Everybody clapped their hands, including the third wife and her retinue. 'Aysha joined in, but soon came back up with her servants, *with the help of Baba Dahdah, of course*, leaving the third wife and her retinue behind to die in the well.

Thus 'Aysha got rid of all three of them. Time passed and 'Aysha would not talk to the prince. One day, as they were sitting in the courtyard, the pitcher and mop were washing the floor. *In this house, everything worked on its own, with Baba Dahdah's help, may God protect you and all of us!* The pitcher and mop began to fight. The mop came to complain to the mistress, saying: 'Didn't the pitcher start it? 'Aysha remained silent. The mop continued: 'Who is in the right? Please mistress, in the name of Baba Dahdah, answer.' 'Aysha replied: 'Since you are begging me in the name of my father, I'll be the judge. The pitcher is wrong.'

Hastily the prince turned to her, saying: 'Throughout all these years you haven't uttered a word. Please speak, in the name of Baba Dahdah.' She replied: 'Baba Dahdah is so dear to me, and I owe him everything. I promised him not to speak unless I was begged in his name.' Suddenly the wall split apart and Baba Dahdah appeared, saying: 'My dear little daughter, you did what you wanted with your rivals with my help. I cannot help you any more; you have a husband. I need to go to the holy shrine at Mecca to rest and live there until I die.' With that, he disappeared.

'Aysha and her husband lived safely and procreated until death did them part.

X

The Women of the Moon

God is omnipresent.

Once upon a time there was an old woman who was poor but eked out a living by spinning wool. Each and every morning she would rise early and go to the souk to sell her wool. One evening, there was a full moon and it was so light that she thought morning had come. So she wrapped herself in her silk veil and went to the souk. But it was all closed. She found four other women who had made the same mistake. So they decided to spend the time until dawn broke together, chatting about their lives. One said: 'Why don't we talk about the good old days, when we used to wear fine clothes even in the kitchen?'

The first one started: 'I was pampered and spoilt in my parents' house. On my wedding day I was taken to the bridegroom's house and I sat in the middle of the guests

164

like a queen, with the drums playing. Now, in the middle of the courtyard stood an impressive plum tree, with tempting fruit so red that every pregnant woman would crave for them. I did nothing but admire it all evening. The party went on until dawn. When everybody had left and everything had become quiet, I slipped out of the room, on the pretext of relieving myself, and picked a couple of plums from the tree. When I was about to eat them, my new husband came out to join me, so I stuffed them in my cheeks. "What's happened to your face?" he asked me. I answered: "It's my tooth; it's aching badly." He answered: "I'll call the dentist, then." *If she had been clever, she would have taken them out while he was away, but she didn't think of it.* So the dentist came and opened my mouth. He discovered the two plums. My husband nearly died of shame! He paid the dentist and divorced me on the spot.'

The second woman said: 'He had good reason to divorce you. In my case, my husband had none. On my wedding day I was taken to the groom's house, and there was a nice strong smell of *mlukhiyya* [a stew made with Jew's Mallow] wafting around. *Tradition had it that brides were not to eat that day in the bridegroom's house or he would die. It is usually the hennana, who puts henna on the bride's hands, who brings her dinner in a basket from her parents' house.* The drums were beating, but the smell was so strong that I was obsessed with how to get some of it. When everybody had left and the house had become quiet, I slipped out of the room, on the pretext of relieving myself, and went to the kitchen. A big pot full of *mlukhiyya* and meat stood on the range. So as not to dirty my hands, I put my head right inside the pot to eat. Putting my head in was easy . . . I licked it up until I'd had enough. When I tried to pull my head out, it wouldn't come. I tried and tried, to no avail. When I failed to return, my new husband came out to find me. He discovered me with my head stuck in the pot. He tried to get me out, but he couldn't. Then his father came, his brother and his mother. My head wouldn't budge! So the coppersmith was called and melted down the pot to set my head free. My husband paid him, divorced me on the spot and sent me back to my father's house.'

The third one said: 'There was a good reason for it; but in my case, there was none. I got married to a nice handsome young man. We were happy and contented. One day, he came back home with a big red pumpkin and asked me to do a *mitzawra**. I agreed to do it. When he left, I put on my *khama* and *rihiyya* [wrap and black face veil], put the pumpkin on my head and took it to visit all the saints' tombs: Sidi Ben 'Arus, Sidi Bel-Hassan, Sidi Mehrez, Sayyda Manubiyya, Sayyda 'Arbiyya, Sidi Brahim al-Riahi, and so on, until the sun set. I came back home and sank exhausted to the floor. When my husband came back, he asked: "Did you do the *mitzawra?*" I answered: "Can't you see for yourself? My feet are sore and I have no energy left. I have visited all the saints, as God is my witness. You told me to take the pumpkin on a visit!" He

* In Arabic, *mitzawra* is the name of a dish but also means a round of visits.

166

replied: "What are you talking about? I asked you to cook a *mitzawra*. So you've been out gallivanting all day? How could I have honour with my wife *hamla* [promiscuous] all day in the street! You are divorced!" ' *Respectable women were not to be seen on the street, only prostitutes wander freely.* 'So he sent me back to my father's house.'

The fourth woman said: 'That was a good reason for divorce. But in my case, there was none. I had been happily married and contented for some time when my husband came back one day with a cock and told me he had a guest for dinner. He asked me to cook it in its entirety and leave it ready on time. So I took the cock and put it in the pot – whole, feathers and all. I added some vegetables, oil and tomato, and steamed the *couscous*. When it was ready, I served it in a *tabsi* [pottery serving dish]. At sunset he came back from work and asked me if dinner was ready. Fortunately his guest was waiting outside. I answered: "I cooked it in its entirety, just like you wanted." So he lifted the straw lid and discovered the cock with all its feathers, comb and spurs. He hurried out and apologized to the man, saying: "I'm sorry, the dinner is not ready. My wife is on her deathbed." Then he came in, divorced me and sent me back to my father's house.'

The last woman said: 'That was a good reason for divorce. In my case, there was none. I was married to a man and we lived in one room. One day he came back with a guest. So he asked me to put on a head scarf and stay in the bed recess out of the way, as was tradition, so as not to come face to face with a stranger. The two men sat

167

down to eat, and I felt I needed urgently to relieve myself. What was I to do? Now, my husband had a nightcap he usually wore in bed. So I did it in that. As I was afraid it would smell, I threw it out through the curtains, aiming for the courtyard, but I missed, and it landed on the man's face. That was it . . . My husband saw the man to the door and came back to divorce me.'

With that, the sun rose and all the women sold their wool and went back home.

XI

Shadli Ben 'Adli

God is omnipresent.

Once upon a time there was an old woman whose husband died and left her with three daughters to look after. Like many old women, she earned her living spinning wool. She was very poor, and if she could afford lunch she had to go without supper, and vice versa.

One day, as she was selling her wool in the market, a handsome young man wearing a *jibba* and *burnous* of extreme elegance approached her, saying: 'Who spins this wool for you?' She answered: 'My daughters, may God bless them.' He asked: 'Would you give me the eldest in marriage?' She answered: 'But we are poor, and not of your rank.' He replied: 'Only God is truly rich. I still want to marry your daughter.' They agreed to celebrate the wedding the next Thursday. He said: 'I will send a donkey

169

carrying a trunk containing jewellery and finery for the bride. She should mount the donkey and order him, "Take me back to where you are fed with barley." ' Before taking his leave of the old woman, the young man gave her a thousand riyals. Thrilled, the woman hurried to the vegetable market and filled her baskets with every luxury she and her daughters could want.

Arriving home, she was received with great surprise. The daughters exclaimed: 'Where has all this come from!' She replied: 'From God the Merciful. By the way, I have given your eldest sister away in marriage. We must prepare for the wedding next Thursday.'

The following Thursday, a donkey carrying a trunk arrived at their door. The mother hurried to unload it. Soon the bride was clothed in her wedding dress and decked in the finery the groom had sent for her. She was finally wrapped in her silk veil and sent off on the donkey. The donkey walked and walked until he came to an orchard, then a splendid house. He went through the first open door, then another and another, until he had passed through seven doors and came to a courtyard paved with marble. There he left her. The young bride found herself alone in the middle of a beautiful traditional house. She made for the sitting-room, took off her veil and sat down to wait. Suddenly, a donkey's head came rolling to her feet. The young bride screamed with horror. When she did so, the donkey's head blew on her and she found herself back in front of her mother's house, crying and shaking. Her mother and sisters exclaimed: 'Whatever's the matter?' She replied: 'I found myself all alone in a huge house, when suddenly a donkey's head covered in blood rolled at my feet. No sooner had I screamed than I found myself back here.' 'May God protect you!' said her mother. 'After all, we haven't lost anything. The thousand riyals were a gift from God.'

Two weeks later, the handsome young man approached the old woman again, asking her for the hand of her second daughter. The old woman acquiesced, thinking that maybe her second daughter was his destined wife. Again he gave her a thousand riyals to celebrate the wedding, and again a donkey came to fetch the bride the following Thursday. Exactly the same thing happened. The second daughter found herself back home again in front of her mother's house.

The old woman resolved not to give her last daughter in marriage if he should come to ask for her hand. But the youngest daughter begged her mother to accept. On the next occasion, the handsome young man came to ask for the hand of the youngest. The old woman accepted willingly, and again he gave her a thousand riyals to celebrate the wedding, and again a donkey came to fetch the bride the following Thursday. The young bride found herself, just like her sisters, in a splendid house. The courtyard was paved with translucent marble with a fountain in the middle, the rooms were vaulted with inner chambers and bed alcoves, upholstered with cushions. She took off her veil and put it away in a chest. She found a silver bucket and a golden one which she filled with jasmine and roses. Then she opened the chest of drawers and took out two embroidered towels, and sat down to wait.

Suddenly, the donkey's head came rolling, covered in blood. The youngest daughter exclaimed: 'God bless you!' and hurried to wash it, and perfume it with jasmine and roses. Then she dried it with the towels and took it to rest in the inner room. Then she went to the kitchen and found that dinner was cooking by itself. She helped herself and sat down to eat her fill. It was almost midnight; she felt tired and weary and went straight to bed.

A new day is born and he who prays for the Prophet will be blessed. When she woke up, she saw the most handsome man she had ever seen, dressed in a *jibba* and *burnous*, leaving the house. She did not utter a word. An hour later, there was a knock on the door. She opened it. Three black female servants came in, saying: 'We have come to serve you.' The three servants each set about a different kind of housework: cooking, cleaning and washing. At noon, lunch was ready. The mistress sat down to eat at leisure. Later, the servants entertained her with stories, songs and dancing until sunset. At dusk, she heard a voice saying: 'Put out the lamps, draw the curtains. Your master has returned.' Suddenly, the lights went out and the handsome young man came straight into the inner room. The mistress carried on normally, had her dinner and went to bed. Every day she put on a splendid new dress embroidered with sequins and went happily through the same routine, presiding over her household *with no mother-*

172

in-law and no burden, a situation to be envied. She was lucky God had willed it so.

Now let us return to her sisters. On the wedding day, the two sisters waited and waited for the younger sister to return, but she did not come back. They were puzzled, and curious to know what had happened. The first week passed, and the second, but still the younger sister failed to return. They were jealous and decided to break up her marriage. They summoned Azuzet es-Stut (may she be damned!) and told her: 'Next time the sultan's wife auctions off her old caftan, bring it to us.'

A week later, the old witch came back with a luxurious, expensive caftan. The sisters commanded her to take it to their younger sister, saying: 'If your husband really loves you, he must buy you this.' The old witch did as she was told. She came to the house and knocked on the door. A servant opened it. The old witch explained that she came on behalf of the mistress's sisters and mother to pay her a visit. 'Let her in,' said the mistress. She was eager for news of her family. The old witch told her all was well, and accepted an invitation to stay for lunch. A large table was set with sweet and savoury dishes. The two women ate their fill, helped themselves to tea and cakes, and chatted. Just before the old witch made to leave, the mistress rose to her feet, went to the chest and filled a cloth with fine clothes, tied it up and gave it to the old witch. The old witch said: 'By the way, your sisters and mother greet you and say to you that if your husband really loves you, he must buy you this caftan.' 'How much is it?' the mistress

enquired. 'Five hundred riyals,' the old witch replied, and
with that she left.

When the master came back, the woman was low in
spirits. She didn't even have dinner. How could she
explain this to her husband? He never addressed a word
to her. Suddenly she heard him address the lamp: 'You,
lamp, why is your mistress so upset?' The lamp replied:
'Her mother and sisters have upset her and sown doubt
in her mind about her marriage.' He replied: 'Tell her to
laugh her morose ideas away. Tomorrow is another day,
her wish will be fulfilled.' As soon as she heard this the
mistress was reassured and became her old self again. She
sat down to eat. The following day she found five hundred
riyals under her pillow.

When the old witch came back, she gave her the money.
The old witch informed her that her mother was ill. That
evening, she informed the master through the servants
and sought his permission to visit her old home. He
recommended she should take the donkey, look after it
well and be sure to return before sunset. The next morning the mistress took two baskets of provisions and set off.
The donkey plodded on slowly until they reached the
house. When they arrived, she tied the donkey up, gave
him some water and barley and went into the house. She
found it full of relatives come to enquire about her
mother's condition. She sat down with the women and
chatted. One of them said: 'What is your husband like? Is
he handsome?' She replied: 'I don't know him. He comes
home in the dark and leaves before dawn. We don't speak

174

to each other.' The women were shocked and exclaimed: 'How come? How can you live with a man you don't know? How can you live with a man who doesn't speak to you?'

The young woman went back home. The following day she awoke to the news that her mother had died and she had to go back again. The master gave the same instructions, recommending her to take the donkey, look after it well, and be sure to return before sunset. But the young woman, distraught at her mother's death, forgot all about the donkey once she had arrived. The children played with it and teased it unkindly. The women enquired again about her husband. 'Did you talk to him? Do you know his name?' The young woman said no. That evening, the young woman went home determined to speak to him.

At dusk, she heard a voice saying: 'Put out the lamps, draw the curtains. Your master has returned.' Suddenly, the lights went out and the handsome young man came in straight to the inner room, coughing and unwell. She joined him in the room, enquired about his health and asked him: 'What is your name?' He replied: 'What is more important to you, my name or my body?' She insisted: 'Your name.' He repeated his question: 'What is more important to you, my name or my body?' 'Your name.' As she spoke, she did not realize that he was being swallowed up by the earth. He repeated the question: 'What is more important to you, my name or my body?' She insisted, 'Your name.' He replied: 'Shadli Ben 'Adli,' and the earth closed over him. Immediately the three slaves hurried to beat her and cast her out of the house. She put on a man's clothes, gathered provisions and decided to look for him.

She walked and walked, crossing country after country, until she grew tired and hungry. She found a pool of water, drank from it and washed her face. When she saw her reflection in the water she exclaimed: 'How beautiful I am! But unlucky!'

She heard a voice: 'You who are admiring yourself in the water, lift the marble slab and see what's underneath.'

When she lifted the slab she found a staircase. She walked down and found an extremely beautiful young woman. She enquired: 'What are you doing here?'

The young woman replied: 'Don't ask. My father is an ogre. He is coming to visit me today. Come and help me and tell me all about yourself.'

She agreed to help her and she confided to her the secret about searching for her lost husband. The young woman promised to help her in her search, explaining that her father was the king of the ogres, and that nothing escaped his attention. A huge *couscous* was prepared for the ogre. When he came, his daughter hid her in a rolled-up mat, but he sensed a human presence and exclaimed: 'I can smell humans! Come to me, all of my possessions.' Each and every one of his possessions rushed to him, except the mat. He enquired: 'Where is the mat?'

His daughter answered: 'It is sick and tired out.'

He answered: 'Leave it to rest.'

176

After he had dinner, his daughter came to him and asked: 'Father, have you heard about Shadli Ben 'Adli?'

He answered: 'What? How did you come to hear that story, buried here under the earth?' He slapped her on the face and put her eye out.

When the ogre left, the sister came out of hiding, apologizing: 'I'm sorry I got you into trouble.'

She replied: 'No harm done: I will recover. Take this walnut and this almond and go and find my younger sister. She will be able to help you.'

She walked and walked miles around until she found a pool of water, drank from it and washed her face. When she saw her reflection in the water she exclaimed: 'How beautiful I am! But unlucky!'

She heard a voice: 'You who are admiring yourself in the water, lift the marble slab and see what's underneath.'

When she lifted the slab she found a staircase. She walked down and found an extremely beautiful young woman. She enquired: 'What are you doing here?'

The young woman replied: 'Don't ask. My father is an ogre. He is coming to visit me today. Come and help me and tell me all about yourself.'

She agreed to help her and she confided to her the secret about searching for her lost husband. The young woman promised to help her in her search, explaining that her father was the king of ogres, and that nothing escaped his attention. A huge *couscous* was prepared for the ogre. When he came, his daughter hid her in a rolled-up mat, but he sensed a human presence and exclaimed:

'I can smell humans! Come to me, all of my possessions.'
Each and every one of his possessions rushed to him,
except the mat. He enquired: 'Where is the mat?'

His daughter answered:'It is sick and tired out.'

He answered: 'Leave it to rest.'

After he had dinner, his daughter came to him and
asked: 'Father, have you heard about Shadli Ben 'Adli?'

He replied: 'You know what happened to your sister
when she asked me the same question. But because you
are so dear to me I will answer. Whoever wants to get to
him needs one of my robes, one of my sticks and one
portion of my supper. The portion is for the ants when
they swarm, the stick is to help get through the mountains
covered in thorns and thistles, and the robe is to escape
from the other ogres.'

She answered: 'Who cares?'

After a week, when her father was due to come again,
she prepared for him a clean robe, a new stick and new
shoes. When he started his meal, she shouted: 'Don't eat
that, there's a hair in it.' So he spat it out. Then she said
to him: 'You must get rid of this old robe and stick. I've
got new ones for you.'

He replied: 'You are right, I need to change into a new
robe.' He took off the old robe and put on the new one
and left with the new stick.

She called her out of her hiding place and said to her:
'Now you can start your search. Take this hazelnut and
use it in case of necessity and go, may you be blessed.'

She kissed her goodbye and left.

The young girl walked and walked, crossing country after country until she came to a mountain covered with thorns and thistles. She struggled through it with the help of the magic stick. Then suddenly she was surrounded by ants. She threw them the ogre's morsel of food and continued on her way. She met with lions and tigers but none of them molested her because she was wearing the magic robe. She walked until she came to a grave where her destined husband was buried, as the ogre had explained to her. She was to cry until she filled seven jars and seven drinking cups with her tears, which would break the spell on him. She sat down on a bench and started to cry and cry until she filled the first, then the second and so on. She remembered her father's death and cried . . . As she was filling the seventh, a procession of people passed by and asked for water to quench their thirst. She said to herself: 'Maybe I should buy a serving-girl to help me through.' So she gave them some water and got a black servant in exchange. Explaining to the girl that she was to fill the last jar with tears and wake her when it was full, she lay down to rest. Exhausted by her crying, she immediately fell into a sound sleep. The serving-girl only had to think of her own problems to cry her eyes out and soon filled the last jar to the brim.

Shadli Ben 'Adli had promised he would marry whoever broke the spell. So when the last tear was shed, the grave opened and he rose from it as beautiful as the moon. He saw the woman lying there, more beautiful than he had ever imagined. He enquired: 'Who is this?' The black girl answered: 'A beggar who came to ask for alms.' He asked: 'Was it you who cried over me?' She said: 'Yes, indeed.' He said: 'Then you shall be my wife in this world and the next.'

The sleeping woman woke up to find herself alone. She realized what had happened and lamented her fate. Then she got to her feet and started to walk until she came to a city which was in turmoil with the king's impending marriage, and rumours that the king's spell had been broken by a black girl. She made her way to the palace to ask for food, and was taken on as a maid.

She worked for some time until one day she saw the new bride and recognized her. She decided to take her revenge. She took out the first daughter's gift, the walnut, and broke it. When she broke it, there came out of it a tray of amber and goldfinches. She put it on the patio for the black bride to see. When she saw it she coveted it and enquired: 'Whose is this?' The servants answered: 'It belongs to the new servant.' She asked for her to be brought before her. When she asked the servant to name her price, she replied: 'A night with your husband.' The bride was taken aback but eventually gave in.

On that night, the black bride prepared the coffee with a sleeping potion in it and served it to her husband so that he would be incapable of doing anything. To test its effect, she burned his heel but he did not react. The woman was then allowed to come up to his apartment. Seeing him unconscious, she tried to shake him awake and explain what had happened. But he would not wake up.

A week or so later, the young woman took out the daughter's second gift, the almond, and broke it. Out of it came a priceless robe. She spread it out in the sun for the black bride to see. When she saw it she enquired: 'Whose is this?' The servants answered: 'It belongs to the new servant.' She asked for her to be brought before her. When she asked the servant to name her price, she replied: 'A night with your husband.' The black bride was taken aback but remembering the beautiful robe, eventually gave in.

On that night again, the black bride prepared a coffee, put in it a sleeping potion and served it to her husband. Before allowing the servant into his apartment, she burnt his heel to test the effect of the potion. The king did not react. So she called the servant up to his apartment. The same thing happened again.

A new day is born and he who prays for the Prophet will be blessed. The king went to his vizier complaining about his sore feet and inexplicable exhaustion. The vizier enquired: 'What did you eat last night?' The king answered: 'Only the usual coffee and cake before going to bed.' The vizier answered: 'Well, next time don't drink it, and pretend to fall asleep.'

A week later she took out the hazelnut and broke it. Out of it came a priceless crown studded with emeralds and rubies. Again, she left it for the bride to find and the same thing happened. But this time she took a stick to

181

strike him awake. That very night the king didn't drink his coffee so when the woman came he was wide awake but pretending to sleep. She cried to him and started to beat him. He stood up and enquired: 'Are you telling the truth? Was it really you?' She said: 'Indeed.' She went to the bathroom and bathed and when she returned he gave her a priceless nightgown, and they passed the night in married bliss.

A new day is born and he who prays for the Prophet will be blessed. When the black woman came to knock, he opened the door and asked his new bride to decide what her fate should be. She said: 'I want four she-camels, two hungry and two thirsty, to tear her apart.' And so it was done.

The order was given to celebrate the wedding, seven days and seven nights of festivities. The king and queen lived happily for years until one day the queen yearned for her mother and sisters. She sent messengers to her sisters and they all gathered happily at their mother's house. All the daughters lived safely and procreated until death did them part.

XII

The Crazy Elderly Woman

God is omnipresent.

Once upon a time there was an old woman who was married to a perfume merchant in Souk al-'Attarein. She had seven daughters. All of them got married and moved to their husbands' houses. After having a house full and bustling with children, she found herself all alone and became demented. Her husband was a perfume maker and kept in his house provisions of amber, jasmine, rose water and musk. One day, the old woman took all the amber into the courtyard and poured rose water over it, turning it into a paste like Turkish delight. She moulded black dolls and gave them each a name and a task: 'Mabruka! your duty is to open the door to your master; Mas'uda! your duty is do the washing-up; Zohra! your duty is to take charge of the kitchen, etc. Then she sat down

183

clicking the beads of her rosary and chanting al-Latif. The merchant came back at lunchtime. He knocked on the door. The elderly woman asked Mabruka: 'Open the door for the master,' but Mabruka did not move. The old woman started to shout. The merchant forced the door open, and, realizing what had happened, he ordered her to leave the house. She said: 'Never mind, I will take my bits and pieces and stay with my most affectionate daughter.'

Her daughter gave her a warm welcome and expressed her delight at having her to stay with her and give her some help. The daughter had many children and was up to her ears in washing. Thinking of a way of helping her, she parcelled up all the white sheets and the white linen and took them to the *qarwi* [dyer] round the corner and asked him to dye them brown and black!

When her daughter realized what had happened, she threw her out. She said: 'Never mind I will stay with my affectionate daughter.' And she went to her second daughter.

XIII

The Dog with The Seven Chains

God is omnipresent.

There was a widower who had seven daughters. They had
no one in the world except Almighty God. One day a crier
went round the village announcing the time had come
for the pilgrimage. The father's heart yearned to make
the pilgrimage. In those days, it took a whole year to
accomplish. He called his eldest daughter and said: 'My
heart has long yearned to visit Mecca the Holy. Can I rely
on you to look after all your sisters during my absence,
and not to open the door to any stranger?' 'Aysha the
youngest said: 'You may go with an easy mind. I shall be
the man of the house.' The father prepared provisions
for a year's journey and laid in for them everything they
would need. As protection, he bought them a watchdog

and put seven locks on the door, telling each girl not go beyond the threshold.

'Aysha fed the dog and pampered him. Azuzet es-Stut, the old witch, noticed the helpless girls and decided to eat them. One day she came to the house and knocked at the door. One of the girls answered. 'Who is it?' 'I'm your old aunt, come to visit you.' 'We haven't got an old aunt,' she replied. 'Yes, you have. It's your father's fault for not telling you, may God forgive him.' The dog said: 'Woof, woof. My master put me in charge of his daughters. You won't get your hands on them. Over my dead body!' 'Aysha the youngest warned her sisters: 'On no account open the door!' The ogress mumbled: 'Damn the dog!' and went away.

The following day she came back and knocked again. 'I'm your dear aunt. Open the door. I'll keep you company and tell you stories.' The dog replied: 'Woof, woof. My master put me in charge of his daughters. You won't get your hands on them. Over my dead body!' 'Kill the dog!' the old witch urged the girls. 'Aysha warned them: 'Don't listen to her; she's an ogress.' The girls turned a deaf ear and killed the dog and buried it in the entrance hall. Soon the ogress came back. 'Open the door, my dear ones!' The dog's bones replied: 'Woof, woof. My master put me in charge of his daughters. You won't get your hands on them. Over my dead body!' The girls took the skull and bones of the dog and burned them to ashes. 'Aysha gathered the ashes, buried them in a hole, and hid in the larder. The old witch was allowed into the house.

The first night she won their confidence by telling them stories until they fell asleep.

The following day she ate them one by one. She addressed the first one, saying: 'Where shall I begin with you?' She answered: 'With my ears, which didn't listen to 'Aysha's warning.' With that, the witch chewed her down to the bones. She then addressed the younger one: 'Where shall I begin with you?' 'With my teeth,' she suggested, 'which bit my little sister 'Aysha.' With that, she chewed her up. She then addressed the third one. 'Where shall I begin with you?' 'With my hand, which hit my little sister 'Aysha.' She too was swiftly gnawed away. She then turned to the fourth one. 'Where shall I begin with you?' 'With my foot, which kicked my little sister 'Aysha.' With that, the old witch ate her up. Her remaining two sisters met the same fate. The old witch left the house. 'Aysha came out of her hiding-place, gathered together her sisters' bones, crying and wailing. She then locked the door and settled down to wait for her father's return.

When the year was up, 'Aysha prepared cakes and sweets for the pilgrim's return. When he finally arrived she met him on the doorstep and wished him: 'May your pilgrimage be accepted and your sins absolved.' After three days of seclusion, *as is customary on returning from the pilgrimage,* he asked: 'Where are your sisters?' She explained: 'My dear father, they disobeyed your orders and opened the door to a cunning ogress, who ate them all. I warned them time and again, but they wouldn't listen. They tied me up and killed the dog. The ogress eventually ate them all.' He replied: 'Bless you, who obeyed, and damn them who disobeyed!'

With that, we left them, and we have never seen them again.

XIV

Long Live The Beldi

God is omnipresent.

Once upon a time there was a Beldi married to four wives: one from Tunis, one from Gabes, one from Jerba and a black woman. His Beldi wife, a Beldi from the bottom of the jar, was radiant, with good smooth light skin, good breeding and manners and 'a touch of class'. His other wives were dark and green with tattoos, wearing their *mellia* [regional bedouin dress]. After a few years of marriage he grew tired of their jealousy and heavy expenses, so he decided to make things easier for himself by divorcing three wives and keeping one – but he didn't know which one to keep. So he consulted an elderly man and said: 'Uncle, I have four wives, and I've had enough of their continual quarrelling and the expense of maintaining four

189

households.' The old man answered: 'Test them with four questions, and keep whoever gives the best answers.'

The wives from Jerba and Gabes were bedouin peasants, wearing *mellia* and green with tattoos. The black wife was coal-black with thick lips and a wide, negroid nose. The Beldi wife was fair, with a radiant face, of good breeding and with a touch of class.

He asked the Jerbi woman: 'What is your favourite dish?'

She answered: '*Terfis* and *terfus*.'

'What is your ideal house?'

She answered: 'A house with a cellar.'

'What is your favourite name?'

She answered: 'Yahya Bin Danfus.'

'How would you tell night from day?'

She answered: 'When the cattle sleep and the cockroaches come out.'

He addressed the black woman: 'What is your favourite dish?'

She answered: '*Assida* with okra.'

'What is your favourite name?'

She answered: 'Mabrouka Hafnawiyya.'

'Your ideal dwelling?'

She answered: '*Bayt kummaniyya* [The servants' quarters].'

'How would you tell night from day?'

She answered: 'When the master asks for the chamber-pot.'

Then he addressed the bedouin from Gabes. 'Your favourite dish?'

She said: 'Chicken *couscous.*'

'Your favourite dwelling?'

'A mud hut without a door.'

'Your favourite name?'

'Muhammad Hajjaj.'

'How would you tell night from day?'

'When the cattle sleep and the ewes rise.'

Finally he addressed the Beldi wife. 'What is your favourite dish?'

She answered: '*Ftat 'al-Mri.*'

'Your favourite dwelling?'

She answered: 'A two-storey house with a courtyard.'

'Your favourite name?'

She answered: 'Muhammad and Ali.'

'How would you recognize night from day?'

She answered: 'When the *muezzin* calls to prayer in the Prophet's holy dwelling-place, peace be upon Him.'

He said to himself: I'll keep the Beldi and divorce the others.

And they lived happily ever after.

XV

The Beldi and The Sharecropper

God is omnipresent.

There was a Beldi who had an orchard in Jebel Wuslat, and he hired a sharecropper to work it. *In those days owners did not work their own land but had sharecroppers and factors to do it.* The sharecroppers would take one fifth of the crop and the factors would supervise the workers and labourers. The sharecropper would represent the owner of the land in all deals in the market. One day a sharecropper came to Tunis and headed for the owner's house, as usual. *In those times it was usual for the sharecropper to stay with the owner when he came to town on business.* He arrived late, knocked on the door and was let in. They gave him a meal. *In those days the food was kept fresh outside, under an upturned copper basin, for the barrow boys who brought produce regularly from the orchard, because there were no vans at the time.*

He ate his fill, had a glass of tea, and stayed up until four or five in the morning when he left for the market. He bought and sold and came back to share the profits with the owner: one fifth for himself and four fifths for the owner. The sharecropper stayed with the owner three days and three nights. The owner gave him hospitality and entertained him. He took him to the Café Chantant [cabaret café], to the cinema, the *karakuz* [Punch and Judy show] and so on. The man was delighted. Then he took him to the souk to help him buy clothes. He bought an overall for himself and scarves, lengths of colourful *mellia* cloth and embroidered slippers for the women. Then he went to Souq al-'Attarein [perfumers' souk] and bought amber and musk and kohl. He filled a bag and got on his donkey and rode off. Before he left the owner said to him: 'Mabruk,' or, 'Meftah,' *for those were common names of the peasants,* 'next time you come, bring us fresh eggs and fresh chicken.' The sharecropper answered: 'Certainly.' The owner went on: 'And bring us fresh *ghee* and butter.' 'Of course,' the sharecropper answered: 'Don't forget the *tabbuna* bread [baked in a clay oven].' The sharecropper answered: 'I won't.' The owner went on and on . . . The sharecropper agreed with every request and set off.

Three days later, he reached Jebel Wuslat. He got off his donkey and shouted: 'You, the Beldi, you're always asking me for this and that. To hell with all that! You can't reach me here! Fuck off!'

SA'DIYYA

I

Lulsha

Once upon a time . . .

Once upon a time there was a silk merchant who was
married to his cousin and they doted on each other. One
day, he came and said he wanted to pay a visit to Sidi
Belhassen, the local saint, on the customary visiting day.
She said: 'Yes, of course.' So the merchant went to pay
his usual visit to the local saint. There he met one of his
friends, who asked him a favour. 'I have many jars of oil,
which I would like you to look after for me. Then I will
collect them later.' The merchant answered: 'Willingly!'
In olden times, houses had huge store-rooms.

The merchant's friend brought forty jars and lined them
up in the store-room. Now, they had a maid who became
suspicious at the sight of the forty jars. 'I must uncover

195

the mystery,' she thought. On the same evening, the family stayed up late but there was a power cut. The maid suggested they should use some of the oil to make lamps. When she lifted the lid of the first jar she discovered a red *shashiyya* [man's skullcap], and realized there was a thief inside every jar. She emptied one of their own oil jars into a large cauldron and brought it to the boil. Then she uncovered every jar and poured some boiling oil into each one. All forty men died instantly. Now, they were to have risen from the jars at their master's signal with a couple of pebbles, and swarm through the house, stealing everything. So when he threw the first pebble, no one responded. When the second and third pebbles still brought no answer, their master understood what must have happpened. The maid went to report to her mistress what she had done. The following day, the master of the thieves came to his friend's house to claim his jars as if nothing had happened. He carried away forty jars containing forty corpses. This fuelled his anger and he swore to take his revenge.

The merchant, appalled at what had happened, said to his wife: 'We're not safe anymore in this town. We have to move. We'll sell the house and move away.' *A new day is born and he who prays for the Prophet will be blessed.* He put an advertisement in the paper which came to the notice of the master of the thieves, who decided to keep a watch on them. The merchant sold the house and bought two she-camels, and made ready to depart. The following day they gathered together provisions and all his heart's desires and set off early, the merchant leading and his wife behind. They travelled and travelled. The master of the thieves followed them surreptitiously on a camel. The merchant's camel sped on ahead, but his wife's was slower, and the master of the thieves caught up with her, and grasped her camel's tail to hold it back. Her husband was unaware of this and continued on his way, calling out from time to time without turning round: 'Are you still there? Come on!'

By now, the merchant's wife had fallen far behind. The master of the thieves caught hold of her and tied her to a tree. 'You will die there. You have murdered my men.' Then he went to collect some wood to burn her. In the meantime, a salt-pedlar passed by. She cried out to him: 'Save me, please save me! My enemy is going to kill me! Your good turn will be rewarded.' The old man untied her and put her in one of his donkey's panniers with a cover over her. When the master of the thieves came back, there was no trace of her. He climbed on his camel and rode away. A few miles further on he met the salt-pedlar and asked him: 'Old man, have you seen a woman?' Pretending he was deaf, he answered: 'Eh? What?' The man gave up.

The salt-pedlar arrived home and unloaded his panniers. To calm his wife's surprise at the sight of the woman, he recounted what had happened. She took pity on her and decided to adopt her as her own daughter. The younger woman lived with them, helping to cook and clean and run the house. After a while the merchant realized that his wife had disappeared. He looked for her, then gave up, *as men and time are not to be trusted.* The salt-pedlar's house was close to that of the Sultan. One day, the Sultan's son's dove escaped and he followed it from roof to roof until he came to the old pedlar's house. He saw the young woman of exceptional beauty, *praise to God who created her with such beauty,* hanging out the washing on the terrace. He stood spellbound. 'Where has she come from? To my knowledge, the old woman has no daughter.'

The old woman was in the habit of paying courtesy calls to the palace, so on the next occasion she visited, the prince told her: 'I want your daughter.' The old woman answered: 'What daughter? I have no daughter.' The merchant's young wife had asked her to keep her existence secret. The prince warned: 'Either you tell me the truth or your head will roll.' The old woman recounted to him the young woman's story. The prince said: 'Ask her if she will marry me.' The old woman answered: 'I will tell her.' When she came back to the house, she informed the young woman of the prince's intention. She answered: 'I won't hear of it as long as my enemy is still alive.' Astonished, the old woman replied: 'How could you turn down the prince?' She answered: 'Go and tell him my answer.' So the old woman went back to the palace and recounted what had happened between her and her adopted daughter. 'I will provide three lions on the right and three on the left, and soldiers to protect her.' The old woman reported back to the girl, who eventually agreed to marry the prince, on condition that she wore a black dress and that there would be no celebration. Her enemy, the master of the thieves, searched everywhere for her to no avail, but he promised himself that she would not get away from him. The prince and the girl were married. As promised, three lions were placed on her left and three on her right, with soldiers to protect her. Time passed, and they lived happily.

The master of the thieves was now in the same town. News reached him that Miss So-and-So had married the Sultan, *as news travels like wildfire in a small town.* So he prepared to carry out his plan of revenge. It was summertime, so he made up a big pitcher of lemonade and began to distribute it to the soldiers, with little cakes. He did this over several days until he gained their trust and gratitude. One day, he enquired: 'Why are there so many of you on guard duty? What are the lions for?' They answered: 'Our master the prince is protecting his young bride from an enemy she fears.' He asked nonchalantly: 'An enemy? By the way, where are her apartments?' They replied: 'Over there,' pointing to a building.

On the following afternoon, the man came back with the same pitcher of lemonade and cakes. This time he included a sleeping potion. He distributed the lemonade and the cakes as usual to the soldiers. All of them drank and passed out. Then he turned his attention to the lions and threw them poisoned joints of meat. They too passed out. He sneaked up to the roof of the girl's apartments and began to make a hole. Then he dropped down inside.

199

The girl was taking a nap. He shook her awake and ordered her to accompany him. She protested: 'How can I come with you, dressed in my petticoat? Let me dress.' She went to the room next door where her husband was sleeping. She tried to wake him but couldn't. In her panic she didn't know what to do. Suddenly the wall split apart and a bedouin woman appeared, saying: 'How can I help you?' The girl answered: 'My enemy has caught up with me.' The bedouin answered: 'I will wake your husband, but promise me that if you bear a girl you will give her to me. If you bear a boy you may keep him.' The girl gave her promise, so her husband was woken up, together with the soldiers and the lions. Soon the man was torn to pieces.

The town was all lit up at the news and the prince's wedding was celebrated belatedly. Seven days and seven nights when no fire was lit and no food was cooked except in the sultan's house. God willed it and his young bride became pregnant. Nine months later a baby girl was born as beautiful as the moon. Praise God the creator for creating her with such beauty. The baby crawled, tottered, held to the wall and walked. In real life a child grows up in a year or two, but in just a couple of words in a tale. Little Lulsha turned five and was sent to school. Her mother forgot all about her promise to the bedouin. Every day after school she was met by the old bedouin woman who would kiss her and tell her to remind her mother of her promise. The girl was too young to remember. One day the bedouin pinched her hard on the arm, leaving a mark so that she would remember.

The girl was now fourteen. Her mother was bathing her when she found the mark on her arm. She enquired: 'Who hurt my little darling?' The girl said: 'Oh, Ummi, that reminds me. There is a woman who always kisses me when I come out of school and asks me to remind you of your promise.' The mother was devastated at this and kept silent. That night, she cried her eyes out. The following day, after she had got her daughter ready for school, she told her: 'When this bedouin approaches you again, tell her, "I'm yours." '

The bedouin came as usual to meet Lulsha, who repeated her mother's words to the woman. 'Close your eyes,' the bedouin ordered. Lulsha closed them. When she opened them again, she found herself in a strange place. She cried and shouted for her mother. The bedouin soothed her with gold, diamonds and pearls. Lulsha calmed down and gradually got used to the place. One day the bedouin opened seven rooms for her: one full of diamonds, one full of pearls, one full of gold, and so on until she got to the seventh, which she forbade her to open.

Lulsha's presence filled the bedouin's life with joy. She entertained her with stories and riddles. One day the woman asked her to massage her scalp. As she was doing so, she found a twist of paper in her hair. 'What's this?' she enquired. The old woman explained: 'It's called Burn-me-with-Fire. Put it back.' Lulsha pretended to do so but hid it in her bodice. Then she found another twist of paper. 'What is this called?' she enquired. 'Thorns-and-Thistles. Put it back.' Then she found another one. 'What's this called?' she asked. 'Throw-me-behind-the-Seven-Seas. Did you put them all back?' Lulsha said: 'Yes, of course,' but she was lying.

One day the bedouin woman informed her that she was going on a trip, warned her not to open the forbidden room, and left. Lulsha thought to herself, 'I wonder why she doesn't want me to open this room. She's given me everything: rubies, pearls, diamonds. What is in this room? I must unravel the mystery.' She went straight to the room and opened it. It was a long room. There was a flash of light which she followed. At the end of the room she discovered a fine handsome young man lying on the floor with a heavy stone on his chest. She approached him. 'Hello!' As soon as she said this, he breathed his last. In panic Lulsha rushed from the room and closed it. As soon as she closed the room, she saw a cloud of smoke, the wind rose and the sky grew dark. Lulsha remembered the twist of paper. She threw down the Thorn-and-Thistle one. 'You have betrayed me,' the bedouin cried. 'Take this,' giving her a lock of her hair, 'and roll it into a cigarette and light it if you are in danger.' Lulsha took it, and cast the Throw-me-behind-the-Seven-Seas paper. The bedouin was soon out of sight.

Lulsha went into the different rooms collecting gold, diamonds and pearls, then put on her wrap and went out. She walked and walked until she grew tired and sleepy, she found a stone and sat down to rest. Worn out by exertion she sank into a deathlike slumber and it was not until the following morning when the sun rose that she came to her senses. She woke up to the sound of a shepherd's call. She went to him and said: 'Would you like to exchange my clothes for yours?' 'Are you mad?' he asked. 'I'm serious,' she replied. The shepherd could not but be tempted. He took off his outer clothes and gave them to her. She gave him hers in return and changed into his, rolling up her long hair under a turban, and went back to her seat.

As she sat there, the king's messenger passed by and dropped a letter he was carrying into a puddle. He started to cry, fearing the king's wrath, thinking aloud: 'My head will roll for this!' She approached him saying: 'Don't you worry, I will write you another one.' 'Could you really?' he asked. 'Indeed I could.' (Remember she was speaking as a man, disguised in the shepherd's clothes.) He went and brought her a sheet of paper and an envelope. She copied the letter in her own hand. The messenger was delighted and took it to the king. When the king opened it he was amazed at the elegance of the handwriting. He turned to his vizier saying: 'This letter is not like others. I must find out about it. Call the messenger back.' The messenger was brought before the king. 'Tell me the story behind this letter.' The messenger answered: 'My Lord, I must confess that I dropped the letter in a puddle and a shepherd offered to copy it for me.' The king commanded the shepherd to be brought to him immediately.

She was still resting when the king's guard came to fetch her. They took her to the baths, but fearing she would be found out, she insisted on being left alone to bathe. After bathing, she was dressed in a fine robe befitting a royal scribe. The king took to him (her) at once, and didn't want to be parted from him, even for an instant. The king's wife, as soon as she set eyes on him, felt a burning desire for him. She sent him her maid, saying: 'Could you return the passion of one who burns for you?' He answered: 'I would rather be damned than betray my Lord's trust.' The king's wife was enraged by this answer. 'How dare he turn down someone of my rank? I know what I can do. I shall take my revenge.' She confided in the vizier that the new scribe had made improper suggestions to her.

The vizier was jealous of the scribe's favoured position, so he told the king one day: 'I don't trust the scribe; he has a shifty look. In fact, I think he's a woman.' The king answered: 'Really?' The vizier continued: 'I have long sensed it; only God knows. Let's scatter jasmine flowers on his bed.' *Jasmine will wither in the presence of a woman, but not of a man.* The vizier crept into the scribe's room one afternoon and scattered jasmine flowers on his bed. When the scribe returned to sleep in the evening, she found the flowers and realized the intention behind it. So she gathered up the blooms and left them on the windowsill. When she awoke in the morning, she scattered the still-fresh flowers back on the bed, and went off to her duties. The vizier wasted no time and rushed into the scribe's room to see the result of his scheme. To his surprise, the jasmine flowers were all fresh. He reported it to the king, who said to him: 'I told you he's a man.'

After a while, the king's wife sent her maid again to the scribe saying: 'Would you return the passion of one who burns for you?' Again he answered: 'I don't want your passion; I won't risk my life for it. I would rather be damned than betray my Lord's trust.' This made the king's wife even angrier. She raged 'How dare he disobey me? I shall take my revenge.' So she called the vizier and confided that the scribe was still foisting his attentions on her.

The vizier approached the king, saying that he was still convinced the scribe was a woman. 'I shall spread thorns and thistles in his bed. A man wouldn't pay any attention, but a woman will wake the next day tired and with pains in her back and sides.' *Women are always more delicate than men.* The king agreed to the scheme. The vizier crept into the scribe's room and spread thorns and thistles in his bed. When she came in and went to bed, she sensed something rough, so she decided to sleep on the sofa. The next day, she resumed her duties as usual with no word of complaint about a sleepless night. The king and the vizier gave up.

Two years passed. One day, the king's wife, still harbouring a passion for the scribe, contrived a plan. She instructed her servants that when they heard her cry out, they were to break into the apartments. She crept into the scribe's apartment, saying: 'I have come to you in person this time. Would you return my passion?' He answered: 'I would rather be damned than betray my Lord's trust.' Outraged, the king's wife started to cry for help. All the servants came running and broke in through the window. The news reached the king, who rushed to the scene. 'Your beloved scribe,' she said, 'made advances to me.' The king was enraged and ordered him to be beheaded. 'How dare he have designs on my own wife? He shall die.'

A new day is born and he who prays for the Prophet will be blessed. The vizier was entrusted with carrying out the sentence. Before doing so, he asked the scribe if he had any final request. The scribe said he wanted to smoke a last cigarette. His wish was granted. The scribe rolled a cigarette around that special lock of hair, lit it and inhaled deeply. The second time he inhaled, the sky turned dark, a strong wind arose and the bedouin made her appearance in the air. The crowd gaped in astonishment. The bedouin descended and pulled off the scribe's turban, allowing her beautiful long hair to fall loose to her feet. She snatched her up, saying: 'You stupid donkey! My daughter has been with you for two years and you didn't know if she was man or woman!' With that, she rose into the sky and flew off with her. The king shouted: 'Bring her back to me! Bring her back, bring her back!' But the women were soon out of sight.

By seeking constantly throughout the two years, the bedouin had found a suitable husband for Lulsha, and the wedding was celebrated seven days and seven nights. Lulsha was eventually reunited with her natural mother, and they all lived safely and procreated until death did them part.

II

Rdah

Once upon a time – as God is everywhere, Listeners, may we all be guided to goodness and to make the Shehada [declaration of faith in Islam].

Once upon a time there lived in Tunis a childless king who had always yearned for a child to fill his house with joy. He prayed day and night to God to grant him a child. One night an angel came to him in a dream, asking him: 'Do you want a daughter with a misfortune but who survives, or a son with a misfortune who dies?' He turned on his side and exclaimed: 'God forbid!' But the angel appeared again, explaining: 'I am a messenger sent from God to fulfil your wishes.' His wife the queen noticed his agitation and enquired: 'What's wrong with our lord, his sleep is disturbed and his bed is upset?' He recounted what he had seen and she advised him: 'A daughter. We

are rich and powerful and can overcome any misfortune.'
So when the angel returned, the King asked him for a
daughter. The angel answered: 'When you rise in the
morning, go to the water-butt facing Mecca and you will
find a date. Give half to your wife and eat the rest yourself;
burn the stone as incense and keep it a secret.'

He did so, and his wife became pregnant. A seamstress
was summoned and the baby's layette was prepared. One
evening the queen gave birth to a bouncing little baby
girl as beautiful as the moon. Praise the creator who
created her with such beauty. The baby crawled, toddled,
held to the wall and walked. In real life a child grows in
a year or two, but just in a couple of words in a tale. Out
of concern for her seclusion, the king had a glass palace
built for her, suspended between earth and sky, to prevent
any misfortune befalling her, but 'whatever is written shall
be'.

For forty days mother and baby were pampered and
spoilt. Then the baby was taken to the palace with her
maid. Thus the girl grew up knowing nothing and no one
but her mother and father and the maid. One day the
servant fell ill, and the princess Rdah had to eat her meat
off the bone, which the servant had always removed for
her. Not knowing what it was, she tapped it on the floor,
which broke open, being glass. For the first time ever she
saw the outside world through the hole and people going
to and fro. 'So there are other people besides my parents!'
she exclaimed. As she marvelled at the sight, she heard a
bedouin woman shouting. The princess enquired what

was wrong. The woman answered: 'God protect us! Are you human or spirit?' 'A human,' the princess answered. 'May God protect your beauty! Will you allow me to come and visit you?' The request was granted and she came up into the glass palace. When she saw the princess's long flowing hair, she praised Allah and said: 'Glory to Allah the exalted creator! What beautiful hair you have! The only thing missing is musk oil to perfume it.' 'Where can one get it?' the princess asked. 'Your father is the king and could get you anything.' With that, the woman left.

The following week, Rdah's face turned as pale as straw and she fell ill. Her father was summoned urgently to visit her. When he came and enquired about the cause of her illness, she answered petulantly: 'I want some musk oil.' No sooner had she uttered this than the king slapped her on the face angrily, saying: 'Who put that idea into your head?' She didn't answer, fearing to tell him about the woman coming to visit her. Her father came back to the palace, angry and full of foreboding. The queen met him, enquiring about her daughter's health. He answered: 'There is nothing wrong with her health, but I fear this is the beginning of her misfortune.' 'Tell me what has happened.' He answered: 'Your daughter is now asking for musk oil to be brought to her. You know how its perfume can be smelt for miles around and it is bound to attract attention to her.' 'Have you gone mad?' the queen exclaimed. 'How could she know about it?' asked the king. The queen answered: 'Our daughter is well read. She must have read about it in her books. You shouldn't

210

have hit her. Get it for her and apologize.' So the king
sent his vizier to get it and took it with him when he next
went to visit her, warning her to use it sparingly.

Hmid al-Hilali, a member of the Beni Hilal tribe, had
a cousin of exceptional beauty, but he couldn't take her
as his bride because she was his foster-sister. He always
marvelled at her beauty and asked: 'How on earth could
I ever find anyone else as beautiful as you?' He was already
married to a girl from the same tribe. One day, his cousin
told him of the rumours about a woman of exceptional
beauty living in Tunis. He said: 'I will find her.'

He was a handsome bedouin Arab. He put on his *burnous* and headcloth, picked up his rifle and set off. He
travelled and travelled and travelled, emptying one land
and filling another and no land can be filled except by
our dear almighty God, until he came to a group of
bedouin singers, 'Ghanaya'. A woman among them asked:
'Have you come for us, O handsome young man, or are
you visiting other lands?' 'I have neither come for you nor
am I visiting other lands. Tell me about Rdah, who has
driven suitors mad with her beauty.' She answered: 'An
evil fate must have driven you all this way. If you seek
Paradise it is close at hand; but Hell lies at the end of the
path you have chosen.' He answered: 'Had I wanted wheat
I would have eaten it at home.' He turned his horse
and rode off. He went on and on, emptying one land and
filling another, and no land can be filled except by
almighty God, until he came to another gathering of
bedouin singers, 'Tabbala'. The dancer of the group,

211

seeing his beauty, enquired: 'O handsome young knight, have you come for us, or are you heading for other lands?' He answered: 'I have neither come for you nor am I heading for other lands. Tell me about Rdah who has driven men mad.' She said with a wink: 'Paradise is close at hand; but Hell lies at the end of your path.' He said: 'Had I wanted wheat I would have eaten it at home.' And he rode off.

As he drew closer to Tunis, the perfume of musk oil now wafted stronger and stronger and Hmid's heart throbbed more wildly. He arrived at Bab Bhar, in the centre of the city. He approached a Jewish shoemaker and enquired 'What is this perfume?' The Jew answered:

'It is the perfume of Rdah, Mother of Beauty.
Her breasts are like two golden apples,
Her locks, dressed in sixty-six plaits,
Are perfumed with musk oil.
Her lips are coral-red and her teeth white as pearls.
Her cheeks are like pomegranates.
She is not as tall as a palm tree nor too short to be seen.
Her skin is neither as white as milk nor brown as a berry.'

On hearing her description, Hmid's heart pounded with love and tenderness. He asked where he could find her. The Jew answered: 'Just there,' pointing to the glass palace. Hmid turned his horse and headed for the palace.

Rdah walked about her apartment, dressed in a fine transparent silk petticoat, letting down her long hair loose

and perfumed with musk oil. That day, she had decided
to bathe, so she sent Dadah to fetch some water and heat
it for her. When Dadah reached the spring outside the
palace she was amazed to find a handsome young man
mounted on a horse. She stood marvelling at his beauty
and forgot about the water. When she came to her senses,
she hastened to draw the water and return to the palace.
Rdah scolded her, asking: 'What kept you?' Dadah replied:
'A handsome young knight, mounted on a fine horse,
who fixed me with piercing eyes until I could bear his
gaze no longer.' Rdah told her: 'Go and ask him where
he comes from.' So Dadah went and asked him: 'Who are
you and where do you come from?' He replied: 'Give my
greetings to your mistress and tell her I am Hmid al-
Hilali of the Beni Hilal tribe, whose prowess in battle is
legendary.'

Dadah went back and reported what she had heard.
Rdah covered herself in her wrap and went down to look.
Their eyes met. He told her: 'I was destined to come all
this way to woo you, despite warnings. My heart will always
beat for you, even if I should repent.' She replied: 'Your
folly is boundless. How dare you ask for a treasure you
can never aspire too, a mighty tree you could never climb.'
On hearing this, he turned his horse to leave. She added:
'Are you angry or running away? Anger is unworthy of
noble people.' He replied: 'I am neither angry nor running away, and indeed, anger is unworthy of noble people.
It's of no consequence; only Destiny can decide. If Destiny
delivers you into my hands, even if you resist, you are

213

bound to give in.' She invited him to follow her, and they spent three days and nights together . . . On the third day she gave him her necklace as a token of her troth and sent him to see her father.

Hmid took the necklace and travelled with it to his own land. He went straight to see his cousin and related to her what had happened. She asked him: 'Could you describe her to me?' He repeated the Jew's description. She told him: 'Bring her to me so I can rejoice at your marriage.' He gave her the necklace and told her: 'I have to go to [let's say] France [or America] to order the furniture. Give this to 'Ammar and Khaleifa and send them to ask the king for her hand on my behalf.'

Hmid went back to see his wife, who had heard of his plans, and asked her to prepare some *mesfuf* quickly before he set off. She got it ready and served it to him. Usually she prepared it with butter, sugar, nuts and milk, but this time she served it plain and he remarked on it. 'Nothing is better than sweet *mesfuf* to give one strength to face the day, but yours today is bitter.' She replied: 'No one can either bear or want a cup of bitterness. You are taking another woman in my place; we must go our separate ways.'

His cousin took charge of the painting and decoration of the house in readiness for the wedding. She summoned 'Ammar and Khaleifa and gave them the necklace and asked them to go and visit the king in person. They put on their best clothes and set off. They arrived in the city and headed for the palace, asking for an audience. 'Have you come to make a complaint?' They replied: 'Certainly not. We have come on a private matter.' So the king was informed that two bedouin peasants wanted to see him. He told the footman to show them in after he had finished with the legal affairs of the kingdom. As soon as they were shown in, 'Ammar and Khaleifa greeted the king and threw the necklace before him. The king was taken aback. *Tradition had it that whenever a daughter gave away her necklace, it meant that she accepted the suitor.* Beside himself with rage, the king summoned the vizier and told him to throw Rdah out in rags, like a dog.

Now Dadah came to see her mistress, scolding her for her ingratitude, saying: 'My lord has spoilt and pampered you in a glass palace, away from prying eyes, and you pay him back by choosing an uncouth bedouin peasant.' When Rdah saw the two men, she understood. She found herself outside, dispossessed and stripped of all her belongings.

Rdah, being the king's daughter, had always lived a sheltered and leisurely life. The two men took her and on the way tried to molest her. She resisted, but they took turns in abusing her. She was of the city and not used to the scorching sun. She got sunstroke, and by the time they reached the village she was almost dying. *Where would she escape from her father's wrath.* Hmid al-Hilali's cousin immediately took care of her and nursed her. He sent a messenger to announce his return. By now Rdah was dying. She called Hmid's cousin and told her: 'I have a secret; I want to confide it to you.' The cousin said: 'Tell

215

me; I promise to keep it forever.' She said to her: 'A bird of the land cannot live over the sea, and silk and cotton are for the nobility and merchants. I am soft and he is rough. We are poles apart. That is my real grief. I fell sick from no illness and he is finished without being killed.' And she sighed her last.

Hmid's cousin grieved and wailed over her death. She buried her in an inner room and decided to find him a new bride. She had a beautiful slave girl named Nour al-Sabah. She got her ready for the wedding and carried on with the preparations for the planned celebration.

Rumours of Rdah's death reached Hmid, so he looked from afar through his binoculars to see if there were any signs of mourning in the village. But he was glad to see that the place was all decorated and lit up. He set off and arrived back in the village. He went straight to his cousin and asked if Rdah was there. She answered: 'Indeed, she is to be your bride, just as you wanted.' So she showed him to the bridal chamber but when he lifted Nour al-Sabah's veil he turned to his cousin. 'This isn't Rdah! Tell me where she is!' She replied: 'I can't lie to you any more. Rdah died, and I had her buried in there.' Hmid went to see the tomb, crying: 'He who dies with the sun will be resurrected by the rain. I want no one but my beautiful Rdah. If I can't have her back I will die.' And he fell down dead. *So Destiny united them and Destiny separated them.* So his cousin, weeping, opened Rdah's tomb and laid them to rest together.

There we left them, and they were never seen again.

216

III

Hmid al-Mitjawwil

Listeners, may we all be guided to goodness and to make the Shehada. *Once upon a time...*

Once upon a time, there was a childless king who had always yearned for a child. He prayed to God night and day to grant him a child who would complete his happiness. One night an angel appeared in a dream and asked him: 'Do you want a boy with a misfortune but who lives, or a daughter with a misfortune who dies?' He turned away and said, 'God forbid!' The angel appeared again. Seeing his agitation, his wife enquired what was wrong, and he told her of his vision. She said: 'Ask for a boy. We have power and money and can overcome any misfortune.' So when the angel appeared again, the king asked for a boy. The angel said: 'Go to the water-butt facing

217

Mecca. You will find a date; eat half of it and give the other half to your wife.'

God willed it so, and she conceived. Nine months passed. The queen went into labour and gave birth to a bouncing healthy boy as beautiful as the moon. The news was received with great rejoicing and celebration. The boy crawled, toddled, held to the wall and walked. He was spoilt and pampered. A wet-nurse was summoned to look after the child, then a nanny, then a tutor. The prince was instructed in all the arts and sciences and in chivalry, as befitted his rank.

Now the prince had grown into a handsome young man, but he began to display a cruel streak and his arrogance, given full rein, turned to despotism. No woman was safe from his attentions; wives, young girls and even old maids were dishonoured, to the indignation of husbands, fathers and brothers. People complained to the king, but he wouldn't hear a word against his beloved only son. Outraged, and seeing no other solution, the men turned to an old witch to put an end to his evil excesses. Two men were chosen to go and seek her help. They told her: 'The prince has abused our wives, sisters and mothers, and we don't know how to put a stop to it.' She replied: 'Is that all? I can rid you of him, and erase every trace of his existence from the country.' They came to an agreement about her fee, and left.

The old witch went back to her room and dressed herself in a green robe. She took a green stick and went out. She came to a path he habitually took and sat down with

her legs stretched out in front of her and waited. Soon
the prince passed by on his horse, at a gallop, with his
vizier. Ignoring her presence, he made his horse jump
over her, catching her foot as he did so. She cried out:
'Ouch! My foot!' and started wailing. The vizier came back
and enquired: 'What has happened? What are you wailing
about?' She replied: 'Your honoured master's horse is the
cause. He trampled me and ignored me, and left my toes
bleeding. I will never get over it. He is as haughty as if he
had conquered al-Hajja Mkada.' The vizier continued on
his way. When he caught up with the prince, the latter
asked: 'What kept you, father's vizier?' He replied: 'What
kept me was that wailing old woman who told me, "He
trampled me and ignored me, and left my toe bleeding.
I will never get over it. He is as haughty as if he had
conquered al-Hajja Mkada." ' He asked: 'What did you tell
her?' The vizier replied: 'I told her to wait, and we'd be
back for her.' The prince said: 'Thank you, vizier, for your
initiative.' With that, he turned his horse and headed
back. But when he came to where the woman had been,
she was nowhere to be seen. He hunted around, but to
no avail.

So he went back to the palace, and took to his sickbed.
All the physicians and magicians of the kingdom were
summoned, but each and every one said that he was suffering from mere melancholy. The king was perturbed, fearing that his only son might die. He tried everything to
make him laugh – acrobats, jugglers, conjurors – but without success. All the old story-tellers in the kingdom, men

and women, were called to entertain him but the old witch refused, saying: 'If he wants me, let him come to me. After all, young people should respect their elders.'

On hearing this, the prince pulled himself together and went to see her. She asked him: 'So now you are infatuated with the black-eyed beauty you have heard about? I will direct you how to find al-Hajja Mkada, but promise me that you will go without a companion. Promise me that you will go unarmed.' As soon as he heard this, the prince rushed back to the palace, hurriedly gathered together provisions and all his heart's desires, and informed the king and queen he was leaving. The king declared mourning throughout the kingdom: no one was to celebrate a wedding, or a circumcision, no rejoicing whatsoever was to take place.

Hmid al-Mitjawwil (for this was the prince's name) walked and walked and walked. He beheaded anyone he met who was unable to tell him of her whereabouts. Eventually he grew tired of beheading people and decided to do otherwise. He approached a shoemaker and sat chatting with him for a while. He left him a purse of gold and disappeared. The shoemaker was overjoyed at such a windfall. The next day, the prince came back to see the man and left another purse of gold. On reporting this unexpected godsend to his wife, she suggested he should ask the man to come and dine with them.

So, on the next occasion the shoemaker saw the prince, he invited him to dine. When he came to the house, the shoemaker's wife asked him: 'I understand you are looking

for al-Hajja Mkada?' He replied: 'Indeed I am.' She reproached him, saying: 'What has driven you to this? Your very
life is at risk.' The prince answered: 'My life is in God's
hands. I don't need your advice.' She continued: 'In this
country, the hangman's noose awaits anyone who ventures
to talk about her or say where she is. But I will direct you.
My husband will be carrying an oil-can. Follow him, and
when he collapses, do not stop to help him but continue
on your way until you come to the palace where she lives.'
The next morning, the prince did as he was told. When
he came to the palace, he found a horse-trough and a
bench. He tied up his horse and lay down to rest on the
bench.

Al-Hajja Mkada was wandering about in her palace when
Dadah came to inform her that Hmid al-Mitjawwil was
outside. The princess replied, with a smile, 'He is destined
to be my husband. Go to the store-room and make some
honey dough.' Dadah hurriedly made the cakes and came
back with them to her mistress, who told her: 'Go and
waken this sleeping beauty. Give him these honey-cakes
and tell him, "Eat these, and leave. This is not a place for
a playboy like you."' Dadah went down and wakened
Hmid al-Mitjawwil, reporting to him what her mistress had
said. He said: 'Give my greetings to your mistress and tell
her I don't want your pastries; it's a different sort of honey-
cake I want . . .' Dadah went back to her mistress and told
her what he had said. The princess took a quick bath, put
on a silk petticoat. As she walked about her apartment,
the perfume of musk wafted all over the place. She sent

Dadah downstairs to invite the man to join her in her sleeping chamber. He greeted her, saying:

'You who have broken every young man's heart . . .
News of your beauty reached me one day
And at once I set off without delay.
For two years I wandered around and around,
But no one would tell me where you could be found.'

She replied:

'I am al-Hajja Mkada, daughter of the prophet 'Issa,
My beauty is flawless and my fame spread afar.
Had I not feared disgrace, the mere sight of my face
Would distract the poor pilgrims away from God's grace.'

They spent three days and nights in illicit bliss, then she gave him her necklace as a token of her troth, and he rode away. The following day the prince sought an audience with the king. In private, he gave him the necklace and told him he was Hmid al-Mitjawwil, son of his highness the king of Tunis. He gave him a warm welcome and immediately gave orders to celebrate the wedding, seven days and seven nights.

The prince's father was still in mourning for his absence, so a messenger was sent to him to say that his son was safe and sound. Three days after the marriage was celebrated, the prince and his new bride took leave of the king and travelled back to the prince's land. A second celebration of the wedding took place. The whole kingdom was painted and decorated and lit up in their honour. And they lived safely and procreated until death did them part.

IV

The Birthmark

Listeners, may we all be guided to goodness and to make the Shehada. *Once upon a time . . .*

Once upon a time there was a perfume merchant who was married to his cousin. She was loyal, faithful and dearer than life to him. One day, as he was working in his shop, a man passed by selling a bird which could sing and tell stories. He said to himself: 'Why not buy it for my wife to keep her company?' He bought it, and bought for it a golden cage and two bowls, one gold and one silver, and took it home to his wife. He filled one bowl with rose water and the other with bird-seed. Of course, the bird could talk. Each and every day his wife would get up in the morning, see to her household chores and then sit and listen to the bird, entertaining her with stories. She grew very fond of the bird.

224

One day, a group of fellow-merchants decided on a business trip. The merchant was asked to join them. He went home and informed his wife about the trip. She said to him: 'How can you think of leaving me alone, a helpless woman?' He answered: 'Such is life . . . I have to make a living. After all, you've got your bird to keep you company.' She said: 'May God protect you.' She prepared a year's provisions for him. *A new day is born and he who prays for the Prophet will be blessed.* He bade her farewell and left.

The expedition reached Baghdad. They would buy and sell during the day and gather at night to play cards, dominoes and chess, and to chat. One evening the topic of women's fickleness was raised. One of them said: 'No one could even dream of seeing my wife's fingernail.' Another added: 'It would be easier to reach heaven than to catch a glimpse of my sister.' The merchant intervened, saying: 'No matter what you say, there will never be a woman as virtuous as my wife. She has never stepped across the threshold and no man has ever seen her toe.' One of them answered: 'Who do you take her for! Let us bet on it.' The merchant said: 'Done! Let us play a game of cards.' They played, and the other man won. He said to him: 'Does she have any distinguishing mark on her body?' The merchant answered: 'Yes, she has.' The other merchant asked: 'What if I discovered it?' The merchant answered: 'Then you may do as you please.'

The man took ship and sought out an old witch, told her the story and asked her to help him reach the woman, otherwise he would lose all his fortune and become a

225

slave to the brother. They came to an agreement, and he directed her to the woman's house.

The old witch dressed herself in a green robe, covered her head with a green shawl and painted her stick green and went to see the woman. She knocked on the door and posed as her aunt, but the woman was surprised to hear that she had an aunt. The old witch explained: 'Your father, God rest his soul, cut me off from my sister, so we weren't able to see each other. Now he is in God's care, and I have forgiven him.' She started to cry and sob. The woman was taken in by her sweet words and let her in. She entertained her to tea, and then she left. The old witch would come and visit her every day. One day, she came and invited her to attend her supposed daughter's henna ceremony, which would be incomplete without her presence, now that they had been reunited, thank God. The woman answered: 'You know my husband is away and I cannot go out in his absence.' The witch replied: 'How can you disappoint your cousin like that? Don't you want her to be happy?' She eventually talked her into it. The woman put on her finery, took out her silk and silver veil and was about to go out when the bird intervened: 'Mistress, put your silken veil away in the chest and your gold in your jewel-box, and let me tell you the story of the *muezzin*.' The old witch said: 'Is this the time for telling stories? Damn the bird!' The woman answered: 'I must listen to my bird's story.' The old witch left in a rage.

The bird started his story: Once upon a time there was a pious *muezzin* who used to make a living calling people to pray. One day, as he was calling people for the morning prayer, a dove flew down and settled on his shoulder. He stroked her gently, but soon the dove picked him up in her beak and flew off to a distant land. On arrival, the dove changed into a beautiful maiden as beautiful as the moon, praise the creator who created her with such beauty. She soon advised him that she had made him the king of that land in place of her recently deceased husband. The *muezzin* thanked Allah the merciful for his *qasm* [allotted share] and lived happily for years treated with the love and respect due to a king. One day the queen discovered that he was not faithful to her anymore. When she confronted him with it, he said: "You are getting too old for me!" Grieved and hurt in her pride, she changed him back into a *muezzin* and blew him off to his original place, and fate turned against him. When he realized his change of fortune, he regretted it, and stood days on end waiting for the dove to come back.' The bird continued: 'Mistress, if you leave your house you will regret it too.' She folded her veil, placed it in the chest and declined the invitation.

The old witch left in a rage. She went to see the man who was waiting to carry the woman off on his horse, and related what had happened, saying: 'It's an impossible task. Did her husband mention anything distinctive about her?' He answered: 'Yes, she has a birthmark.' She replied: 'Don't you worry. I will tell you what it is.'

She came to visit the woman on a scorching hot afternoon and suggested they should take a refreshing shower, explaining: 'I can see your hair is dirty. Let me give you a good wash, scrub your back and pour the water over you, just like your mother would have done, God rest her soul.' And she started to cry. The woman heated some water and they went into the kitchen. As she was taking off her clothes, the old witch noticed her birthmark: a slice of watermelon, green on the outside and red in the middle, with black pips, visible on her thigh. As soon as she saw it, she took to her heels to find the man. Immediately he heard, he went back to find her husband and tell him that he had had his wife, proving it by describing the mark on her thigh. 'From now on I claim your fortune and you become my slave as agreed.' The merchant opened a doughnut shop to survive, dressed in rags and fried dough-nuts, barefoot.

The woman was surprised at the old witch's disappear-ance but the bird told her: 'You are so naïve.' Time passed until one day he told her: 'Do you know that my master is now in Baghdad, a slave to a fellow-merchant, making doughnuts for a living?' She immediately disguised herself in men's clothes, gathered provisions and all her heart's desires, and asked her bird if he wanted anything from there. He told her: 'On your way back across the Red Sea, call out three times for Morjan, my cousin, and tell him: "Yaqut greets you and asks you how he can escape from his cage and leave this foreign land." '

A new day is born and he who prays for the Prophet will be blessed. She gathered together provisions and all her heart's desires and took ship. In Baghdad she sought out her husband and enquired what had happened. He related the whole story to her. She told him: 'I have not been brought up to disgrace my family,' and told him all about the old witch. She redeemed her husband and they sailed away together. When they came to the Red Sea, she called out: 'Morjan, Morjan! Yaqut greets you and asks you how to escape and leave this foreign land.' Morjan replied: 'Why don't you just bang your head against the wall?' *Obviously the woman couldn't understand the message.* When they arrived back home the bird was delighted to see them. After they had had a meal and drunk tea, the bird enquired: 'Did you talk to my cousin?' She answered: 'Of course I did.' He asked: 'What did he say?' She replied: 'Bang your head against the wall.' They had a good night's sleep. The following morning she got up to find the bird dead in its cage. She wailed and cried and mourned him: 'My poor bird. He was my only companion and adviser.' The husband intervened: 'All this for a bird! I will buy you another one.' He reached out for the bird and threw it on the rubbish heap. The bird flew off. There we left them and we have never seen them since.

V

Walha and 'Aysha

My tale is one of wonder. May our prayers and yours be offered up for the beloved Prophet, peace be upon him! Listeners, may we all be guided to goodness and to make the Shehada. *Once upon a time . . .*

Once upon a time there was a silk merchant who had two daughters called Walha and 'Aysha. The two girls were of exceptional beauty. The merchant had a nephew who wanted to marry 'Aysha, but the merchant swore he would only give her in marriage to a suitor who could offer him three loads of gold as a bride-price, even if he were a Jew. The nephew was poor and humble and couldn't satisfy the father's greed and provide for his cousin. Walha, the elder girl, advised her cousin to travel and make his fortune and come back to claim her younger sister. For her part, she would not allow her younger sister to marry before her.

So the young man went to see his uncle and informed him he was going to France to seek his fortune. He made his uncle promise not to give 'Aysha to anyone else in the meantime.

One day, a rich Jew arrived, mounted on a fine horse, and asked for 'Aysha's hand, offering the required three loads of gold. The father was tempted, and agreed to give her in marriage. 'Aysha cried and wailed, but what could she do? *Such was the fate God had ordained for her.* The marriage took place, and 'Aysha soon took to her husband. He was kind and gentle, and showered her with gifts and attention.

Her cousin worked hard night and day to save up and came back to claim her. He found Walha grinding corn and singing this song: 'O cousin, what happened to you? A man has come to take her from you.' The cousin was saddened by the news, but swore not to give up. Walha offered to help him win 'Aysha back.

'Aysha's husband, Khaleifa, was very rich and owned huge estates. The cousin approached one of his shepherds, who told him everything he wanted to know about his master's wealth, his lands and his wife, who was kept locked up in a palace, and her blind mother-in-law kept the key. The shepherd was in the habit of massaging the old lady's head to help her fall asleep each evening. The cousin offered a purse of gold to the shepherd in exchange for his clothes, and went to the old lady in his place. As she drifted off to sleep under his soothing touch, he was able to steal the key to the palace. 'Aysha's husband was away on a trip. The cousin slipped into her room, surprised her and asked her to come with him. But 'Aysha refused, saying that she was now married and loved her husband. The cousin managed to catch her and carry her off.

On his way, he met the husband coming back on his horse, carrying quantities of meat and bottles of wine. The Jew quickly rescued his wife and tied her abductor to a tree. Then they sat before him, grilling the meat, eating and drinking. Gradually they became drunk and helpless. The cousin managed to untie himself and reached out for the Jew's sword. He stabbed him and slapped 'Aysha on the face to wake her. Then he bundled her on to the horse and made off.

When they arrived at his uncle's house, he was met by Walha, who soon took charge of her sister, slapping and scolding her, and saying: 'Shame on you! You're a disgrace to your family. You let down your cousin for a Jew, and indulged in drinking.' Then she locked her in her room for three days.

After the customary three months' period of mourning had passed, 'Aysha was wedded to her cousin. And they lived safely and procreated.

VI

The Bedouin and The Trousers

Once upon a time . . .

Once upon a time there was a rich bedouin who came to settle in Tunis. He was recommended to Ummi 'Aysha the matchmaker to help him find a wife.

Ummi 'Aysha welcomed him and gave him some water to wash his feet. 'Meanwhile, I shall prepare you some food from your provisions,' she said. She opened his bag. To her surprise, it was full of gold, not wheat. She gaped, and went back to him, saying: 'You must go and wash in the baths.' 'What baths?' he asked. 'Well, the public baths where anyone can go for a wash and massage,' she answered. 'But wait here.'

She went to the old city and bought him a fine traditional *burnous* and *jibba*. She tied them up in a cloth, added a silver box containing jasmine-scented *tfal* [washing clay] and gave him two gold Louis from his own money. One was for the bath and one for the barber, she instructed. The young bedouin went to the bath. At first he was received coolly, but when he showed the gold coins the attendants rushed to serve him.

Ummi 'Aysha the go-between took good care of the young bedouin for seven days and seven nights, feeding him and looking after his needs and teaching him Beldi manners. One day, she said to him: 'I must now find you a fine bride.' He said: 'That's a good idea.' She went to ask for the hand of the daughter of a modest Beldi family who, on hearing about the bedouin's extreme wealth, agreed to celebrate the marriage the following Thursday.

On the wedding day, the bedouin was taken to the bridal chamber and left with the bride. The bedouin had never worn trousers or been to an indoor toilet. Ummi 'Aysha had made him many pairs of trousers and put them away in the chest. When he needed to relieve himself, he took off his trousers and made for the bathroom. The bride was shocked. The bedouin, thinking she was shocked to see his trousers exclaimed: 'I have got seven other pairs in the chest!' The bride ran out of the room and asked immediately for a divorce.

VII

The Old Witch and Satan

Once upon a time . . .

Once upon a time, the old witch and Satan would bet on causing a couple to divorce. The old witch would say: 'You can't!' and he would reply: 'Of course, I can! I'll show you.' He found a pretext to make them quarrel. They argued and argued all night, but she ended by sleeping in his arms. Satan lost his bet.

It was now the old witch's turn. She put on her green robe and shawl, painted her stick green, took her rosary and went to the couple's house in the early afternoon. She knocked on the door, pushed it ajar and spoke to the woman through the crack. 'It's time to pray; will you allow me to make my ablutions here?' The woman was taken in and allowed her to enter the house. The old witch made her ablutions, and said her prayers. The woman invited her to stay and lunch with her. When they sat down to eat the *couscous*, the old witch said: 'My daughter, I'm afraid I have got into the bad habit of eating with two spoons. Would you mind?' 'Not at all,' replied the mistress of the house. She brought another spoon and they began to eat. The old witch helped herself alternately from two different parts of the dish, so that it looked as if two guests had been eating. The husband arrived shortly and joined them. When he sat down, the old witch turned to the young woman and asked: 'Where is your guest?' 'Guest? Which guest?' she answered. 'The one who was eating here with us just now,' the witch replied. 'But there was no one else!' the woman protested. The witch turned to the husband and pointed to the second spoon, saying: 'Look, here is his spoon, and there [pointing to the door of the room] are his slippers!' In fact, the old witch herself had surreptitiously dropped the slippers from under her robe on entering. The young woman was aghast, but her husband lost his temper and pronounced her thrice-divorced on the spot. The old witch left laughing in triumph.

VIII

Qamar al-Zaman

My tale is one of wonder. May our prayers and yours be offered up for the beloved Prophet, peace be upon him! Listeners, may we all be guided to goodness and to make the Shehada. *Once upon a time . . .*

Once upon a time there lived a sultan – *and there is no sultan but Allah* – who had a son called Qamar al-Zaman. He had the prince taught and instructed in all branches of the arts and sciences and in chivalry. Qamar al-Zaman came of age to marry. The sultan sent his vizier to consult the prince, but he would not agree to it. The sultan sent the vizier back on the same mission on several other occasions, but the prince persisted in his refusal. This angered the sultan, who decided to send him into exile in a distant abandoned palace, with the vizier for sole companion.

237

This palace was in fact inhabited by two demonesses, Queen Morgana and Queen Maymouna. When Qamar al-Zaman and the vizier went to sleep, the two demonesses came out of their hiding-place and marvelled at the prince's beauty. 'Praise to God!' said Maymouna, 'who created such beauty!' Morjana replied: 'Fancy a father sending such a handsome boy into exile just because he didn't want to get married!' 'Let's have some fun,' suggested Maymouna.

In a faraway land lived Husn al-Wujoud, the only daughter of a king, who also turned down all the suitors who sought her hand. Maymouna suggested Husn al-Wujoud would be a suitable bride for Qamar al-Zaman. They left Qamar al-Zaman sleeping and flew off to the land of Husn al-Wujoud. They gave her a sleeping-potion and carried her back to Qamar al-Zaman's palace, and laid her by his side. When he woke up he found the beautiful maiden beside him. He tried to wake her up: 'Sleeper, sleeper! Wake up!' But she wouldn't answer him. So he took off the ring with his seal and slipped it on to her finger. With that, he was put back to sleep. Husn al-Wujoud woke up to find herself lying beside a handsome stranger. 'Who can this fine young man be?' She shook him: 'Sleeper, sleeper! Wake up!' But he wouldn't answer her. She took off her ring and slipped it on to his finger. With that, Husn al-Wujoud was put back to sleep and carried back to her palace.

Qamar al-Zaman woke up the following morning and looked for his partner of the night before. 'Where is the beautiful maiden who was in my bed last night?' he asked the vizier. 'Which maiden? There was no maiden,' replied the vizier, bemused. Qamar al-Zaman recounted to him all that had passed during the night. 'Dear child!' exclaimed the vizier. 'Take care not to repeat this story to anyone. They will say the sultan's son has gone mad.' 'But I haven't!' he protested. 'I have told you nothing but the truth.' The vizier, concerned, went to tell the sultan. Everybody was now convinced that the prince was suffering from hallucinations.

Qamar al-Zaman's face turned as pale as straw and he slept in a consumptive bed. All the physicians and the magicians of the kingdom were summoned, but they all said he suffered from mere melancholy. The king and the court did all they could to cheer him up and dissipate his gloom, but for all their efforts he remained silent and brooded over what had happened the previous night.

Husn al-Wujoud woke up the following morning and looked for her partner of the night before. 'Where is the handsome youth who was in my bed last night?' she asked her mother. 'Which youth? There was no youth,' replied her mother, bemused. Husn al-Wujoud recounted to her all that had passed during the night. 'Dear child!' exclaimed her mother. 'Take care not to repeat this story to anyone. They will say the king's daughter has gone mad.' 'But I haven't!' she protested. 'I have told you nothing but the truth.' The queen, concerned, went to tell the king that the princess was suffering from hallucinations.

Husn al-Wujoud's face turned as pale as straw and she slept in a consumptive bed. All the physicians and the magicians of the kingdom were summoned, but they all said she suffered from mere melancholy. The king and the court did all they could to cheer her up and dissipate her gloom, but for all their efforts she remained silent and brooded over what had happened the previous night.

The news of Qamar al-Zaman's illness travelled to the village where lived a traditional bedouin healer, who set off at once to tend the prince. When he came before him, he said: 'Confide in me, and tell me the whole story.' Qamar al-Zaman recounted to him what had happened the previous night. The healer replied: 'Your cure is in my hands. I will bring her back to you, but you will have to come with me.'

The prince gathered his strength, took leave of the king and set off with the bedouin. They crossed country after country, crying out: 'Here is the healer of your afflictions, but the cure is in God's hands.' At last they reached the land of Husn al-Wujoud. The bedouin asked to attend the princess. Qamar al-Zaman disguised himself as the healer's assistant and went in with him to her chamber. As soon as he entered, she recognized him and came to her senses. Qamar al-Zaman, overjoyed to have found his beloved, rushed to the king and asked for her hand. The wedding was celebrated, seven days and seven nights of festivities. At the end of this time the prince sought his father-in-law's permission to take her back to his own land for a second ceremony.

240

A new day is born and he who prays for the Prophet will be blessed. The prince and princess boarded a ship and set sail for Qamar al-Zaman's land. They sailed and sailed until they reached an island, where they put in to rest. They sat down under a palm tree and Husn al-Wujoud laid her head on the prince's lap and dozed off. Qamar al-Zaman noticed the pearl necklace she was wearing and undid it to take a closer look. As he did so, a bird swooped down and snatched it from his hand. The prince ran after the bird as fast as he could, getting further and further from Husn al-Wujoud until he had lost his way completely.

Husn al-Wujoud waited and waited, and when he failed to return, thought, 'He must have abandoned me.' She disguised herself as a man, sealed up her jars full of jewellery and settled down on a rock. Now this island was not far from Qamar al-Zaman's father's land. As she sat there, the king's messenger passed by and happened to drop a letter he was carrying in a puddle. He cried and wailed: 'I fear my head will roll for this! What shall I do?' 'Don't worry,' replied Husn al-Wujoud, 'I'll write you a new one.' She fetched pen and paper and copied out the letter. Relieved, the messenger continued on his way to the palace.

Qamar al-Zaman tried to retrace his steps, but without success. He decided to find work and settle down. He found an old man who tended a market-garden and asked him to take him on. The old man was alone in the world and welcomed the idea of adopting a son. 'You will be my son, my child, and we will share whatever God sends us.'

241

Qamar al-Zaman soon settled into the work, praying: 'O Almighty God, help me to find my lost bride, Husn al-Wujoud.' He explained to the old man that the ship bringing him back to his father's land had left its last port of call without him, and it would not come back until the next year.

The king's messenger arrived at the palace with the letter. On reading it, the king was amazed at the beauty of the calligraphy. 'Who wrote this? Bring him to me!' he exclaimed. Frightened, the messenger rushed back to find the 'man' who had helped him. Husn al-Wujoud was soon brought before the king and made his court scribe. Honoured and feted, the scribe soon gained the king's favour and attention, and was asked to marry the king's daughter. Husn al-Wujoud replied: 'I shall never refuse you your wish.' Back in her room, Husn al-Wujoud cried and wept over her dilemma.

The festivities were held to celebrate the wedding. On the wedding night the 'bridegroom' ignored his bride and slept apart. The following day, the bride's mother enquired how the bridal night had passed. 'He didn't come to me, but slept on his own,' she explained sadly. 'There, there, don't fret, my child. It was only the first night after all,' replied her mother, 'he must have been shy.' The second and third nights passed in the same way. The bride's mother grew concerned and advised her daughter to say to him: 'The Prophet sent you a gift. Do you take it or leave it?'

That night the bride did as she was advised and said to

her groom: 'The Prophet sent you a gift. Do you take it
or leave it?' Husn al-Wujoud burst into tears when she
heard this. 'Confide in me,' urged the bride, 'and tell me
the whole truth.' 'I am a woman just like you,' Husn al-
Wujoud replied. 'I promise to get my husband to marry
you as well, when I find him.' Behind closed doors, they
vowed eternal friendship. The following morning the
mother was comforted to hear that the marriage was consummated.

Meanwhile, Qamar al-Zaman continued to work hard
for the old man, praying that he would be reunited with
his beloved. One day, he surprised two birds fighting over
a necklace. One of them swallowed it. The other struck
it, and it fell to the floor, dead. Qamar al-Zaman rushed
to pick up the dead bird, open its crop and remove the
necklace, which he sealed in a jar. He heard that the ship
had put into port again and they were looking for him.
He rushed to the old man to bid him goodbye. 'My destiny
is accomplished. I must go,' he announced. 'My dear son,
don't let me die in this land of infidels. I feel my hour
has come.' The ship was to be in harbour for a month.
Qamar al-Zaman was hoping the old man's condition
would improve before he had to leave, but Fate caught
up with him and he died. Qamar al-Zaman buried him
and carried out all the mourning rituals as befitted a son.
By then the ship had left and Qamar al-Zaman had been
left behind again.

*A new day is born and he who prays for the Prophet will be
blessed.* He resumed work, praying to Almighty God to

reunite him with his beloved. The following year, the ship called again, with Husn al-Wujoud on board. They were eventually reunited, but Husn al-Wujoud recounted her story and asked him to pose as her brother. She said to him: 'The princess has kept my secret and I promised her you would take her as a wife.' 'But I can't do that!' he exclaimed. 'You are my only wife.' 'It must be,' she insisted.

Qamar al-Zaman was received as an honoured guest for three days and three nights. In private, he took the princess as his second wife. After some time, Husn al-Wujoud obtained permission to take her bride to her father's land, together with her supposed brother. When they arrived, they were warmly welcomed, and all three settled there together. There we left them, and we have never seen them since.

IX

The Fisherman's Daughter

My tale is one of wonder.
May our prayers and yours be offered up for the beloved Prophet,
peace be upon him! May the old witch Azuzet es-Stut be damned!
Listeners, may we all be guided to goodness and to make the
Shehada. *Once upon a time . . .*

Once upon a time there was a fisherman from Kelibia
who was poor but managed to make a meagre living. He
was happily married and had a daughter called ʻAysha.
ʻAysha's *mʻallma* [mistress in a traditional learning institution for girls] was a widow and always enquired about
ʻAysha's parents and whether they were happy. ʻAysha
always answered that they were happy, thank God, and
loved each other. The *mʻallma* was jealous and wanted to
get rid of the wife, to take her place. So one day, she put
a scorpion in a small box and gave it to ʻAysha, instructing

her to empty it in the *couscous* jar in the pantry. One day, the fisherman's wife made her husband promise that if she died, he would wait until 'Aysha was as tall as the nail she had driven into the wall before remarrying. The husband said: 'May God grant you long life.' She replied: 'Our span is in God's hands.'

A week later, the *m'allma* told 'Aysha to ask her mother to give her some *couscous*. When 'Aysha's mother went to get the *couscous*, she was bitten by the scorpion and died. 'Such is the fate that God has decreed,' the man thought, resignedly. The daughter grieved for her mother's death but was immediately taken in by the *m'allma*, who looked after her, bathing her and changing her clothes. One day, she asked her: 'Why doesn't your father remarry?' She replied: 'I don't know. I will ask him.' When she came home that day, she asked her father: 'Why don't you find another wife?' He answered: 'I promised your mother I wouldn't remarry until you reached that nail up there.'

On the following day, 'Aysha related this to her *m'allma*, who soon made plans to visit her home on the pretext of offering to clean it. When she came to the house, she went straight to the nail and lowered it. She cleaned the house, cooked the dinner and waited for the fisherman's return. When he came back, she served him a delicious dinner and said: 'You really ought to have a woman to look after you and your daughter, you know.' He said: 'I promised my late wife, God rest her soul, not to remarry until little 'Aysha was as tall as that nail in the wall.' She said: 'Let's try her.' When they did, to his surprise, 'Aysha

246

came up to the height of the nail. 'Aysha said: 'Now you can remarry, and my *m'allma* is the right person for you.' So the father and the *m'allma* eventually got married and she moved in with them.

The *m'allma* also had a daughter called Hafsa. Hafsa was pampered and spoilt and taught embroidery and lace-making, and little 'Aysha was always asked to do the dirty jobs: cleaning, and washing the floor. From early morning till nightfall, 'Aysha would sweep the floor, do the washing and cooking; who cares the loving mother is in the grave. She would cry her eyes out remembering her dead mother. *We were neither thanked nor praised.* Her stepmother maltreated her and spoilt her own daughter. One day, the fisherman came back home as usual with fish for dinner. 'Aysha, as usual, was told to gut and clean them. As she started the job, one of the fish spoke to her. 'Set me free and I will make you rich.' 'Aysha took the fish and threw it in the well. When her stepmother counted the fish she found one missing. She questioned 'Aysha about it. She answered: 'As I was washing it, it fell down the well.' Her stepmother gave her a good hiding and shut her up in the washhouse on the roof with a bag of corn to grind. Her father tried to reason with his wife, but she wouldn't back down.

So little 'Aysha found herself upstairs, weeping and wailing, in the dark. She became thirsty and started to whine. Suddenly the room lit up and she found a well made of silver with a golden chain. When she let down the bucket to draw water, she heard a sheep saying: 'Little 'Aysha, give me some water.' Before she drank herself, she gave him some. So he said: 'May you have the softness of my fleece.' As she was about to drink, a gazelle appeared, asking: 'Give me some water.' She gave her some, and the gazelle answered: 'May you have my eyes.' Again, as she was about to drink, there appeared a rose, saying: 'Give me some water.' She gave her some, and the rose said: 'May you have my perfume and my bloom.' Again, as she was about to drink, a cypress tree emerged asking: 'Little 'Aysha, give me some water.' She gave her some, and the cypress tree said, 'May you have my height.' As she went to drink again, a jasmine blossom appeared, saying: 'I'm thirsty: give me some water.' She gave her some, and the jasmine said: 'May your tears, every time you weep, be pearls and jewels streaming down your face.' At last, little 'Aysha was able to quench her thirst and the fish appeared, saying: 'Didn't I tell you you would be rewarded for setting me free?' The fish spent the rest of the night finishing 'Aysha's tasks for her: picking over the grain, grinding and sifting it.

Her stepmother got up early in the morning and went up to see if 'Aysha had done what she had been told to do. When she opened the door she was amazed at what she saw. She exclaimed: 'Where did all this come from? Tell me!' 'Aysha said: 'I don't know. I have spent the night working at the grain.' The stepmother did not believe her and beat her cruelly. As she wept, tears of pearls and gemstones streamed down her face. This fuelled the stepmother's anger, and she went straightaway to her own daughter Hafsa, instructing her to do what her sister had done. She gave her some fish to clean. As she started her task, one of the fish spoke to her. 'Set me free, and I will reward you.' 'Aysha's stepsister answered: 'Never! I want to enjoy your flesh.' The fish leapt up, saying: 'You will regret it.' 'Aysha's stepsister was then given a second task, to pick over and grind the grain in the washhouse on the roof. She was dragged there, weeping and wailing, and locked in. She started the job, unwillingly, then felt thirsty, so she drew some water from the well. As she was about to drink, a sheep appeared and asked: 'Give me some water, Hafsa.' She replied: 'Not on your life. I'm thirsty – I drink first.' So he cursed her: 'May you have my wool matted with burrs.' As she went to drink a second time, a gazelle appeared, saying: 'Give me some water.' She replied: 'Never!' The gazelle cursed her: 'May you have my behind for your face!' As she went to drink, the rose appeared, saying 'Give me some water.' She replied: 'What? Give you water when I'm thirsty myself?' So the rose cursed her: 'May you have my thorns.' As she went again to drink, the cypress tree appeared, saying: 'Give me some water.' She answered: 'Never!' So the cypress tree cursed her: 'May you have my thorns and brushwood entangling your feet when you walk, and serpents and scorpions streaming down your face when you cry.' As she was about to drink, the jasmine blossom appeared, saying: 'Give me some water.' She refused. So the jasmine cursed her: 'May you have my greenness.' As she was about to drink, undisturbed at last, she felt a change coming over her. So she cursed her mother: 'It's all my mother's fault, damn her!'

Early in the morning, her mother hurried upstairs to see the result of the night's work. She was shocked at what she saw. She lamented over her daughter's horrible transformation and wept bitterly until her heart broke and she died.

Little 'Aysha was spoilt and pampered by her father, and many suitors came to ask for her hand. She chose the finest one, and her father gave orders to celebrate the wedding with seven days and seven nights of festivities. And they lived happily and procreated until death did them part.

X

The Bird Without Wings

Listeners, may we all be guided to goodness and to make the Shehada. *Once upon a time . . .*

Once upon a time there was a silk merchant whom God granted seven sons and one daughter. The girl's mother took good care in giving her a good upbringing, teaching her modesty and propriety and all the domestic skills – embroidery, knitting, sewing, cooking – and the girl never set foot outside. She sat every day embroidering on the terrace. One day, the prince's bird flew off so he followed it from roof to roof, until he came near where the girl sat engrossed in her embroidery. He saw her and marvelled at her beauty. The prince's face turned as pale as straw and he took to his bed. All the court physicians were summoned to cure him, but they all said that he was suffering from depression. Story-tellers were brought to entertain the prince but he refused access to see any of them and asked instead for the old witch. When she came, he confided his secret to her and she promised to bring the girl to him.

The old witch dressed herself in a green robe, put on a green shawl, picked up a green stick and went out to search for the girl's house. When she arrived in front of the house, she sat on the doorstep. The maid was washing the floor and accidentally splashed the old woman. The old witch shouted: 'What have I done to you, a pious old woman like me?' 'Forgive me! I didn't mean to,' the maid exclaimed. *Old women were respected in those days.* On hearing the commotion, the mistress went out to investigate. She saw the old witch, who complained to her about the incident. So the mistress of the house invited her to come in and change her wet clothes.

Now, out of concern to keep her secluded, the merchant had had a private apartment built on the upper floor for his daughter's use. The old witch came in, changed into dry clothes offered by the mistress, and enquired whether the woman lived on her own. The mistress replied: 'I have my daughter, God bless her, who lives upstairs.' Soon the sons and the father came back from work to have supper. The old witch was invited to join them, as custom dictated that guests present at mealtimes should be fed. Over the meal, she entertained them with tales of the Prophet, *God have mercy on him,* and jokes. When night fell, the old witch made as if to leave. But the mistress of the house and her daughter were greatly entertained by her company and

252

begged her to stay three days and nights with them, as was the tradition established by the Prophet, *God have mercy on him*. So she stayed three days and three nights with the girl in her private apartment before leaving.

A week later, she came back and everybody gave her a warm welcome, offering her gifts. By now she had become almost a member of the household, respected and revered. One day, she came to the house and informed the merchant's wife: 'My daughter, my only daughter, is getting married on Thursday and I want her sister, your daughter, to attend her *henna*.' The mistress apologized, saying: 'She's not allowed out. Her father and brothers would kill me if she stepped across the threshold.' The old witch convinced her that nobody would need to know: they could take her in the evening and come back in the early morning, before the men of the house were up. The mistress persisted in refusing, but the old witch eventually talked her into accepting. On Thursday evening, the girl put on her best clothes and finery and went out.

Her mother gave her a handkerchief full of sand to mark her path in case she lost her way, as she had never before ventured outside the house. The girl and the old witch walked and walked until the girl was exhausted and enquired: 'Haven't we arrived yet?' 'Soon, my dear,' the old woman replied. Eventually they came to a house and went in. She found a handsome young man waiting for them. The girl soon understood she was trapped. But she hadn't forgotten to sprinkle the sand along her way. The old witch took a purse of gold from the man and left.

The young man welcomed her and invited her to dine with him. Meanwhile, the girl's mother began to worry when her daughter did not return as planned, and paced anxiously up and down.

The young man and the girl ate and talked and laughed, and she did not let on that she realized she had been taken in and that her family's honour was at stake, concentrating instead on forming a secret plan of escape. He said: 'It's time to sleep.' She said: 'Indeed,' and asked him to leave her while she put on the nightgown they had given her. Then she asked to go to the bathroom. The prince, not trusting her, said: 'I'll show you the way.' She answered: 'Don't you trust me? I'm not about to run away from such a handsome young man.' But he suggested: 'Let me tie you with my *shemla* [cummerbund] so that you can't run away.' He did so, and she went to the bathroom with the *shemla* tied around her ankle. As she returned, she found two doves settled in the courtyard. She hurriedly untied the *shemla* and attached it to the two doves, and ran away in her nightgown.

The prince waited and waited while the girl ran and ran, following the trail of sand until she reached her home. Her mother, seeing her dressed only in a nightgown, feared the worst, but the girl reassured her: 'Nothing had happened *al-hamdulilloh* [thanks to God], I am my mother's daughter I have not been brought up to disgrace my family. I had to abandon my clothes and jewels; a small price to pay.'

When she failed to return, the prince pulled the *shemla*

and to his great disappointment discovered two doves at the other end of it. He immediately went back to the palace, his face turned as pale as straw and he took to his bed. All the court physicians were summoned and they all said that he was suffering from depression. The king, concerned about his only son, said: 'Name what you want and I will have it brought for you.' The prince answered: 'I want to rule for three days.' The king replied: 'The kingdom will one day be in your hands, sooner or later.' The prince announced that he had had a dream, and he would give a reward to whoever could best interpret it for him. The dream was:

> *A bird without wings and beak took to the air.*
> *It came to me decked in finery and left in a petticoat.*

All the members of the different merchants' guilds came to give their interpretations of the dream. Finally came the turn of the girl's brothers. The topic had been discussed at home. The girl suggested the following inter-pretation to her favourite youngest brother and asked him to relate it to the prince. 'If it hadn't flown it would have brought shame on seven brothers' *shashiyya* [red knitted caps] and their father's. Propose, and do not sully the honour of the merchant's family.'

A new day is born and he who prays for the Prophet will be blessed. The youngest brother's turn came; he sought permission to speak to the prince privately. This was granted, and he recounted his interpretation of the dream

255

saying: 'If it hadn't flown it would have brought shame on seven men and their father. Propose, and do not sully the honour of the merchant's family.' On hearing it, the prince hurried to his father and asked him to go and ask for the hand of the merchant's daughter. The king did so and the wedding was planned for the following Thursday. The order was given to celebrate the wedding with seven days and seven nights of festivities.

Now the girl did not trust the prince, and feared that he had asked for her hand only to take his revenge on her. So she asked a Jewish pastry-cook to make her a life-size marzipan doll, filled up to the neck with pistachio syrup. When it was ready, she dressed it in a replica of her own wedding outfit and veil, and asked to have it brought with her to the bridal chamber. On her wedding-day a carriage was sent for the bride. The doll went with her. When she came to the bridal chamber, she sat it in her place in the centre of the room and hid herself behind the curtains. The groom came to welcome her, saying: 'You made fun of me; I swear by the land which bore your father and mine. I will strike off your head.' And with a single blow, he struck the head off. As he did so, a drop of the syrup splashed into his mouth. He exclaimed: 'You are as sweet in death as you were in life! My life is not worth living.' And he went to decapitate himself. But the merchant's daughter shouted: 'Don't do it!' The prince was surprised and exclaimed: 'This is another one of your tricks!' She replied: 'Surely it is better to marry me honourably than to seduce and abandon me?' He replied:

'You are the queen among women. You shall be my wife in this world and the next.' He kissed her on her forehead and they lived safely and procreated until death did them part.

XI

The Silk Merchant and his Neighbour

Once upon a time . . .

Once upon a time there was a handsome master silk merchant who lived next door to a beautiful married woman. The merchant desired the woman, and the attraction was mutual. One day, the woman went to the Turkish bath and had her body hair removed, the hair of her head tinted with henna, *dabgha wa harqus* [beauty spots] applied, her teeth polished with *swek* [tooth-stick] and her eyebrows dyed. Thus prepared, she perfumed herself and put on her best clothes covered herself with her *sifsari* [full length silk veil] and went to see the silk merchant.

She greeted him and he welcomed her warmly, saying: 'What can I do for you, madam? Your every wish will be fulfilled.' 'I want a fine *fouta* [an African wrap skirt],' she replied. He suggested: 'I will weave you one with silk and

258

gold stripes, to match your beauty.' 'How much?' she asked. 'It's free for you, if you come into the back shop with me . . .' 'When will it be ready?' she asked. He replied: 'This very afternoon.' 'Then I might as well wait,' she answered.

The merchant abandoned what he had been doing and set up his loom for her *fouta*. The woman let her *sifsari* fall and sat in front of the weaver. She gradually lifted the hem of her dress, showing her bare legs and thighs. The merchant looked up and caught sight of her most intimate places. Agitated, he began to sing a popular song, which went: 'Don't stop, don't stop, just let me enjoy it.' She tried to engage him in conversation, but he just went on weaving and singing, and she went on gradually lifting her skirt. After some time, she decided to go home and return in the afternoon to collect her *fouta*.

The weaver went on weaving, impatient to eat the fresh fruit, and daydreaming of the beautiful woman and the merriment the afternoon held in store for him. He waited and waited, but the woman failed to return; so he decided to go and deliver the *fouta* himself. He went next door and knocked. To his surprise, it was the husband who answered, but he came out with a stick and beat the merchant mercilessly, to punish him for attempting to seduce his *hurma* [wife, therefore forbidden].

XII

The Peasant and the Beldi

Once upon a time . . .

Once upon a time there was a king, *and there is no king but Almighty God,* who lived in Tunis. One day as he sat on the verandah of his palace he heard a woman beggar asking for alms. He leaned over the parapet to have a closer look at her and was amazed at her beauty under her ragged appearance. 'Praise to God the Creator who created such a beauty as fair as the moon,' he exclaimed. He hastily called his black servant and asked him to summon her to him. When she came before him he said to her: 'Such beauty is not meant to be hidden under rags. You should be honoured and raised to the ranks of kings and queens. Will you marry me?' The woman was delighted and answered: 'I will be more than honoured. He who wants to be generous needs no advice.' He then called his

260

mother and asked her to prepare her for the wedding the following Thursday.

The young woman was taken to the baths, where many slave girls attended to her, washing her and dressing her hair. Thereafter, the celebration of the wedding lasted for seven days and seven nights. The king was delighted with his beautiful new bride and was blissfully happy.

When the wedding was over, the young bride never agreed to sit and share a meal with him saying she wasn't hungry. 'She must be shy,' he explained to his mother. 'Let's give her time to get used to it.' Two weeks passed and still the young bride would not eat with her husband. The king was worried that his bride wasn't eating, and yet she didn't seem to be losing weight. 'I must unravel the mystery,' he thought. So he decided to watch her.

Now there was a big cupboard in the bride's apartment. While no one was looking, she would take some of the food and hide it in the cupboard. When nobody was around, she would go to the cupboard and take out some food, saying: 'God bless your generosity!' and then start to eat. The king watched her for three days and realized what she was doing. Appalled, he thought: 'Curse the woman! I can't live with a beggar.' He summoned her to his council-chamber, saying: 'I wanted to make a civilized human being of you, but it's useless. You were born a beggar; you will die a beggar. I have kept your rags – put them on and go. You were not made for such an honour. "What's bred in the bone comes out in the blood." '

261

XIII

The Innocent Virgin

Once upon a time . . .

Once upon a time there was a man who wanted to marry
an innocent virgin with no sexual knowledge. So he sought
the help of the local matchmaker. One day she came and
told him: 'I have found the one you are looking for. Her
father, out of concern for her seclusion, has used the
"seven locks".' Delighted, the man went to ask for the
daughter's hand. Her father consented to marry her to
him and they came to an agreement.

On the wedding night, when they were alone in the
bridal chamber, the man, wanting to test her 'innocence',
asked her the following question: 'Do you know what this
is?' exposing himself to her. 'Oh! yes,' she answered. 'It is
a cock!' Appalled, the man sent her back in shame the
very same night to her father's house.

A week later he called the same matchmaker and asked her to find him a completely innocent virgin. When asked the same ritual question, the new bride gave the same answer as the first one. She was repudiated too.

The third bride answered: 'I don't know,' to the question put to her to test her innocence. The man was delighted. 'This is the one I am looking for; I must be gentle with her', he thought to himself. That night the marriage was not consummated. Three days later, he said to her: 'I'll teach you what this is', pointing down to that which was between his thighs, 'this is a cock!' 'Is that what you call a cock!' she answered scornfully. 'My paternal cousin's *wild 'ammi* is this big!' showing her forearm, 'my maternal cousin's *wild khali* is this big, my neighbour's is this big . . .'

XIV

The Woman with Two

Once upon a time . . .

Once upon a time there was a man who wanted to marry
a woman with two. Every time he sent to ask for the hand
of a girl, he made it a condition that she must have two.
All the girls replied that they had only one, and so they
were not eligible for marriage. There was a cunning young
girl who heard about the man and decided to trick him.
'I have two,' she said. And so the marriage was celebrated.

It was customary for the young bride to be prepared
for her wedding by an attendant, a *hennana* who would
tint the bride's hair and hands with henna and shave off
all her body hair. This girl had asked the *hennana* to leave
half of her pubic hair unshaved. On the wedding night
the marriage was consummated, but the bride allowed the

bridegroom to see only half her body, and saved the rest for later. *How could she hide it, when both her legs were apart?*

One day the husband informed his bride that he was leaving on business and that he wanted to take the spare one with him to play with! The young bride said, 'Of course!' Before he left, she caught a bird, put it in a tin, and gave it to him, and told him to be careful with it. Delighted, the husband set off with the tin in his pocket.

One evening, he felt horny and reached for the tin in his pocket. 'It's always useful,' he thought, 'to have two.' And he opened the tin. The bird flew away. He ran after it, but eventually had to give up. In the meantime, the young bride shaved the rest of her pubic hair. Soon the husband came back, saying: 'Something terrible has happened. I've lost the spare one.' The girl shouted: 'How awful I told you to be careful.' He answered: 'Thank God you've still got one left.' And they enjoyed the newly shaved one together.

XV

The Woman with Three

Once upon a time . . .

Once upon a time there was a man who wanted to marry a woman with three. Every time he sent to ask for the hand of a girl, he made it a condition that she must have three. All the girls replied that they had only one, and so they were not eligible for marriage. There was a cunning young girl who heard about the man and decided to trick him. 'I have three,' she said. And so the marriage was celebrated.

It was customary for the young bride to be prepared for her wedding by a *hennana* who would tint the bride's hair and hands with henna and shave off all her body hair. This girl had asked the *hennana* to leave all of her pubic hair unshaved. On the wedding night the marriage was consummated. 'What is your first one called?' the bridegroom asked her. '*Al-mghafghaf* [the bushy one],' she replied. They enjoyed the bushy one for weeks and weeks, until he felt like a change. 'Let's have the other one,' he said to her, 'tonight.' The young bride had her pubic hair removed, leaving a single tuft of hair. That night, they enjoyed the new one. 'What is your second one called?' her husband asked. '*Bu qussa* [the one with the fringe],' she replied. Again, they enjoyed the one with the fringe for weeks, until he felt like a change. 'Let's enjoy your third one tonight,' he suggested. That day the young bride had her pubic hair all removed. That night they enjoyed the newly shaved one. 'What do you call this one?' he asked jokingly. '*Al-fartas* [the bald one],' she answered. 'I think I like it best,' he replied. And they enjoyed the bald one from then on.

XVI

Women Are Fickle

Once upon a time . . .

Once upon a time there was a rich man who was happily married to a wife who loved him. He called her Lilla and she called him Sidi.* Then one day, his wife came and said to him: 'Why don't you will me your fortune, if you really love me? We don't know what Fate may have in store for us. If you were to die, I would be lost without you and unprovided for.'

He replied: 'There'll be time enough for that.' But the woman persisted and nagged day after day until he agreed to do so; after all, he could trust his own wife. So he signed all his property over to her. Some time later, her attitude towards him changed completely. Some days she would cook for him and some days she would refuse. He

* Lilla and Sidi are terms of endearment and respect.

268

enquired: 'Why are you being so difficult?' She replied:
'If you don't like it, you know what you can do. After all,
the house is mine, and everything in it.'

One day, he came back from work as usual and knocked
on the door, but his wife shouted: 'Help! A stranger is
breaking into my house.' The man begged her to open
the door, trying to reason with her, but she wouldn't. He
gave up. But soon his wife put on her veil and made for
the *qadi*'s house: her husband followed her. Now, the *qadi*
was known to be a womanizer. When they came before
him she complained: 'This stranger is harassing me. He
says he has a claim on my property.' The husband intervened: 'But I signed it over to you in the first place!' She
replied: 'What are you talking about? I don't even know
you.' The *qadi* pronounced judgement against him and
he was flogged mercilessly.

A few weeks passed. The man sat in a café, sad and
weighed down by his predicament. A friend of his noticed
his gloom and enquired: ' What's the matter? What's both-
ering you?' He explained: 'I'm my own worst enemy. I was
happy and contented until I signed all my property over
to my wife. She led me a merry dance and the final straw
was when she threw me out of my own house.' His friend
replied: 'You must be mad! How could you trust a woman,
and sign over your fortune to her? Don't you know God
has made them from a crooked rib?' The husband replied:
'She sweet-talked me into it.' His friend recommended:
'Why don't you seek the help of the *qadi*'s wife? She is
known to be fair and able to redress wrongs. She knows

her husband is a womanizer and will always decide in favour of a woman and then have her. I'm sure she would welcome the chance to get her own back on him.'

The husband bought a few kilos of fish and went to see the *qadi*'s wife. She talked to him through the door-grille (*women could not come face to face with men outside the family*) and he recounted what had happened. She replied: 'Come back and see me in three days.'

As it is the tradition to cook *couscous* on Fridays, the *qadi*'s wife informed her husband that he was going to have chicken *couscous* that evening. She prepared a nice rich chicken *couscous*, as well as a plain and simple one with the left-over grain. Towards sunset, she set the table with the chicken *couscous* and sat waiting. Her husband came back, lifted the lid of the dish and was delighted by the smell of the *couscous*. Then he went to change his clothes. Meanwhile, his wife substituted the plain *couscous* for the chicken one. After saying his evening prayer, the *qadi* sat down to eat. But when he lifted the lid, to his surprise there was no chicken and the *couscous* was poor and coarse. He enquired angrily: 'Where's the chicken *couscous* I just saw?' The wife replied: 'You're crazy. There was no chicken.' He insisted: 'But there was!' She replied: 'That's all we have.'

Beside himself with anger, the *qadi* rushed off to complain to her father. Meanwhile, his wife replaced the chicken *couscous* on the table. When the *qadi* came back with her father, they were astonished to find such a delicious meal laid out. The father told him off and left.

But when the *qadi* came back, lo and behold, there was no chicken *couscous!* He rushed back again to his father-in-law, explaining that he now had grounds for divorce. This time, the wife's father and brothers came to settle the dispute once and for all. Meanwhile, she had changed the dishes over again. When they arrived, she feigned surprise and said she feared he had gone mad, as there had never been anything but chicken *couscous.* So the father and brothers took the law into their own hands and bound and beat him and left. The wife ate her fill of the chicken *couscous* in front of his very eyes.

Every day, she came to ask him: 'Chicken *couscous* or plain *couscous*?' and he answered: 'Plain *couscous*.' She would say: 'Then you're still not cured of this madness.' To this question, he answered one day: 'Chicken *couscous*.' 'There you are,' she answered, 'now you are coming back to your senses. You must be fair and forswear always judging in favour of women, regardless of justice.' She branded him on the forehead and untied him.

On the appointed day, the wronged husband returned. The *qadi*'s wife told him to go and appeal against the *qadi*'s decision. So the man came before the *qadi* and presented his appeal. The *qadi* asked for the 'bitch' to be brought before him and flogged one hundred lashes. The *qadi* then asked her: 'Whose property are you claiming?' She explained tearfully: 'Sidi's, it's all his.' The husband joyfully recovered his fortune and his wife was thrown into prison on the *qadi*'s orders. From then on, the *qadi* judged

271

impartially and never favoured women unfairly. He had learned his lesson!

XVII

The Chief of the Tribe's Daughter

Implore God's oneness and he who has sinned implore his pardon.

It was commonplace among bedouin tribes to fight over cattle and property, and he who was stronger won. One day, a chief's house was invaded by his enemies, who killed him and looted and destroyed his household. Only his daughter managed to escape with her baby brother, with God's grace.

She walked and walked, crossing country after country, until she saw a light in the distance. She hastened towards it and found a friendly tribe. 'My folk are all dead,' she said. 'I am the only survivor, and this is my younger brother.' 'You are most welcome to stay with us, if it suits you, and become like one of my daughters,' said the head of the family. 'I am very grateful. May God bless you and your family,' she replied. 'Aysha was taken to the women

273

of the house and soon took her place among them. She would help the daughters in carding wool and spinning and drawing water from the well. One day, as she went collecting wood, God guided her steps to a cauldron full of gold coins. Delighted by this gift from God, she hid it in her bundle of firewood and went back, saying nothing of her windfall to anyone. She dug a hole on a nearby hillside and hid it, thinking to give it to her brother when the time was ripe.

'Aysha's brother was now ten. She summoned him, saying: 'If I gave you a hundred dinars, what would you do with it?' 'I'd buy balloons for all the children of the neighbourhood,' he answered. 'He's still young and frivolous,' she thought.

Five years later, she asked him the same question. 'I'd buy some land and start a business,' he replied. 'He's beginning to understand life,' she said to herself. The following day she told the people of the tribe: 'It's time for me to move on.' Saddened, they all said with one voice: 'We shall miss you.' 'My brother is now grown up,' she explained, 'and he must start to earn his living.' The head of the household gave her his blessing and she and her brother left. That day they all wept and there was an air of sadness about the family.

They walked and walked and finally settled in a distant land. Soon she made friends with the neighbours and enquired whether there was any land for sale. One kind neighbour directed her to a landowner who had a large estate to sell. She hastily went to see the man, bought the land and signed the papers. 'Aysha was now in possession of a large estate and her brother became well known and respected in the neighbourhood as a merchant.

A few years later, as 'Aysha was taking a walk, she came across a young girl as fair as the moon, but dressed in rags. 'Who are you?' she asked, approaching her. 'What guided your steps here?' 'I am an orphan and have no one but Almighty God.' 'Would you like to keep me company?' asked 'Aysha. 'I live with my younger brother and there is a place for you in our generous home,' said 'Aysha, thinking of the kind people who had taken her in. The girl was delighted and both women walked back as true sisters. When they arrived, 'Aysha washed and dressed her, and she became even more beautiful.

The newcomer was of marriageable age. 'Aysha thought of a match with her brother. She asked her: 'Why don't you two marry? I want you to attract my brother's attention.' A word of praise from his sister and a seductive glance from the young girl sufficed to make the brother propose. 'Aysha received the news with rejoicing and called the neighbours to prepare for the ceremony. The marriage was celebrated with much show and the young couple settled happily together. A year later, a baby boy was born and he was named after his deceased grandfather. 'Aysha spoilt and pampered the baby.

As time passed, the new bride grew tired of her sister-in-law and jealous that her husband never did anything without consulting his sister. But 'Aysha continued with the same kindness of heart and generosity and the brother

275

respected and loved her for it. Knowing there was no way out of it, the young wife sought the help of 'Azuzet es-Stut, the old witch. 'I want to get rid of her, but my husband is very fond of her and won't hear a word against her.' The old witch answered: 'I know just the thing for it.' Then she gave her the egg of a water snake and instructed her to give it to her sister-in-law to swallow whole, as a token of her love for her brother.

The following day, the young wife approached 'Aysha, saying: 'Do you say you love your brother?' 'Indeed, I am ready to give my life for him.' 'Then swallow this egg whole to prove it.' 'Aysha answered: 'What's so difficult about swallowing this egg whole for my dear brother's sake?' And she swallowed it.

A month later 'Aysha felt something strange in her belly. Day after day her belly grew bigger. She started to worry, but in the meantime her sister-in-law started to draw her husband's attention to his sister's belly. 'I have something awful to tell you. Your sister is pregnant,' she came and said one day. 'Do not be angry with her.' The brother didn't want to hear anything about it. 'If you don't want to believe me, put your head on her belly when she sits in the sun and you will soon feel the baby moving.' The following day her brother watched 'Aysha waddling along and sitting down in the sun. He went up to her and hugged her, pretending to be affectionate. He then put his head on her belly and felt something moving. 'It must be true,' he thought. 'What am I going to do? What a disgrace! Just when I have become well known among my fellow-merchants . . .' He went back in with a heavy heart.

He was fond of his sister and the idea of killing her to wipe out the shame was repugnant to him. He thought of another idea. 'I am thinking of buying a new estate. Why don't you come along to see it?' he said. 'You go on your own. I feel too tired to walk,' 'Aysha replied. 'You know I can do nothing without your precious advice,' he said. 'Then we should take the money with us, in case we like it,' 'Aysha said.

The following day they set off early in the morning, taking a waterskin with them. The journey was long and tiring and it was scorching hot. 'Aysha stopped now and then to rest and swallow a drop of water. 'How much further is it?' she asked. 'We'll soon be there,' her brother reassured her. It was sunset when her brother finally said: 'We're there.' By then 'Aysha was exhausted and asked to rest and soon she sank into a deep sleep. Her brother emptied the waterskin in the sand, covered her with his *burnous*, mounted his horse and set off.

It was morning before 'Aysha awoke to the scorching sun, and found herself alone. She realized what had happened. She invoked God, saying: 'O God, who created me, do not abandon me.' She cried and wailed, realizing that her brother had eventually found out about her pregnancy. 'Aysha rose to her feet and appealed to God to guide her steps to a shelter. She walked until early afternoon and then sat down to rest. Tired and weary, she covered herself with her brother's *burnous* and sank again into a deep sleep. A while later, a horseman was passing by and noticed the *burnous* flapping in the wind. He dismounted and uncovered the sleeping woman. He carried her to his horse and rode off to his estate nearby. When 'Aysha came to, he asked her: 'Tell me your story. What brought you here?' 'My brother,' she said, 'driven by his wife. I don't understand what is happening to me.' The young man took leave of her, went to see an elderly man and reported what had happened. 'She is enchanted. She must have swallowed a water snake's egg,' he explained. 'But I can undo the spell for her. Bring me two lamb's lungs, and bring her to me.' The man did as he was told. The old man put the two lungs on to fry. The smell of the fat would drive the snake out of the woman's belly, he said. As he did so, the woman groaned in pain and the snake appeared. The woman was aghast at what she saw, but finally relieved. The snake was embalmed, just like a human corpse. 'Aysha nailed the snake on a wooden board and asked the old man to write the following line on it: 'A catastrophe from a most beloved sister.' *Because she loved and spoiled her and married her to her brother, she was paid back in this way.*

After she had rested, she asked to leave. The young man proposed to her: 'Will you marry me?' 'Aysha answered: 'Aren't I too old for you?' 'You are still young, and will live years and years. Leave it to God to punish them for their deeds.' They married, and he did his best to spoil her, to make up for the hardship she had endured. She gave him two children.

278

Now, her brother had left some money with her when he abandoned her. Having known thirst, 'Aysha decided to build a well with it. 'I want to build a well for thirsty travellers.' Her wish was fulfilled and a well was built near her estate.

Let's now come back to 'Aysha's brother, who, after he had abandoned her, came back home with a heavy heart, and nothing was ever the same again. He looked for the money that 'Aysha must have hidden, but could find no trace of it. Soon they became poor and wretched, and his wife made his life hell. One day, he left her. He walked and walked until he came near the well. He stopped to drink and refresh himself. 'Aysha saw him and recognized him. Her heart filled with longing and she made a move to speak to him, then refrained. She called her elder son and asked him to go and invite the man to join them for lunch. 'You shall be our guest,' the young boy said to him. The man was taken to the house. 'Aysha mentioned nothing to her husband about recognizing her brother. They ate and had tea, and the man thanked them and made to leave, but 'Aysha intervened and said: 'Where are you heading on this scorching afternoon? You should stay overnight and set off early tomorrow morning.' The man thanked her for her hospitality and accepted the invitation.

'Aysha cooked dinner that night and instructed her elder son to ask her to entertain them by telling stories, and to insist she did so. After dinner, the son begged his mother: 'Please, mother, tell us a story.' She said: 'What do you want me to tell you?' 'A story, anything,' he said. She replied: 'Then I'll tell you the story of the Cares of my Heart.' The woman related her story from the very beginning to the end: how she ran away with her little brother, devoted her life to bringing him up, and so on and so forth. When she came to the part about the water-skin and how her brother abandoned her in the middle of nowhere, her brother shouted: 'My sister?' and clasped her to his breast. 'Forgive me sister! I sinned against you.' They both cried bitterly; then he told her that it was all his wife's fault, the bitch. Her husband sympathized with him and asked him to stay. But his sister advised him not to abandon his wife and children. The brother made up his mind to kill her or divorce her, and bring his children to live with his sister. They gave him a horse and he set off. When he arrived at his orchard he was met by his little children, crying and wailing. 'What's the matter with you?' he asked. 'Mother is dead!' they sobbed. 'Thank God!' he thought to himself. 'She was struck down by the Hand of God rather than mine.'

He retrieved the money that his sister had hidden and bought a piece of land near hers, took his children and settled there. There we left them, and never heard from them again.

XVII

The Sparkling Maiden

My tale is well ordered. May our prayers and yours be offered up for the beloved Prophet, peace be upon him! Listeners, may we all be guided to goodness and to make the Shehada.

Once upon a time there was a rich merchant who had two sons. They all worked in the father's silk business in Souk al-Wusta [a quarter in the old town]. One day, the towncrier announced that it was the season for the pilgrimage to Mecca. The old merchant's heart longed to make the pilgrimage. He called his two sons, who were both married and whose wives had conceived on the same day, and informed them that he was going to Mecca, and told them to take charge of the business.

He set off on pilgrimage. *In those days, it took a whole year.* In the meantime, the sons' wives gave birth to two little girls, one dark and ugly and the other fair and as beautiful as the moon. Three days after the grandfather returned from Mecca, he was presented with the two baby girls to choose names for them. On seeing the beauty of the fair one, he praised God and called her *Sharqat wa Dhawat* [The one who shines bright]. Looking at the other one, he called her *Za'frana* [Saffron].

Fate caught up with the old man and he fell ill. On his deathbed, he called his elder son and asked him to look

after his younger brother, and keep his shop stocked for
him. With that, the old man died.

The elder son kept his promise to look after his brother
and make sure he always had stock to sell. But his wife
objected, saying: 'He must now stand on his own two feet.'
The husband replied: 'But I promised my father I would
supply him with goods to sell.' The wife eventually persuaded her husband to stop helping his brother.

The younger brother sold all his stock and was not able
to replenish it. So he started selling his own property.
Little by little, it all went: the shop, the land, the house,
the furniture. The elder brother bought it all; each has
received his God's allotted *qasm* [share]. One day he came
and said: 'You have no right to this house any more; it all
belongs to me. There is a small dilapidated house nearby;
why don't you go and live there?' So the younger brother
took his wife and his daughter and left. They moved into
the miserable house and led a very modest existence there,
looking after their daughter Sharqat.

The two girls, Za'frana and Sharqat, turned fifteen and
were put into the care of a *m'allma*, to teach them domestic
arts. Za'frana was spoilt and her meals were always brought
to her by a black slave, whereas Sharqat had to carry her
own lunch with her. The *m'allma* was fond of Sharqat
because she was modest and shy and never spoke loudly.
She would spoil her with cakes and candy. One day,
Sharqat came to the *m'allma* saying: 'I had a dream last
night.' The *m'allma* replied: 'A good one, God willing.'
Sharqat answered: 'I had a vision that one day, as I was

sitting, someone brought an ivory ship with golden oars saying it was for the daughter of the poor and needy merchant.' The *m'allma* replied: 'It's a gift from God.'

Za'frana went back home crying, and told her mother to ask her cousin Sharqat if she could buy her dream. Sharqat's uncle had never taken any further interest in his brother's affairs since he bought him out. His wife told him: 'Go and ask Sharqat if she could sell her dream. After all, they are poor and will be glad of whatever we care to give them. A hundred dinars will keep them happy.' The husband replied: 'How can I go and ask for such a thing when I haven't even enquired after them for years?' The wife eventually talked him into it. So he went to visit his brother and his family. They gave him a warm welcome and he eventually brought up the object of his visit. Sharqat refused. Her uncle said: 'What if I gave you a hundred dinars?' She replied: 'The answer is still no. I will not sell my dream.' 'Five hundred, then,' he said. She said: 'No.' He offered to leave her half his fortune in his will. This time she accepted. The notaries were called and drew up the will. Thus, Sharqat sold her dream.

Now, the prince, son of the king of Morocco, arrived in the country by sea and said he would not disembark unless Sharqat, whom he had seen in a dream, came to meet him. Her uncle hurried to see her and ask her to go and meet the prince in place of his daughter. But she refused, saying: 'I have sold the dream to your daughter. She must go and meet him.' He replied: 'How can I send him a dark, ugly girl? He would be put off.' She answered: 'It's nothing to do with me any more.' He begged: 'I will leave you the rest of my fortune as well, if you will only do it.' She answered: 'Agreed,' and the notaries were called to amend the will.

Sharqat's father was overjoyed to recover his fortune. *A new day is born and he who prays for the Prophet will be blessed.* She had a beautiful dress made and went to meet the prince. The prince said he would offer the ivory ship with the golden oars to Sharqat, if she would wait on him at dinner. The uncle hurried to his brother's house begging Sharqat to come and wait on their guest the prince. She replied: 'Why don't you ask your own daughter?' He answered: 'But he has already seen you. I am prepared to leave you half the ship if you will go.' She said: 'Agreed.' So the notaries were called back again and drew up a new will. Sharqat went to her uncle's house dressed as a queen and waited on the prince, who offered her his royal armlet with the marriage contract inscribed on it.

The prince asked to see Sharqat before the wedding took place. The uncle hurried to his brother's house and begged Sharqat to come and stand in for his daughter again. She said she would do it on condition he left her the other half of the ship as well. They agreed, the notaries were summoned and the new will was written out. This time, the prince offered his ring and expressed his wish to attend Sharqat's *qassan al-Dlal,* when according to Beldi tradition, her hair would be cut for the first time to signify the end of her spoiling by her parents. In fact her hair had never been seen, as tradition had it that a girl at puberty should bind her hair in an *'oksa* [bun] and never show it to her kinsmen. *When I was young I remember being slapped by my mother just because I ventured to cut a fringe which was a fashion at that time. They used to be tough with us.* Anyway, the following day Sharqat sat in the middle of a chanting crowd of women, and her hair was cut. The prince took a lock of her hair and left. Za'frana was also undergoing the same ceremony, but in private.

On the wedding-day, Sharqat and Za'frana were dressed identically in dresses and jewellery provided by the bridge-groom. The carriages came for them and they set off. Now, the uncle's wife had prepared very salty lamb cutlets for Sharqat's lunch. So on the way to her bridgegroom's house, she felt very thirsty, but her uncle's wife, who was accompanying her, refused to give her any water. The journey was long and tiring and it was hot, which made her even thirstier. The uncle's wife said she would let her have some water on condition she could blind her in one eye. Sharqat was so thirsty that she agreed, but her aunt only gave her a drop of water, saying she could have more if she would let her blind her in the other eye. Thus Sharqat lost the sight of both eyes. A few miles further on, Sharqat asked her to stop the carriage to let her relieve herself. As she got out, in all her finery, her aunt told the coachman to drive on, and she was left behind.

The coach arrived at the prince's palace, which was all lit up and decorated for the festivities. Now the prince had been adopted by his aunt, who was in charge of the whole event, and very impatient to see his bride, who was said to be exceptionally fair. Za'frana was now taken to the bridal chamber, completely veiled, as was the tradition, to meet her groom. When he came and lifted the veil, to his disappointment he discovered a dark, ugly girl. 'Are you Sharqat?' he exclaimed. 'Indeed I am,' she answered, and it is your country's climate which has transformed me.' Saddened, the prince went out and asked the musicians to stop drumming. He went to his chest and took out the lock of hair he had taken from Sharqat's *qassan al-Dlal*, but found it bore no similarity at all to the hair of the girl he had just seen. Disappointed, he remained silent. His aunt went to see the bride and was shocked: 'Has he given up his fortune for a woman like this? But such is his choice; I must accept it.'

Meanwhile, Sharqat heard hooves passing along the road and called out, 'Help!' The donkey's rider turned to discover a beautiful girl dressed as a bride, blindly feeling her way. He asked her: 'Whatever has happened to you, my poor girl?' She related what had happened. He was moved by her story and offered to take her home to his wife. When they arrived at his wretched hovel in the prince's town, they were met by his wife. She took pity on her when she heard the story and offered to shelter her. On finding how poor the childless old couple were, Sharqat offered to sell her bracelet, which had been given to her by the prince. The man took it to the souk to sell. No one could afford such an opulent piece of jewellery except the prince, for his new bride. So the bracelet was brought to the court where the prince sat in judgement on affairs of state. When he saw the bracelet he was astonished. 'This is the twin of the bracelet I gave to Sharqat! This is a mystery.' So he said nothing, but bought it.

The poor man took the money back home to Sharqat, who gave him half of it to renovate the house and buy provisions. She spent some time living with the couple, but eventually grew bored. So she gave him her earrings to sell and asked him to buy her an orchard and two black slaves to keep her company. The man took them to the souk to sell. Who could afford such priceless things but the prince? When he saw them, he was astonished and exclaimed: 'These are identical to the earrings I gave to Sharqat! I must unravel this mystery.'

Sharqat now lived in her orchard with the two black slaves, whose marriage she had arranged. Each and every day, she would stroll around her estate, then rest under an olive tree. The slave couple could understand the language of the animals, and one day they overheard two birds talking. 'You bird of the sea, do you have any news for the bird of the earth?' The female answered: 'I have no news, but I stole a sultana from a street-barrow and they hit me on the beak.' The other bird retorted: 'Damn your greed! You only talk about your stomach. Tell me about the fair young maiden who was blinded by her aunt, instead.' The female answered: 'I have a cure for her. She needs an olive leaf chewed with a drop of blood from each of our claws and placed on her eyes to recover her

287

sight. But she must not forget to heal our wounded claws with the chewed leaf as well.'

As soon as they heard this, the black couple caught the two birds, cut them on the claws, took an olive leaf and chewed it up with the bird's blood. Then they placed the paste on the eyes of their mistress, who quickly recovered her sight. She was overjoyed to see the world again. The old couple and a notary were called to witness her signing over her property to her slaves. Talking to the old man, she said: 'I haven't forgotten you, but be patient.' She asked him to go to the gold souk and select a fine Jewish or Italian jeweller, and bring him home to her. When he arrived, she told him: 'I want you to make me a replica of a gazelle, big enough to hide inside. The eyes must be made of emerald, and do not spare the cost.'

The jeweller went back to the souk and worked day and night for a whole week on the task. Finally the gazelle was ready. He took it to her and was paid generously for his work. Sharqat hid inside the gazelle and asked the old man to take it to the souk and sell it for its weight in gold. Who could afford such a priceless *objet d'art*, except the prince?

The prince bought this exquisite object and put it in his bedroom to admire. In the evening, through the eyes of the gazelle, Sharqat saw her cousin Za'frana come in alone, undress and slip into bed. Later on, a slave girl brought the prince's dinner on a tray and left it on the table for his return. Sharqat left her hiding-place and ate her fill from the prince's dinner. Then she went back.

When the prince came in, to his dismay he found his dinner disturbed. So he went to see his aunt and enquired: 'Who served my dinner?' 'Your slave girl,' answered his aunt. He complained: 'It wasn't properly done.' She answered: 'Don't worry, tomorrow I'll do it myself.' On the next occasion the prince came to have his dinner he found it disturbed again. So he decided to get to the bottom of the mystery himself.

The next evening, the prince came back early and hid behind the curtains before his dinner was brought. As usual, Za'frana came into the room, undressed and slipped into bed. Sharqat came out of her hiding-place and made her way to the dinner-table. She had not even taken the first mouthful when the prince came out, saying: 'Do you need company?' When he saw her face, the prince recognized her immediately and asked her to tell him her story. She related the whole story about her aunt's misdeeds and the old couple's generosity. He promised to take his revenge. Sharqat soon regained her rightful place in the palace, whereas Za'frana was suspended from the chandelier as a punishment.

A new day is born and he who prays for the Prophet will be blessed. The prince introduced her to his aunt, explaining: 'This is the woman I really gave up my fortune for, not the other one. I knew there was a mystery, and I have been through it all with patience.' When Sharqat's aunt saw her niece again, she went pale. The prince asked Sharqat what kind of punishment she wanted to give her. 'I want four she-camels to tear her limb from limb. As for my cousin, I want her to be walled up in a sewer and left to die.'

The prince and Sharqat started their marriage anew. Her father and uncle were summoned to attend the celebrations. Seven days and seven nights of festivities. Sharqat arranged for the poor old couple who had taken her in, to come and live with her in a wing of the palace. And they all lived safely and procreated until death did them part.

IXX

The Salt Pedlar

My tale is one of wonder. May our prayers and yours be offered up for the beloved Prophet, peace be upon him! Listeners, may we all be guided to goodness.
Once upon a time . . .

Once upon a time, there was a childless king who had always yearned for a child. He prayed to God night and day. One night an angel appeared in his dream, asking him: 'Would you rather have a daughter with a misfortune who will survive, or a son with a misfortune who will die?' He answered: 'God forbid!' The angel replied: 'I am a messenger sent to you by God.' He answered: 'A daughter, then.' His wife conceived the following month. Nine months later a baby daughter as beautiful as the moon, praise to the creator who created her with such beauty, was born. She was put into the good care of a nurse, then

291

a nanny. The child crawled, toddled, held to the wall and walked. In real life a child grows in a year or two, but in a couple of words in a tale. A governess taught her handicrafts and to read and write. When she turned sixteen, she was learned in the arts and handicrafts. One day, as she was sitting peacefully embroidering, a bird flew down and started to annoy her by scattering the sequins on her embroidery hoop. She tried to shoo him away, then slipped off her anklet and hit him with it. He picked it up, flew away and headed for a distant castle. As he arrived, he took off his bird-skin, changed into human form and commanded: 'All of you weep with me over the one who hit me with her anklet. O! castle, weep. O! fish in the depths of the sea, listen.' The castle and the fish wept with him. All three wept bitterly. Two or three days later, the bird went back to the scene. The princess was sitting at her embroidery as usual. He started to tease her, and she hit him with her bracelet. He picked it up and flew off with it to his castle. As he arrived he turned into a man and commanded the castle as before. 'Weep with me over the one who hit me with her anklet. Weep with me over the one who hit me with her bracelet. O! castle, weep with me and you, fish, in the depths of the sea, listen.' All of them wept bitterly.

On the third occasion, when the bird teased the princess, she hit him with her earring. This time, she wept so much that she fell ill. All the court's physicians were summoned to cure her, but they all said that she was suffering from mere melancholy. All the story-tellers were called to entertain her but to no avail.

An old bedouin woman in a distant village lost her chicken. She looked for it for three days without success. One evening the chicken mistook the moon for daytime and came out of hiding. The old lady was staying up late. She gave the chicken some corn, and followed it to its hiding-place near the river. As they came up, she saw the water part and a camel emerged loaded with plates, pots and pans. Amazed, the old lady watched as the camel flopped down and the pots and pans washed themselves in the river, loaded themselves back into the panniers, and the camel made his way back into the water. The old woman caught hold of his tail and followed him. They came to a palace. She hid in the entrance hall, and watched as the pots and pans put themselves away. The table set itself with plates, knives and forks. A king and queen sat down to dine. The bird arrived a few minutes later, took off his bird-skin and turned into a human. He took out the princess's anklet, bracelet and earring and started to weep, commanding: 'O! castle weep with me over the one who hit me with her anklet. O! castle weep with me over the one who hit me with her bracelet. O! castle weep with me over the one who hit me with her earring. O! castle weep! O! fish in the depth of the sea listen!' After dinner, the pots and pans and knives and forks gathered in a basket and loaded themselves on to the camel, which made its way again out of the palace. As he left, the old woman followed him down to the river.

On hearing of the princess's illness, she decided to recount her extraordinary experience to her. She obtained permission to visit the princess and told her the true story.

After hearing it, the princess exclaimed: 'That's exactly who I'm looking for! Take me to him.' The old woman expressed her concern about the risky enterprise, but the princess insisted, and decided to run away that very night with the old woman's help. She tied her bedsheets together and climbed down from her window. The old lady led her to the river and left her. When the camel appeared with the pots and pans to wash, she followed him all the way to the palace and hid in the hallway. She saw what the old woman had seen, then she saw the prince appear, take off his bird-skin and command: 'O! castle weep with me over the one who hit me with her anklet. O! castle weep with me over the one who hit me with her bracelet. O! castle weep with me over the one who hit me with her earring. O! castle, weep! O! fish, in the depth of the sea, listen! To his amazement, all started to laugh. The prince angrily demanded: 'How dare you laugh while I am crying?' They answered: 'The one you are crying over is among us.' He asked: 'Where?' They answered: 'In the cupboard.' He went over to her and said: 'My dear, I've cried my eyes out over you.' She replied: 'I have, too.' They sat and talked happily for a while, then he asked her: 'When my parents, the king and queen, come, ask for their forgiveness in the name of God.' She did so, and they were overjoyed to see her. They explained that they

were not human, but jinn, and their son had been put
under a spell which they hoped she could break. They
lived happily together until one day he went to his father
and announced that he wanted to marry her. His father
objected, on the grounds that he was promised to his
cousin. *This is like my story; they separated us, damn the bastards.* The lovers were disappointed and decided to elope.
They travelled, crossing country after country, until they
were exhausted. They decided to stop for a while. She laid
her head in his lap and fell sound asleep. When she
awoke, she found a stone under her head for a pillow,
and the prince was nowhere to be seen. *You see, one can
never trust men. Sometimes they are mere puppets in their fathers'
hands. Maybe we will have some justice in the world to come,
but even God seems to favour men. He promised them* huris
[angels] and there is no mention of male huris *for women.*

She took to the road again, until she met with a
shepherd. She suggested that they exchange clothes.
The shepherd was more than happy to do so, as her
clothes were far finer than his. She changed into the
shepherd's clothes and wrapped his scarf around her face.
She continued on her way until she reached the king's
city, which was all lit up and decorated. She met with a
salt pedlar (*in those days, salt was carried on donkey-back*) and
asked him what the festivities were for. He replied: 'Today
is the prince's wedding-day, and I am to carry this salt to
his palace.' She asked: 'Can I possibly go in your place?'
And she gave him a purse of gold. He readily agreed, and
she led the donkey with the salt to the palace. As she

arrived, the prince called out to her: '*Mallah* [salt pedlar], have you seen the beautiful maiden?' She answered: 'Yes, I have seen an extraordinarily beautiful maiden wearing one golden anklet, looking for her lost love who left without goodbye.' When he heard that, the prince continued to ask the same question and got the same answer again and again. On the wedding-day, to everyone's surprise, the prince asked to go to the bridal chamber accompanied by the salt pedlar. The salt pedlar asked to have his donkey with him. They went in. The prince again asked: '*Mallah*, have you seen the beautiful maiden?' She answered, 'Yes, I have seen an extraordinarily beautiful maiden wearing one golden anklet, looking for her lost love who left without goodbye.' On hearing the answer he went to bed. When he fell asleep, the princess crept out of the room to the garden and hanged herself. When the prince woke up, he called out for *mallah*, but he didn't answer. He went out to look for him. To his sorrow, he found his beloved princess hanging from a tree. He wept bitterly over her and hanged himself next to her.

In the morning, his bride woke to find him gone. She went out to look for him and discovered them both, hanging side by side. She pushed them apart and hanged herself between them.

The king, the queen and their entourage woke up to the servants' cries coming from the garden. The king and queen mourned their son. Time passed, and a jasmine plant and a honeysuckle grew out of their graves, separated by a thistle. One afternoon, as the king was sitting

296

in his garden enjoying the cool breeze, he heard: 'O! jasmine, O! honeysuckle, what is this thistle doing between us?' The jasmine answered: 'Almighty God willed it so, *hukm Allah.* In life we could not be united and in the hereafter we were kept apart.' When the king heard this, he pulled up the thistle. And whenever there was a breeze, the jasmine and honeysuckle tenderly intertwined. There we left them and we have never seen them since.

XX

The Frivolous

Once upon a time . . .

Once upon a time, there was a merchant who was married and had two daughters. Fate caught up with his wife and she died. The merchant was left to look after his daughters alone. He would go out in the morning to work and come back in the afternoon. A kindly neighbour offered to come and wash and dress the children every day while he was out. The girls grew up lacking *hishma* [modesty], *tarbiyya* [good education] and manners. Even when they reached fifteen (their mother being in the grave), the girls would still play around riding on each other's shoulders, shouting at the top of their voices, lacking a mother's guiding hand. Their father tried to discipline them, but to no avail.

A fellow-merchant had two sons of marriageable age, so

he went one day to his friend and suggested they should arrange a marriage between their children. The girls' father welcomed the idea and they came to an agreement. The neighbour was called again to prepare the brides' trousseaux. The girls themselves were unable to help, never having been taught the domestic arts. On the wedding-day she dressed them and did their make-up. A carriage was sent to bring the girls to their bridegrooms' house. When they arrived, the elder daughter asked her husband to carry her on his back. He was shocked, and scolded her. The younger sister did the same, but her husband picked her up and carried her around the court-yard. The mother-in-law was scandalized at this, but said: 'They are still young; I'll teach them how to behave.'

On the seventh day after the marriage, she took them to the Turkish baths. Seeing her use a depilatory, they enquired what it was. The mother-in-law said: 'It's like a garment you put on all over!' She washed them and dressed them and took them back home. The following day, while the men of the house were out, the two girls decided to try it out for themselves. They undressed, smeared the cream all over their bodies and started playing around naked, shouting and carrying each other on their shoulders. Suddenly, their father-in-law came back unexpectedly and was shocked at what he saw. He hurriedly entered his room muttering: 'If you do not feel ashamed you can do what you want; there is no more shame and respect in this house.' The two young husbands were summoned to discipline their wives. The eldest slapped his wife and dragged her inside their room. The younger tried to do the same, but his wife would not submit to it.

The mother-in-law tried hard to teach them modesty, submission and decorum. The elder was amenable to instruction and soon learnt her lesson. The younger wouldn't, and so she was repudiated and sent back in shame to her father's house.

XXI

The Wicked Mother-in-Law

Once upon a time . . .

Once upon a time there was a young merchant who married a girl from a respectable Beldi family chosen by his mother. *In olden times the in-laws were very powerful and girls were expected to behave modestly. Mothers-in-law took control of the household.* This merchant had two sisters who were very spoilt. The newlywed daughter-in-law was treated like a maid and given the dirtiest tasks, sweeping and cleaning the floor. But she always kissed her mother-in-law's hand and called her Lilla [mistress]. The mother-in-law had the key to the store-room. When dinner was ready the mother-in-law would serve the food, the men first then the women. The women would sit to eat and look for any excuse to send the bride on errands: bring the salt, we forgot the water, etc. While they ate their full, the poor daughter-in-law remained hungry but never complained about her mistreatment; Beldi custom prevented her from speaking out.

The girl grew thinner every day, but she was the daughter of a respectable family which considers it most important for a girl not to show arrogance or disrespect towards her elders. The young husband saw that his wife was pale and subdued. One day he smuggled some cakes to his wife and fed her. But his mother discovered it and accused him of being henpecked. The bride grew thinner, fell sick and died.

The young merchant got married for the second time and his new bride, after a few months, followed the first to the grave. The third newlywed bride, after a few months, grew thinner. The young husband noticed it and this time reported it to an old fellow-merchant and complained about his mother and sisters' treatment of his wives.

The old man advised the young merchant how he could teach his family a lesson. He asked him to feign an argument with his wife and repudiate her and take his effeminate apprentice to pose as a new wife. The young merchant pretended to have an argument with his wife and repudiated her. A week later, his mother suggested she should find him another wife. The young man said this time he would make the choice himself. The first day the new bride came to the house, she took charge of the kitchen. She would pick up the best of the food and eat while the others watched. When they sat down to eat, she found any excuse to send her mother and sisters-in-law in turn to run errands.

One day, the the women decided to go to the Turkish baths and asked the daughter-in-law to prepare some nice soup for their return. After they left, the daughter-in-law took a big jar of grain and emptied it into a huge cauldron, added tomatoes and water and put it on the fire. When the women came back from the baths, they were outraged to discover she had used the whole year's provisions of semolina. Shocked, they begged the young man to repudiate the horrible girl and take back his former wife, and they would gladly serve her. So his former wife came back and regained her rightful position and the two women had learnt their lesson.

XXII

Women's Wiles

Listeners, may we all be guided to goodness and to make the Shehada.
Once upon a time . . .

Once upon a time, as God is all-knowing, there lived in Tunis a master merchant, who had put up a sign on his shop saying: 'Men's wiles are sixteen times more powerful than women's.' The daughter of *amein al-Tujjar* [the chief of guild], a highly educated girl, was passing by one day and saw the sign. It angered her, and she thought to herself: 'I will teach him a lesson.'

A new day is born and he who prays for the Prophet will be blessed. She went into the shop, greeted the merchant and burst out sobbing bitterly. The merchant was surprised and asked: 'What's the matter?' The girl only cried louder. He asked her: 'By God, what's your story?' She replied:

'Am I one-eyed?' He answered: 'One-eyed? I swear your eyes are more beautiful than a gazelle's.' She continued: 'Am I bald?' letting her white veil fall from her hair. 'Bald?' he queried. 'Your hair is like silk, and so black that the night is jealous.' 'Am I lame?' she asked, lifting her skirt to show her fine white legs. By then the merchant was gaping and his mouth was watering. 'Lame?' he echoed. 'Yours legs are straight and white as marble columns.' She continued: 'I am the daughter of the king, and every time a suitor comes to ask for my hand, my father the king turns him down, saying: "My daughter is one-eyed, bald and lame." ' 'Does he really?' the merchant exclaimed. 'Well then, I'll come tomorrow and ask for your hand.' With that, the chief of guild's daughter left.

The master merchant spent a restless night, dreaming about the beautiful girl. As soon as he saw the first streak of dawn of the new day he rose and went straight to the public baths. He washed, shaved, dressed smartly and went to the palace. The king was holding court. The merchant asked for an audience with the king. They said: 'Have you come to make a complaint?' He answered: 'Far from it.' They told him to wait until after the court session to see the king. When it was over, the master merchant was shown into the king's presence. He greeted him with due deference and said: 'I have come seeking kinship with your honour.' Surprised, the king replied: 'I have no daughter to marry off.' 'Indeed you have, my lord, and she is one-eyed, bald and lame.' The king replied: 'Since you are prepared to accept that, then I will give her to you, on condition you give two million dinars as her bride-price.' Hearing the two million dinars mentioned, the merchant wavered, then remembered the girl's beauty and answered: 'Gladly. Agreed.' It was decided to celebrate the marriage the following Thursday.

On the wedding-day the master merchant sent a carriage to the palace to fetch his bride, and waited impatiently for its return. When it arrived two slaves lifted out a huge basket covered with a white veil. 'It must be her trousseau,' he thought to himself, and waited for the bride to follow, but she didn't. He went into the bridal chamber to examine the contents of the basket while he waited for the bride. To his astonishment, when he lifted the veil he found the bride sitting in the middle of the basket. 'Who are you?' he asked. A squeaky little voice replied: 'It's me, your bride!' He felt an immense weight of sadness descend on him, thinking to himself: 'I have been tricked.' He spent a restless night and the following day he went to the souk, opened his shop and sat inside, crushed by his misfortune.

Soon the chief of guild's daughter came in and greeted him. 'Good morning,' he answered. 'May all your days be unlucky!' 'What have I done to you, to cause me such a calamity?' she said, pointing to the sign above: 'Do you really think men's wiles are more powerful than women's? You must change the order of the words on your sign to "Women's wiles are sixteen times more powerful than men's" if you want me to get you out of this misfortune.' So the merchant called a painter and changed the sign.

She said: 'Tomorrow, hire a rowdy band and drummers and ask them to come and play in front of the palace. If the king enquires about them, say they are your folk who have come to congratulate you on the occasion of your wedding.'

The merchant chose the roughest, noisiest band he could find, tattooed and barefoot, and instructed them to go and play in front of the palace. The king was taking a nap and awoke to the sound of a noisy crowd. 'Who are they? What are they doing?' His son-in-law, the master merchant, answered: 'These are my folk, come to congratulate me on my marriage. Each region has its own traditions, and he who denies his roots is a dog. They are my own flesh and blood from Jlass*.' Outraged, the king exclaimed: 'Are you from Jlass, then?' 'Indeed I am, and he who denies his roots is a dog.' The king continued: 'Then we cannot be related in marriage. You must divorce her at once.' The merchant answered sarcastically: 'It isn't that easy. I shall divorce her on condition you give me seven times the amount I paid you.' Turning to his courtiers, the king shouted in disgust: 'Give him what he asks, and turn the pig out!'

A new day is born and he who prays for the Prophet will be blessed; the master merchant opened his shop in high spirits, thinking to go and ask for the hand of the girl he now knew to be the chief of guild's daughter. In the afternoon, he put on his best *jibba* and *burnous* and went to the chief of guild's house. After greeting the man and

* Jlass is the name of an area considered uncivilized by the Beldi

his company, he said: 'I have come to seek kinship with your honour.' He replied: 'She's yours.' The master merchant replied: 'I have one condition, though.' Surprised, the father enquired what it was. 'I would ask to see her first,' he answered, saying to himself: 'He who has been tricked once, shall not be taken in again!' Outraged, the man exclaimed: 'See her! I have no daughter I will allow to be seen by a man!' The company intervened. 'Why not? After all, she is not bald, one-eyed or lame!' The father persisted in refusing, but his companions said: 'This is the opportunity of a lifetime. You must let him.'

The master merchant was eventually shown in to see the girl. When he saw her, he heaved a sigh of relief: 'Thank heavens!' he thought to himself, and said to the girl: 'Once bitten, twice shy!' They were married, the celebration took seven days and seven nights and they lived safely and procreated until death did them part.

XXIII
Al-Maktub/Fate

My tale is one of wonder. May our prayers and yours be offered up for the beloved Prophet, peace be upon him! Listeners, may we all be guided to goodness and to make the Shehada. *Once upon a time . . .*

Once upon a time there was a prince who went out in disguise to enquire about the welfare of his people. When he came to the market he found an old woman selling wool. He asked her: 'Who spins the wool for you?'

She answered: 'My daughters, Hasna [Beauty], Hussayna [Little Beauty] and Kamilt al-Husn (Perfect Beauty), God bless them. They spin the wool and I come to the market to sell it.'

He asked her: 'Would you give me the eldest Hasna in marriage?'

She replied: 'Yes I will.'

309

He told her the marriage would be celebrated the following week. The next Friday he came to her house with
two bags of provisions and the wedding dress, as was the
tradition. She had the bride dressed and made up. He
sent a carriage to take her to the palace. When the bride
was shown to the bridal chamber, he came to greet her.
When he tried to raise her veil he heard a voice saying:
'Don't touch her, O Muhammad, son of the Sultan. She
is not destined for you. She is destined for the dog with
the seven chains.' He dropped the veil, put her back
in the carriage and sent her back to her mother.

A few weeks later, the prince went out in disguise again
and went to see the old lady to ask her for her second
daughter's hand. They came to an agreement and a week
later he sent a carriage for her. But when he again lifted
the veil, he heard a voice saying: 'She is not destined for
you. She is destined for the one swallowed up by the earth
because of his exceptional beauty.' He dropped the veil,
and the same carriage which brought her there took her
back again to her mother's. A week later the prince went
to see the old woman to ask for the hand of her youngest
daughter, Kamilt al-Husn. This time she refused, on the
grounds that her daughters were obviously not meant for
him.

When she went back home, she informed her youngest
daughter Kamilt al-Husn about the match and explained
why she had refused. The youngest begged: 'Let me try, I
might be the one for him.' The following day her mother
relented and agreed to give her to him. A week later, a

carriage was sent to fetch the bride. When she was shown into the bridal chamber he tried to lift her veil and heard the voice saying: 'This is your destined bride. May you prosper and multiply.' He kissed her on the forehead and said to her: 'May you be my destined wife, in this world and in the world to come.' The marriage was consummated and they lived happily together.

A month passed and her sisters had heard no news from her. Curious, they insisted on going to visit her and enquire what had become of her. She was overjoyed to see them, and gave them a warm welcome. They asked for a favour from her: 'Could you ask your husband why he didn't accept us and married you instead?' She said she would, but that she would have to wait until he returned. When the mother told them it was time to leave, they insisted on staying the night to hear the answer the following morning. The mother refused, but the girls were adamant. *In those days, women were not allowed to meet men face to face.* When the husband came back and they went to bed, she asked him: 'Why did you refuse my other sisters and marry me?' He answered: 'Why bring that old story up now?' She insisted on having an answer. He explained that on the first two occasions when he wanted to marry one of the sisters he had heard a voice telling him that they were not for him. The first was destined for the dog with the seven chains and the second for the one who had been swallowed up by the earth because of his exceptional beauty.

A new day is born and he who prays for the Prophet will be

311

blessed. When the two sisters heard the husband leaving, they hurried to hear the answer. 'What did he tell you?' She answered: 'He told me that each of you is destined for someone else; the eldest for the dog with the seven chains and the younger one for the man who was swallowed up by the earth because of his exceptional beauty.' When the two sisters heard this, they exclaimed: 'So that's what it was! Now we must go out and search for our destined husbands.' She answered: 'You must be mad! It's too dangerous.' They answered: 'If you really love us, you will give us provisions and help us.'

They eventually talked her into it. She prepared some provisions for them and all their hearts' desires and bade them farewell. The two girls took to the road. They walked and walked until they grew weary and dejected. When they came to a crossroads they said: 'It's pointless to continue like this together. We should take different roads.' They embraced each other and said if they were destined to meet again they would; if not, there would be no ill-feeling between them.

They went their separate ways. The eldest, Hasna, walked and walked, crossing country after country, until night fell and she grew tired. She saw a light at a distance and decided to head for it and seek shelter for the night. When she arrived she found a big house with seven identical rooms and a big bowl of *couscous.* As she was hungry she went in and helped herself. Around midnight, she heard a rumbling and felt the earth shake. She was frightened to death, rushed into one of the rooms and barred herself in. She was amazed to see a dog being dragged along by four guards, who could barely restrain his frenzy. They gave him the *couscous* and he ate it all up, and drained the water bucket. With that, he collapsed, and the four guards left. When all was calm again, the dog shook off his chains and went around the house, saying: 'Whoever you are, come out of your hiding-place. If you are an old woman, I'll treat you like my mother, if you are an old man I'll treat you like my father, if you are a young woman I'll treat you like a sister or like a wife, or if you are a young boy I'll treat you like a brother. Come out; I swear by God that you will be safe.'

She came out and said: 'I have come all this way for you.'

He said: 'Then you will be my wife.' He went on: 'I am really a prince but I am under a spell. I warn you not to approach me when I am in one of my fits. At sunset, make sure you take your supper with you and lock yourself in one of the rooms, and stay inside.' She followed his instructions and they eventually got married and lived together in this way until she became pregnant. Three months of craving and three months of fleshing out and three months of skin taughtening on the bones. She was praying she would go into labour during the day and not at night, but when the baby was due, she started labour at sunset. She was frightened he might come back before the baby was born, but just as she gave birth she heard him returning, seized her child and locked herself in the room, frightened to death. In his frenzy the dog in the seven chains ate the afterbirth and as soon as he did so, the spell was broken and he turned into a handsome young man. He begged her to open the door. She opened the door, and both were overjoyed to realize that the spell was over. He said to her: 'Thanks to you, my spell is broken and I can live normally. I must take you to my father's land and celebrate our wedding.' He took her to his father's land where a big celebration was awaiting them, seven days and seven nights of festivities.

Now that the eldest has found her destined husband and is happy and contented, let's go back to the second sister, Hussayna. She walked and walked, crossing country after country, until she grew tired and hungry. She found a pool of water, drank from it and washed her face. When she saw her reflection in the water she exclaimed: 'How beautiful I am! But unlucky!'

She heard a voice: 'You who are admiring yourself in the water, lift the marble slab and see what's underneath.' When she lifted the slab she found a staircase. She walked down and found an extremely beautiful young woman. She enquired: 'What are you doing here?' The young woman replied: 'Don't ask. My father is the ogre. He is coming to visit me today. Come and help me and tell me all about yourself.'

She agreed to help her and she confided to her the secret about searching for her destined husband. The young woman promised to help her in her search, explaining that her father was the king of the ogres, and that

nothing escaped his attention. A huge *couscous* was prepared for the ogre. When he came, his daughter hid her
in a rolled-up mat, but he sensed a human presence and
exclaimed: 'I can smell humans! Come to me, all of my
possessions.' Each and every one of his possessions rushed
to him, except the mat. He enquired: 'Where is the mat?'
His daughter answered: 'It is sick and tired out.' He
answered: 'Leave it to rest.' After he had dinner, his daughter came to him and asked: 'Father, have you heard about
the one who was swallowed up by the earth because of his
exceptional beauty?' He answered: 'What? How did you
come to hear that story, buried here under the earth?' He
slapped her on the face and put her eye out.

When the ogre left, the sister came out of hiding, apologizing: 'I'm sorry I got you into trouble.' She replied: 'No
harm done; I will recover. Take this walnut and this
almond and go and find my younger sister. She will be
able to help you.'

She walked and walked miles around until she found a
pool of water, drank from it and washed her face. When
she saw her reflection in the water she exclaimed: 'How
beautiful I am! But unlucky!' She heard a voice: 'You who
are admiring yourself in the water, lift the marble slab and
see what's underneath.' When she lifted the slab she found
a staircase. She walked down and found an extremely
beautiful young woman. She enquired: 'What are you
doing here?' The young woman replied: 'Don't ask. My
father is the ogre. He is coming to visit me today. Come
and help me and tell me all about yourself.'

She agreed to help her and she confided to her the secret about searching for her destined husband. The young woman promised to help her in her search, explaining that her father was the king of the ogres, and that nothing escaped his attention. A huge *couscous* was prepared for the ogre. When he came, his daughter hid her in a rolled-up mat, but he sensed a human presence and exclaimed: 'I can smell humans! Come to me, all of my possessions.' Each and every one of his possessions rushed to him, except the mat. He enquired: 'Where is the mat?' His daughter answered: 'It is sick and tired out.' He answered: 'Leave it to rest.' After he had dinner, his daughter came to him and asked: 'Father, have you heard about the one who was swallowed up by the earth because of his exceptional beauty?' He replied; 'You know what happened to your sister when she asked me the same question. But because you are so dear to me I will answer. Whoever wants to get to him needs one of my robes, one of my sticks and one portion of my supper. The portion is for the ants when they swarm, the stick is to help get through the mountains covered in thorns and thistles, and the robe is to escape from the other ogres.' She answered: 'Who cares?'

After a week, when her father was due to come again, she prepared for him a clean robe, a new stick and new shoes. When he started his meal, she shouted: 'Don't eat that, there's a hair in it.' So he spat it out. Then she said to him: 'You must get rid of this old robe and stick. I've got new ones for you.' He replied: 'You are right, I need to change into a new robe.' He took off the old robe and put on the new one and left with the new stick.

She said to her: 'Now you can start your search; take this hazelnut and use it in case of necessity and go; may you be blessed.' She kissed her goodbye and left.

Hussayna walked and walked, crossing country after country. She came to a mountain covered with thorns and thistles. She struggled through it with the help of the magic stick. Then suddenly she was surrounded by ants. She threw them the ogre's morsel of food and continued on her way. She met with lions and tigers but none of them molested her because she was wearing the magic robe. She walked until she came to a grave where her destined husband was buried, as the ogre had explained to her. She was to cry until she filled seven jars and seven drinking cups with her tears, which would break the spell on him.

She sat down on a bench and started to cry and cry until she filled the first, then the second and so on. She remembered her father's death and cried, she remembered her mother's death and cried, her unhappy days and cried. She cried over her bad luck, her self-sacrifice . . . As she was filling the seventh, a procession of people passed by and asked for water to quench their thirst. She said to herself: 'Maybe I should buy a serving-girl to help me through.' So she gave them some water and got a black servant in exchange. Explaining to the girl that she was to fill the last jar with tears and wake her when it was full, she lay down to rest. Exhausted by her crying, she immediately fell into a sound sleep. The serving-girl only had to think of her own problems to cry her eyes out and she soon filled the last jar to the brim. He-who-was-swallowed-up-by-the-earth-because-of-his-beauty had promised he would marry whoever broke the spell. So when the last tear was shed, the grave opened and he rose from it as beautiful as the moon. He saw the woman lying there, more beautiful than he had ever imagined. He enquired: 'Who is this?' The black girl answered: 'A beggar who came to ask for alms.' He asked: 'Was it you who cried over me?' She said: 'Yes, indeed.' He said: 'Then you shall be my wife in this world and the next.'

The sleeping woman woke up to find herself alone. She realized what had happened and lamented her fate. Then she got to her feet and started to walk until she came to a city which was in turmoil with the king's impending marriage, and rumours that the king's spell had been broken by a black girl. She made her way to the palace to ask for food, and was taken on as a maid.

She worked for some time until one day she saw the new bride and recognized her. She decided to take her revenge. She took out the first daughter's gift, the walnut, and broke it. When she broke it, there came out of it a tray of amber and goldfinches. She put it in the patio for the black bride to see. When she saw it she coveted it and enquired: 'Whose is this?' The servants answered: 'It belongs to the new servant.' She asked for her to be brought before her. When she asked the servant to name

318

her price, she replied: 'A night with your husband.' The bride was taken aback but eventually gave in.

On that night, the black bride prepared the coffee with a sleeping potion in it and served it to her husband so that he would be incapable of doing anything. To test its effect, she burned his heel but he did not react. The woman was then allowed to come up to his apartment. Seeing him unconscious, she tried to shake him awake, explaining: 'I am the one who has loved you so dearly, I am the one cried over you, I am the one who sacrificed her life, I am the one you should have married,' but to no avail. Just before sunrise the wife knocked on the door asking her to leave.

A week or so later, the young woman took out the daughter's second gift, the almond, and broke it. Out of it came a priceless robe. She spread it out in the sun for the black bride to see. When she saw it she coveted it and enquired: 'Whose is this?' The servants answered: 'It belongs to the new servant.' She asked for her to be brought before her. When she asked the servant to name her price, she replied: 'A night with your husband.' The black bride was taken aback but remembering the beautiful robe, eventually gave in.

On that night again, the black bride prepared a coffee, put a sleeping potion in it and served it to her husband. Before allowing the servant into his apartment, she burned his heal to test the effect of the potion. The king did not react. So she called the servant up to his apartment. The same thing happened again.

A new day is born and he who prays for the Prophet will be blessed. The king went to his vizier, complaining about his sore feet and inexplicable exhaustion. The vizier enquired: 'What did you eat last night?' The king answered: 'Only the usual coffee and cake before going to bed.' The vizier answered: 'Well, next time, don't drink it, and pretend to fall asleep.'

A week later she took out the hazelnut and broke it. Out of it came a priceless crown studded with emeralds and rubies. Again, she left it for the bride to find and the same thing happened. But this time she took a stick to strike him awake. That very night the king didn't drink his coffee so when the woman came he was wide awake but pretending to sleep. She cried to him, explaining: 'I am the one who cried over you. I am the one who filled the seven jars. I am the one who wasted her life for you, and now you pay me back by marrying a black slave.' And she started to beat him. He stood up and enquired: 'Are you telling the truth? Was it really you?' She said: 'Indeed.' She went to the bathroom and bathed and when she returned he gave her a priceless nightgown and they passed the night in married bliss.

A new day is born and he who prays for the Prophet will be blessed. When the black woman came to knock, he opened the door and asked his new bride to decide what her fate should be. She said: 'I want four she-camels, two hungry and two thirsty, to tear her apart.' And so it was done.

The order was given to celebrate the wedding, seven days and seven nights of festivities. The king and queen lived happily for years until one day the queen yearned for her mother and sisters. She sent messengers to her sisters and they all gathered happily at their mother's house. The mother was happy to see that all her daughters had finally found their destined husbands and were living happily.

All the daughters lived safely for many years and pro-created until death did them part.

A thousand suitors ask for the hand of a girl but she will only marry her destined partner.

XXIV

Overpowering Desire

Once upon a time . . .

Once upon a time there was a farmer who had three sons. All three were called Muhammad. All of them used to work hard in order to do well. One day, the father fell ill and had to stay in bed. A week later, his condition had not improved and he felt he was dying. So he called his three sons and said to them: 'I believe my hour has come and I have nothing to leave you except the orchard. Muhammad and Muhammad will inherit, but Muhammad will not.' This puzzled the three sons, but they didn't want to aggravate their father on his deathbed. Fate caught up with the father and he died. They observed the forty days' mourning, as was the tradition, and then sat down together to solve the puzzle of their inheritance. They could not find a solution, so decided to seek the help of the *qadi*.

They set off one day early in the morning and made their way to town. They walked and walked until they grew tired and had to sit down and rest. Noticing the tracks of a camel in the dust, one of them said: 'I think a camel has just passed by.' 'It is one-eyed,' said the second, noticing that the grass was eaten only one one side. 'It is loaded with honey and oil,' said the eldest, noticing patches of oil on one side of the path and swarms of ants on the other.

As they moved off again, they met a bedouin Arab. The bedouin asked them: 'Have you people seen a camel?' 'Did it stop to rest here?' asked the first son. The bedouin answered: 'Yes.' The second son asked: 'Is your camel one-eyed?' Surprised, the man said: 'Oh, yes!' 'Is it loaded with oil and honey?' asked the eldest son. 'Yes, indeed! Have you seen it?' asked the bedouin. All three answered: 'No!' The bedouin accused them: 'You must have stolen it.' An argument developed, and they all agreed to take their dispute to the *qadi*.

The bedouin came before the *qadi* and said: 'Master, they stole my camel.' All three denied it. The bedouin explained: 'They identified it to me as being one-eyed and loaded with oil and honey.' The *qadi* addressed the three men, asking: 'How did you know that if you didn't steal it?' The youngest replied: 'I noticed camel-tracks and flattened grass where it had sat down.' The second son added: 'The grass on one side of the path was eaten and untouched on the other side, so I presumed it was one-eyed.' The eldest explained: 'There were patches of oil on one side and swarms of ants on the other, so I presumed it was loaded with oil and honey.' 'How clever of them!' the *qadi* thought, and sent the bedouin away. The three brothers told the *qadi* of their dilemma over the inheritance. The *qadi* withdrew, supposedly to let them eat, but he stayed listening at the door.

The eldest said: 'This is dog-meat.' The second added: 'Whoever cooked it is menstruating.' 'What else could you expect from a *wild hram* [an illegitimate son],' explained the youngest. On hearing this, the *qadi* ran to his slaughterman enquiring: 'Was that dog-meat?' He answered: 'It isn't, it's lamb that was suckled by a bitch.' Then he went to his cook, and asked her 'Are you menstruating?' Surprised, the cook answered: 'I am.' By now, the *qadi* was beside himself. Two out of the three comments had proved to be true. He snatched a knife and ran to his mother, saying: 'By God, tell me the truth. Am I my father's legitimate son?' She answered: 'Your late father used to travel widely, may he rest in peace. One day, a pedlar came with a caravan. He was tall and handsome and as soon as I set eyes on him I was seized with burning desire to lie with him. I have sinned, I gave in to my *nafs* [inner life force], may God forgive me!'

The *qadi* went back to his guests, and asked the eldest: 'How did you know it was dog-meat?' 'From the texture of the meat.' 'And you,' addressing the second son, 'How did you know the cook was menstruating?' 'The food was bland.' Addressing the youngest, the *qadi* exclaimed: 'You are the one who will not inherit. It takes one to know one!'

XXV

The Value of Trustworthiness

Once upon a time . . .

Once upon a time there was a poor pious young man who
was an orphan and lived alone. One day, he felt hungry
but there was nothing to eat in the house. He went out
to the mosque to say his afternoon prayer. He prayed to
God to help him survive. After the prayer, everybody left.
The young man first thought of staying in the house of
God, but then decided to leave. On the doorstep he found
a money-belt. He was overjoyed. 'This is a godsend. Find-
ers keepers!' He rushed back home with it and counted
the money. There were a hundred riyals. He dreamed of
buying the things he had always wanted. Then he thought:
'What if the owner claims the belt? I must take it back to
the mosque.' He went to the mosque and waited on the
doorstep but no one came to claim it on the first day. He

went back the following day, and the day after, but still no one claimed it.

The man who had lost the money-belt hired a crier who toured the town, saying: 'Whoever found a money-belt, I will give him half the amount if he returns it.' The young man heard this, and thought to himself: 'I could keep the money legitimately then.' So he went to find the man and asked him to come with him to his house to collect it. When they arrived, the man counted the money and said to him: 'Now, you want half of it?' The young man answered: 'Whatever you say.' The man said: 'I'll give you a quarter.' The young man said: 'Whatever you say.' 'Then I'll give you an eighth.' 'Whatever you say.' 'Would you be happy with three riyals?' The young man replied: 'That's fine with me.' 'I'll give you one, then.' The young man answered: 'It's up to you. After all, I made no effort for it. Whatever God sends.' The old man said: 'What if I didn't give you anything?' The man replied: 'You don't have to.' The old man said: 'I'll give you three blessings. One, may you acquire a fortune without effort. May you have a house you didn't have to build, and a bride you didn't have to ask for.' With that, the old man left. The young man was disappointed, tired and hungry, but he thought: 'It wasn't my money anyway.' He decided to go out and beg for food.

The old man's predestined hour came and he died. He had a young daughter who, after his death, got into the habit of having a neighbour's wife keep her company overnight. It was sunset that day, and the girl did not come, so she went out to look for her. By then, the beggar had reached her house, and stood at the door and called: 'In the name of God, give me some food.' The door was ajar, so he pushed it open and went in. To his surprise, he found a table set for two with a big dish of *couscous*. He was hungry, and the delicious aroma of the *couscous* whetted his appetite. He reached for a spoonful, then put it back. 'This is not right,' he thought. 'I come into someone's house and eat without permission?' He replaced the cover on the dish and went out.

The young girl came back with her neighbour. When she uncovered the *couscous* she realized that it had been touched. 'Someone must have been in,' she said. 'Fetch your husband.' The neighbour replied: 'But you know he's old and infirm.' The young girl insisted. When the old man came, she said to him: 'You must find me a husband, because I am a poor defenceless girl on my own. My home has been violated.' And she started to cry. The old man replied 'Come, come, my girl. How can I find you a husband at this time of night?' She replied: 'But you must!'

The old man went out. The beggar was still loitering outside, so he approached him, saying: 'Would you like to get married?' The young man answered: 'Are you joking? I haven't even had a bite to eat for four days. How can I afford to get married?' The old man answered: 'Look at me. I am perfectly serious.' The beggar answered: 'Fine.' So he took him to the house. The beggar recognized the house, thinking: 'I've been to this house before.' Two witnesses were called and the marriage contract was drawn up. The girl heated some water [*in those days there were no bathrooms*] and helped him to wash. The old couple left them.

When the bride set the table the beggar laughed. She asked: 'Why are you laughing? Is it because I was the one who asked for your hand instead of the other way round?' He said: 'No. This is the very spoon I lifted earlier, then put it down; but God had ordained that I should eat.' She asked him: 'Tell me your story.' He recounted it. 'I hadn't eaten for four days, so I went out to say my prayers. On the way out of the mosque I found a money-belt. Later I found out it belonged to an old man, and returned it to him. At first he promised to give me half, then a quarter, then an eighth, but in the end all I got was three blessings: a fortune without effort, a house I didn't build and a bride I didn't ask for.'

On hearing this, the girl rushed to the clothes-chest and produced the money-belt. 'Is this it?' 'Indeed it is,' he replied. 'Then it belonged to my father,' she answered, 'and his three blessings have been fulfilled.' He kissed her on the forehead and said: 'May you be my wife in this world and the next. Nothing is sweeter than lawfully acquired wealth.' She said: 'What is mine is yours. Tomorrow you will open my father's shop and take up his trade.' And they lived happily ever after.

XXVI

A Happy Home

Once upon a time . . .

Once upon a time there lived a poor old woman who had three daughters. She earned her living by selling the wool which her daughters spun. Each and every day she would go to the souk, sell however much God had decreed for her, and return home with a basket of provisions. One day, she was approached by a fine, handsome youth, elegantly dressed in a white burnous. He bought all the wool from her and asked her: 'Did you spin this yourself?' 'Oh, no, sir. It's my daughters who spin it, bless them.' 'Would you give one of them to me in marriage?' 'With joy,' she replied. 'The marriage contract will be drawn up next Thursday, then,' he replied, giving her a purse full of money.

Overjoyed, she rushed home to tell them the news and

prepare the eldest for her impending marriage. The following Thursday, a carriage was sent with the wedding dress and veil, as was the tradition. The bride took her place in her new house. On the third day of the marriage she received a basket of provisions. When she opened it she found the grinning head of a corpse. She died of shock. The husband came back and ate her, and threw her head and legs into the larder. A few days later, he went back to see the old woman and told her the sad news of her daughter's death. She enquired as to what had happened. He said: 'Her time had come, God did not grant her a long lifespan.' At that, her mother began to weep and wail.

A week later, the young man presented himself at the old woman's house and asked for the hand of the second daughter. The old woman agreed and the marriage was celebrated without delay. The new bride took her place in her new home and the same fate befell her as her sister. Her mother cried and wept over her and resigned herself to God. A week later the young man came back to ask for the hand of the youngest daughter. This time, the old woman refused. 'She is my sole companion. I don't want to lose her,' she explained to the young man. But 'Aysha begged to be allowed to marry him and unravel the mystery. The marriage was celebrated and 'Aysha took her place in her new home.

The following day, 'Aysha received a basket of provisions. When she opened it she found the grinning head of a corpse. She invoked God's protection, took out the head and decided to grill it and make a *couscous* with it. She made the *couscous* and served it to her husband when he came back. They lived together until 'Aysha conceived. By then she had realized that she was married to an ogre. At midnight he would go out and come back in the early morning with the stench of corpses clinging to him. When she went into labour, the ogre went to inform her mother. Meanwhile, 'Aysha prepared a *zirdab* [makeshift hearth], in front of the house door.

When the ogre came back, he fell into the *zirdab*, and died immediately. 'Aysha, with the help of her mother, gave birth to a male child. She took her son and went back to live with her mother. There was a crier going round the town, announcing that the *qadi*'s wife was in labour and wanted the midwife to help. 'Aysha's mother hurried there, accompanied by her daughter and the new-born baby. With the help of God, the *qadi*'s wife was safely delivered of a boy. 'Aysha and her mother were asked to spend the night with her and attend the celebration the following day. 'Aysha's baby was laid beside the new child to sleep.

At midnight, 'Aysha's son turned to the newborn and devoured it, leaving only the head and legs. Like father, like son – he turned out to be an ogre. He woke his grandmother, saying: 'Granny, granny, I left his head and legs in the cradle.' The grandmother soon realized what had happened. 'Our heads will roll tomorrow,' she thought, shaking 'Aysha awake. They picked up the child, and fled from the house. They walked until they came

332

across the first well in their path. 'He must die, just like his father,' 'Aysha thought, as she flung the baby into the well.

Distressed by the catastrophe which had befallen her, 'Aysha decided to flee from the village, seeking a happy home to shelter her. She walked and walked and walked, and sat on a doorstep to rest. The maid happened to come out to wash the step, and in doing so, splashed her with water. 'Aysha complained and shouted until the mistress of the house came out to see what was going on. 'Aysha explained what had happened and the woman apologized and invited her in to dry off. 'What brings you here?' she asked. 'I am looking for a happy home to shelter me.' The mistress replied: 'This is a happy home, but let me tell you the whole story about my two useless daughters-in-law. They're bone idle. They don't cook or clean. They sit around all day, eating and not lifting a finger. They are as dirty as pigs. I'm sick and tired of them.' 'I'll teach them a lesson,' offered 'Aysha, thinking to herself: 'I was looking for a happy home and here I have found one with more misfortune than my own.' She paid a visit to the eldest son's wife, in her room. To her disgust she found the room in disorder, dirty and unaired. She scolded her, saying: 'What a mess! Why have you let your room get like this? Aren't you ashamed of yourself? How can you expect a husband to love you and keep you if you don't keep his home clean and comfortable?' The daughter-in-law answered: 'I don't know. No one's ever told me how.' 'Well, I'll teach you,' 'Aysha replied. 'Bring me water and a broom.' Then she instructed her in how to clean and tidy up. After she finished she heated some water in a cauldron and gave the girl a bath. In the late afternoon her husband came home and was impressed at the change. The young wife took the lesson to heart and kept the place spick and span from then on.

'Aysha then went on to do the same for the second daughter-in-law. But all her efforts were met with indifference. The young woman refused to give up her slovenly ways. She would sit all day long, chewing and watching the other women of the house doing the domestic chores, and would not offer any assistance. The mother-in-law was dissatisfied and sat every evening in the presence of her son, delighting in her daughter-in-law's laziness and celebrating her lack of domestic prowess. 'She is useless; she can't build a happy home. She's good for nothing ...' Her son grew tired of his lazy wife and soon divorced her. 'Aysha received two silk *futas* in return for her efforts, and left to continue her search.

She walked and walked, crossing country after country. Exhausted, she sat down on the doorstep to rest. Soon, the little maid came out to wash the step, and 'Aysha was accidentally splashed with water. She remonstrated with her, and the mistress of the house came out to see what all the commotion was about. 'Aysha complained: 'They don't respect their elders any more. She's made a mess of my dress.' The mistress answered: 'We'll give you a change of clothes, and you will be our guest for three days and three nights, as the Prophet established the tradition.'

So 'Aysha went in and changed. She noticed a young woman sitting idly chewing gum. The mistress was bustling around, but the younger woman didn't lift a finger. 'Aysha enquired: 'Who is this?' The mistress replied, ironically: 'She's my daughter-in-law, God bless her!' 'Aysha sensed something strange in the girl's demeanour, and decided to observe her. At midnight the girl's eyes turned red, her hair stood on end and she went out. 'Aysha realized that, shortly before this, she had served her husband and mother-in-law coffee laced with a sleeping-potion. 'Aysha followed her. She heard her say: 'Oh, my brother, who fell down the well – I'm hungry.' A voice replied: 'Eat your father-in-law.' 'But he provides for me!' she objected. 'Then eat your mother-in-law.' 'But she waits on me!' 'Eat your husband.' She answered: 'I can't betray him.' 'Eat your guest, then.' 'Not until her three days' hospitality are up.' The voice replied: 'Go and find a dead donkey at Bab Aliwa.' The young woman ran off in the direction of Bab Aliwa in search of her prey.

'Aysha went back to the house and when the morning came she informed the mother-in-law: 'Your daughter-in-law is an ogress.' 'An ogress!' she exclaimed in horror. 'What shall we do?' 'I'll tell you what we'll do,' said 'Aysha. 'We will take her to the baths with a big bowl full of sponges to stuff in her mouth if she should try to eat anyone.' Her husband was instructed to talk her into going to the baths, by an oath if necessary. *Ogresses cannot stand the heat.* A *zirdab* was prepared in front of the house. The young wife refused to go to the baths on the grounds that

335

she was afraid. 'Aysha will accompany you, her husband explained. Eventually she was persuaded. As soon as she stepped into the bath she grew wild. 'Aysha stuffed the sponges into her mouth, one by one, until she finished bathing. Then they walked back home. Just before reaching the threshold, 'Aysha pushed the young woman into the *zirdab*, saying: 'Your brother is an ogre, your brother's son is an ogre, and you are an ogre! I am the one who will rid the world of your evil!' The ogress burned to a cinder.

'Aysha went into the house. She was received with great rejoicing. 'You must stay with us,' the old mistress invited. 'I shall not. I came to seek a happy home, but your misfortune is worse than my own. Let me go back to my home.' 'Aysha settled in the House of God. And there we left her, never to hear of her ever again.

KHEIRA

I

You Who Rebel Against Fate, Rise and Face What God Has Ordained

Declare that there is no God but Allah, and He who has sinned should implore his pardon.

Once upon a time there was a perfume merchant who was married to his cousin. She was dearer than life to him and they lived happily. They were filled with joy and merriment. He called her Lilla al-Nsa, 'the mistress of women', and she called him, Sidi al-Rjal, 'the master of all men'. They manifested a deep love and mutual devotion which defied description. But their happiness was not complete: in her sleep she would heave a deep sigh of unhappiness. This discomforted the husband and he tried to understand the reason for her uneasiness. He could not remember failing to see to her well being. He had

337

always provided fine clothes and jewellery for her to wear and she was well fed. He became preoccupied and worried. This didn't go unnoticed by a venerable old man, who enquired about his anxiety. The husband told him: 'I have a problem. It's my wife ... she always heaves a deep sigh in her sleep. I can't imagine why. She lacks for nothing: clothes, jewellery, money. I provide everything she could possibly want.' The elderly man replied: 'I know the answer. Get a black billy-goat and take it to the house. Keep it out of her sight. When she goes to sleep, after midnight, kill the goat, open it and remove its heart while it is still warm and put it on her chest and listen. You will hear why she sighs.' He replied: 'God bless you.' He did as the old man suggested. *Life was different in those days; wives did not question what their husbands did. There was mutual trust.*

A new day is born and he who prays for the Prophet will be blessed. He brought the billy-goat to the house and hid it in the cellar. On the same night he pretended he was tired and suggested going to bed early. When he was sure she was fast asleep he killed the goat, removed its heart, lit a candle, placed the heart on her chest and asked: 'Why do you sigh?' The heart answered: 'Because of the indignity I have to suffer. I will be a beggar for a year, a thief for a year and a whore for a year.' As soon as the word 'whore' was uttered, the candle dripped on her cheek and woke her. Seeing the bloody heart, she asked what was going on. As he had no secrets from her, he told her what was awaiting her. It sorrowed her and she broke out in lament: 'Time is fickle, why does it harbour hostility to me? How can I disgrace my cousin after such a life of luxury and pampering? I'd rather die than disgrace my beloved husband.' *Indeed no one knows what destiny has in store for us.*

The following day, after her husband went out to work, the indignity of the previous evening was still preying on her mind. So she decided to take her own life. She took out a sharp knife, cut her throat and fell to the floor, unconscious. Her hour had not come yet. *In those days, there were no doctors and no emergency calls.* When she was discovered she was soon washed and laid out and buried. After the last person left, she received a blow and heard a voice saying: 'You who rebel against fate, rise and face what God has ordained for you.'

She rose up from her grave. She had nowhere to go and didn't want to go back to her house. She stood at the cemetery gates and started to beg. When night fell, she took refuge in a mausoleum. The next day she bought a dress and got rid of her shroud. For a whole year she begged. The following year she became a thief. She would steal purses, watches, anything. She grew tired of stealing. In the meantime, she got to know some prostitutes and was soon drawn into their way of life. She had a good voice and became famous and was in great demand for weddings, like Shafia Rushdi in those days.

The husband, after the funeral, came back home, sad and heavy-hearted. He swore he would never marry again after he lost his beloved cousin. The first year passed, then the second, and the third, and he was still alone. Well-meaning neighbours and relatives tried to reason with him and talk him into remarrying: 'It was God's will, *Qadha wa Qadar*, that your wife died; we shall all take our turn, bear it with patience [patience is an article of faith], otherwise you will be damned.' But his heart was broken for ever. They eventually persuaded him to marry again. For the wedding they decided to engage the famous singer to entertain the guests. She had taken a stage name. When she arrived at the house, she recognized her house and her husband. She stood singing before the guests. At the end of the evening she sang an improvised verse which went: 'How strange for me to be here tonight, singing at my husband's wedding in my own house . . .' The husband understood the message, rose to his feet, wrapped his cloak around her and took her to the bridal chamber. He called the witnesses, cancelled the marriage-contract with the new bride and sent the guests away, and they lived safely and procreated until death did them part.

II

Companionship

Declare that there is no God but Allah, and He who has sinned should implore his pardon.

Once upon a time there was a king, *and there is no king but Allah,* who had an only daughter. He was very pious and never missed a prayer. One day, after he finished his morning prayer there appeared a horse's head before him. He greeted him with the respect due to a king and asked him for his daughter's hand. The king refused straightaway. The horse's head warned him that his daughter would turn into a bird for a year, a stone for a year and an ogress for a year if he didn't give her to him in marriage. The king still refused on the grounds that what shall be, shall be. The horse's head would appear every day and repeat the same threat, but the king didn't yield and kept the secret to himself. One day, the daughter got up early and heard her father talking to somebody. She eavesdropped on the conversation. *In those days girls used to be modest, decent and considerate of their elders; nowadays girls are arrogant and callous.* What she heard sorrowed her, but she didn't talk it over with her father. *In olden times, girls were modest; their voices were not to be heard, let alone their complaints and grievances.* She said to herself: 'How can a princess like me, after a life of luxury and pampering, suffer such indignities? What have I done to deserve such a *museiba* [misfortune]. How could I bring shame on my father. I must leave this country as soon as possible.'

She went to her apartments and sat lost in thought. 'I need a confidante and companion to help me through my misfortune.' She remembered their neighbour the carpenter who had three daughters. *In my generation the relationship based on* ma [water] *and* milh [salt] *was similar to that which related brothers and sisters. Our neighbours used to visit us and assist us in sickness and in health, in weddings and in mournings. We shared* ma *and* milh. *Nowadays neither the one nor the other matters any more. No one cares any more about anyone else except his little self.* She said to herself: 'I'll put them to the test and choose the most discreet.' She summoned the neighbour and asked him to allow his eldest daughter to come and spend the day with her. 'It will be an honour,' he answered.

A new day is born and he who praises the Prophet will be blessed. The neighbour's eldest daughter rose early, dressed herself in her best clothes. *In those days, it was quite something for girls to go out.* Then her father took her to the palace. As she entered, she found the princess at her embroidery. She greeted the princess, who returned her greeting and sat her on the floor at her embroidery hoop. *In those days, people used to sit on mattresses on the floor; there were no armchairs and sofas.* The girl sat down without a word, embroidering. Several hours went by in silence. At midday, Dadah came to ask her mistress to lunch, but not the girl. After lunch, the princess came back to her embroidery. Later a tray with tea and cake was brought to her. The other girl sat watching her eat and drink in silence. At sunset, the girl's father came for her and asked if she wanted to stay overnight. She declined. The princess asked Dadah to follow them and hear what the girl would say to her father. As soon as the girl arrived at their house she started to complain about her fast and swore she would never go there again. Dadah overheard what she said and related it to her mistress, who decided that the girl was not to be trusted and taken as a companion and confidante in her misfortune.

The following day she summoned the neighbour again and asked him for his second daughter. Exactly the same thing happened and the second daughter came back home complaining about her long day's fast at the princess's palace. The princess decided again that the second daughter was not to be trusted and taken as a confidante. She decided to put 'Aysha, the youngest, to the test. 'Aysha proved cunning. As soon as she entered and was seated at her hoop, she struck up a light-hearted conversation with the princess and suggested they should work at the same frame, and chat to pass the time away. The whole morning flew by, and Dadah came to summon her mistress to lunch. The girl reproached her for not inviting her too. They all went to have lunch, and then came back to work. In the afternoon, Dadah brought a tray of cakes and tea to her mistress. 'Aysha asked why she was not entertained too. Dadah came back with another tray for her. The princess soon realized that the youngest was lively, talkative and agreeable to be with. At sunset, her father came for her, but she informed him she wanted to stay overnight. That night, they slept in the same bed, and the princess took her into her confidence. She advised her to resign herself to God and to bear it with patience. They vowed loyalty to each other and made a blood-pact by cutting their fingers and mingling their blood. The princess informed her about her future plans to leave the country for another land. They agreed to summon a carpenter to build them a watertight cabin that closed from the inside. When the cabin was ready they had it stocked with provisions – wheat, sugar, oil, *couscous*, everything they would need. One day she called the carpenter, gave him a purse of money and asked him to come back in the evening with his friends and throw the cabin into the water with them inside. That night, after she had dinner with her father, she bade him goodnight and withdrew supposedly to sleep. She crept to the cabin with her companion and they locked themselves inside. At midnight, the carpenter and his friends came with a barrow to transport the cabin. The barrow rumbled along till they reached the shore. The men joined forces, heaved the cabin into the water and left. The cabin was tossed by the waves and the girls could not tell day from night, nor lunch from supper. They would simply eat when they felt hungry. One day, a huge wave tossed them up on the shore of a distant land. The cabin had turned green with seaweed. By now, the girls had run out of provisions. The carpenter's daughter 'Aysha suggested she should creep out of the cabin at dusk and go to find some food. They remained hidden until sunset. The carpenter's daughter disguised herself and went out. She walked and walked, until she came to a mansion. She decided to creep in unseen and steal some food. She came to a table set with all sorts of savoury and sweet dishes, *savoury and sweet delicacies in crystal bowls*. She filled two bags and left the place. She came back to the cabin and shared with the princess what God had sent them.

Back at the mansion, which belonged in fact to the prince, the prince was in the habit of having a table set for himself alone. The servants would set the table and his mother would cast a final glance over it to make sure that everything was in order. That evening the servants set the table and the mother checked that all was in place. When the prince came to have dinner, he found that someone had disturbed it. He summoned his mother, who assured him that she did check it and that perhaps he was imagining it, as he stayed up late. The following day, the same thing happened. On the third day the princess decided that it was her turn to go and find food.

The prince, on the second occasion, seeing the table so obviously in disarray, decided to sit up the following night and wait for the offender. The princess insisted that she would go that night and find food. *It was her fate! She could not escape.* At sunset, the princess left the cabin, following her companion's directions. She crept into the palace and as she was stealing the food, the prince came out of his hiding-place and wrapped his cloak around her. 'There you are! I've caught you.' He summoned his mother and asked her to get ready for his wedding. The princess agreed to marry him on condition he would build her a private apartment which no one else could enter, and bring the cabin that was on the shore into the garden. They came to an agreement. The following day, work began on her apartment, along with the preparations for the wedding, seven days and seven nights of festivities. After a week, when it was ready, she had her companion creep into her private apartment. She would share all her meals with her, down to even a date. The marriage was celebrated. *A husband is for a woman what a lid is for a cooking pot.* The princess's friend occupied an inner room in the apartment. After the prince left, they would share tea and laughter, and nobody was any the wiser. One afternoon, as they were chatting, the princess felt a chill, shook all over three times and turned into a bird. 'Aysha, the carpenter's daughter, cried out, 'May God protect you!' The princess asked: 'Will you keep your vow?' 'Aysha answered: 'He who promises never breaks his word.' The bird-princess flew away. 'Aysha cried and wailed, not knowing what to tell the prince. When Dadah came up, she changed her voice and said: 'Dadah, I have just received a letter. *In those days, pigeons carried letters.* My father has died and it is a tradition in our land to mourn our dead for three years. During this period, I will see nobody and nobody will see me. I want you to bring my meals on a tray and clap your hands to announce them.'

'Aysha spent the whole year telling her beads and moved a chickpea from one pile to another with every day that passed. The bird-princess would come every morning and ask her: 'Will you keep your vow?' and 'Aysha would answer: 'He who promises never breaks his word.'

One day the prince decided to creep into the princess's apartment and cast a secret glance at her mourning. As he did so, he saw the bird-princess and decided to hunt it. He shot it. The bird fell to the floor with a thud. He rushed down the stairs, not to be discovered. 'Aysha jumped to her feet and came to rescue the bird-princess. She pulled out the arrow and nursed the wound with honey and olive oil until it healed.

On the last day of the first year the bird-princess came back to the palace through the window and settled on the sofa where her friend was sitting. She was welcomed with joy and affection, but soon she turned into an icy-cold stone. 'Aysha would pile blankets on top of her and would light many braziers to heat the room. At night she would sleep with her in her arms and count each and every day that passed. There remained a week of the second year and 'Aysha started to worry about her mis-

tress's third ordeal. She called Baba Srur the porter (*in
olden times porters used to be called Baba Srur*) and talked to
him through the closed door. *In olden times women did not
meet men face to face, and even their hands were covered.* She
gave him a purse of gold and a big straw bag and asked
him to take it to the Bab Jabli and leave it there until he
was asked to bring it back in due course. On the last day
of the second year 'Aysha wrapped the stone in a fine
woollen blanket, recited some verses from the Qur'an over
it, embraced it with tears running down her cheeks and
put it in the bag and gave it to Baba Srur.

'Aysha spent the whole year weeping and wailing about
her mistress's plight. She would count each and every day
that passed and prayed incessantly until the last day of the
third year was over. The following morning the prince
asked to be allowed back into his wife's apartment, but he
was told to wait another fortnight to allow the princess to
wash her hands with henna and leave her days of mourning behind her. Meanwhile, 'Aysha summoned Baba Srur
and asked him to bring back the straw bag with whatever
was in it, making sure he wasn't seen. Baba Srur the porter
went to collect the bag but he found an ugly old lady
with prominent teeth and unkempt hair in its place. He
wrapped her in blankets and carried her all the way to
the palace. 'Aysha met him on the stairs, took her from
him weeping and wailing over her and gave her a good
bath straightaway. *A new day is born and he who prays for the
Prophet will be blessed.* She then asked for a substantial meal
to be brought; vegetable broth, grilled lamb and liver, and

fruit. She fed her every day for a week until the princess recovered her strength, stamina and beauty. She then asked 'Aysha to dress her in her best clothes. 'Aysha did so. The prince was overjoyed to see his wife again, *after all, he had been celibate for three years!* He complained that three years were too long to be in mourning. She explained it was the tradition in their country, and that with patience and resignation it was now over. They had dinner and made their way to the bedroom. As she undressed, the prince noticed the scar on her thigh and enquired about it. The princess explained that it was a simple scar but the prince did not believe her and insisted on hearing the whole story, promising he would stand by her, come what may. She related the whole story of her inescapable fate to him and told him about her companion living in her private apartment. 'No power can withhold what Allah gives, patience has brought you through it, patience is beautiful.' *Patience is the key to all problems.* 'Aysha came out dressed in her best and beautiful as the moon, praise to God who created her with such beauty. Seeing her beauty he swore to find her a husband that very night. He went down, summoned the notaries and had the marriage-contract drawn up between 'Aysha and the vizier's son. And they all lived safely and procreated until death did them part.

III

Habb Al-Gtar

Declare that there is no God but Allah, and He who has sinned should implore his pardon.

Once upon a time there was a king who had a son who was very dear to him, but who had no interest in women. In a distant land there was a king who had six daughters but no sons. The last time his wife conceived, she gave birth to a seventh daughter. God willed it so. The king was upset, but his wife said: 'God willed it, what can we do.' The new baby was so beautiful that the king became fond of her, and she grew into a charming and well-educated girl, the centre of attention. Her sisters grew jealous, and decided to plot against her. One day, their father the king informed them that he was going to go on pilgrimage to Mecca and whoever wanted anything brought back should write it on a piece of paper. The

350

sisters seized the opportunity. They went to see their younger sister and told her: 'We have found something precious for you to ask father for.' She asked: 'What?' They answered: 'Habb al-Gtar.' Delighted at the suggestion, the youngest sister wrote it on a piece of paper, folded it and gave it to her father. All the girls wrote down their wishes and gave them to their father.

After carrying out his pilgrimage to Mecca, the king took out the sheets of paper, thinking: 'Now I must see to my dear daughters' wishes.' He bought something for each of them, except the youngest. Each time he mentioned *Habb al-Gtar*, the merchants smiled and said, 'That's not for sale.' The king approached an old man and asked him what could it be. The old man replied: 'Whoever asked for it is either being led into danger or wishes your death. This is the name of a prince who has no interest in women.'

In the afternoon the king went to the prince's palace and sought an audience. He was soon shown in, greeted the prince with the deference due to his rank and gave him the piece of paper, explaining it was his favourite daughter's dearest wish. The prince opened the sheet of paper and smiled, saying: 'She had rather a blade to cut her hair, *it was shameful for maidens to cut their hair*, or a knife held at her throat than see Habb al-Gtar in her palace.' The king left, affronted. As soon as he arrived home, he called his vizier, threatening: 'Your head will roll if you don't bring me a glass of little 'Aysha's blood,' for that was his youngest daughter's name. The news reached her mother. *Mothers are more tender-hearted.* Without understanding what was going on, she hid 'Aysha in a cave, then took a rabbit, killed it, filled a glass with its blood and sent it to the king.

Little 'Aysha lived heartbroken in the dark, empty cave, puzzled by her father's decision to kill her. One day, she called her mother, saying: 'I miss father; bring me something of his as a keepsake.' Her mother did so. 'Aysha, on receiving her father's robe, reached into the pocket and drew out a folded piece of paper which read: 'A blade to cut her hair, a knife held at her throat, rather than see Habb al-Gtar in her palace.' She was devastated by what she read and called her mother: 'My sisters led me into this and I must avenge myself on the prince and purge my father's honour. Tomorrow at first light I shall set off.' At sunrise her mother gave her provisions and saw her off, wishing her Godspeed.

'Aysha travelled and travelled disguised in men's clothes crossing country after country, until she reached Habb al-Gtar's land. She was weary and tired. She knocked on the door of a house and was received by an old woman. She confided that she was a woman and that she needed shelter for the night. The old woman informed her that she was a widow and that she would be glad of the girl's company. The following morning 'Aysha gave the woman a thousand riyals and told her to buy her an expensive dress and later sell her as a slave girl, but only to Prince Habb al-Gtar.

Habb al-Gtar was melancholic and all the court physicians were summoned to cure him of his lack of interest in women, to no avail. The queen was taking a stroll in the market and saw the slave girl up for sale, and marvelled at her beauty. The queen made the highest bid for her at auction, and took her back to the palace with her, saying: 'May my son's cure come through you.'

'Aysha from that day on served the prince dutifully, but he didn't even raise his eyes to look at her. One evening, as he was washing his hands, he saw a face in the mirror and marvelled at her beauty. He enquired: 'How long have you been here?' 'Two weeks, my lord.' He summoned his mother and said to her: 'I want to marry her. Prepare for the wedding.' The queen gave the order to celebrate the wedding. Seven days and seven nights of festivities. 'Aysha went to visit the old woman who had sheltered her and asked her to prepare a horse for her on her wedding-day.

On the wedding-day, 'Aysha sat among her peers, but outshone them all. Habb al-Gtar was overjoyed and impatient to be *tête-à-tête* with his bride. After the guests had left, 'Aysha went to her bridal chamber, put on her nightgown and asked permission to go to the bathroom. The prince waited and waited but she failed to return. He summoned his mother and the order was given to look for her in the palace. The prince threw himself on the bed in despair, and found the slip of paper under the pillow which read: 'A blade to cut his moustache, *in the past, it was shameful for men to cut their moustache*, a knife held at his throat, rather than see little 'Aysha in his bed.' He realized what had happened and summoned the guards to accompany him in his search for 'Aysha.

Meanwhile, 'Aysha mounted her horse and headed for her father's land. She arrived at sunset and went straight to the cave where she used to hide. Early the next morning, a ship full of soldiers docked in the port. A messenger was sent to her father saying: 'Either you hand 'Aysha over to us or we will wage war until we destroy you.' Her father was puzzled; how could he produce 'Aysha when he had ordered her to be killed? He was at a loss to know what to do. His wife confided to him that she had never agreed to kill her own flesh and blood and that consequently 'Aysha was still alive. The king was overjoyed and soon the order was given to celebrate her wedding with seven days and seven nights of festivities. There we left them and we have never seen them since.

IV

The Clever Peasant Girl

Declare that there is no God but Allah, and He who has sinned should implore his pardon.

Once upon a time, there was a king who went out in disguise with his vizier to stroll about the city. They walked and walked until they came to a *saniya* [orchard]. They went in, and found a well and a water-wheel. The king heard the clicking of the mechanism as it turned and said to his vizier: 'What do you think it is trying to say?' Surprised, the vizier answered: 'Trying to say? Do you think water-wheels speak? It is only turning to raise water.' The king replied: 'I grant you three days, at the end of which you must tell me what the water-wheel is saying, otherwise your head will roll.'

The vizier went back home, sad and troubled, dragging one foot after the other (*the eyes are a jar and the lap a*

355

pitcher) and thinking: 'My hour has come.' He went back home with tears in his eyes. This didn't go unnoticed by his daughters, who asked: 'What's wrong, father?' He replied: 'Leave me alone, I am not in the mood for talking.' His youngest daughter, who was his favourite, begged him: 'Won't you tell me what is making your heart so heavy?' He replied: 'Where shall I start?' and he told her of his plight. She comforted him, saying: 'Take it easy. *Chase your morose ideas away; tomorrow is another day; your wish will be fulfilled.* Go and see the farmer working in the *saniya*. He might be able to help you.' The vizier was somewhat soothed.

A new day is born and he who praises the Prophet will be blessed. He got up early and hurried to the *saniya* and sought out the farmer. He found an old man tending some plants, so he greeted him and struck up conversation. He then related his story to him, asking his advice. The farmer's daughter, who had been standing behind him, said: 'I can tell you what the water-wheel says. Relax and be happy, and I will soon let you know.' The vizier was invited to stay three days and nights with them, as was the tradition established by the Prophet. The vizier spent the three days ill-at-ease, eagerly anticipating the answer. On the third day, the farmer's daughter approached him, saying: 'Now go to your king and tell him this:

I used to be a cheerful tree. The carpenter chopped me into planks. Now I weep and wail.

356

At this, the vizier was thrilled, and hurried straight off to the king's palace. He greeted the king with the deference due to him and said: 'Your majesty, I have got the answer.' The king replied: 'Well done! So what is it?' The vizier answered: 'The water-wheel says:

I used to be a cheerful tree. The carpenter chopped me into planks. Now I weep and wail.

Surprised, the king commented: 'Now, this is not your discovery. Someone told you.' The vizier protested, saying: 'Your majesty! How can you disbelieve me?' The king persisted: 'Either you tell me the truth, or your head will roll.' So the vizier said: 'Your majesty, when you set me this test, I went to see the farmer in the orchard and sought his help. His daughter gave me the answer.' The king ordered him: 'Hurry back and ask for her hand on my behalf.'

The vizier went that very day to the farmer and asked for his daughter's hand for his majesty the king. The farmer was overjoyed, but he said: 'I must ask my daughter's opinion.' When the daughter was consulted, she answered: 'I'd be most honoured, but only on condition he builds me a palace on top of his own. When he sits in court, I'd like to watch and listen from my window.' The vizier went back to the king and told him about the condition. The king answered: 'Her wish will be carried out.'

Builders and carpenters and painters worked on the palace day and night. Within a month it was ready. *The order was given to celebrate the wedding, seven days and seven nights, where no fire was lit and no food was cooked except in the king's house.* The wedding was planned for the following Thursday. On that day a carriage was sent to the village to bring the bride, and the marriage took place. The festivities lasted for seven days and seven nights, and the king and his peasant bride were blissfully happy. On the seventh day, the king put on his ceremonial costume and went down to sit in court. His wife drew up a chair to her window and settled down to watch and listen. All sorts of cases passed before him, and she sat through them all. One day, two farmers brought a dispute before the king. The first farmer said: 'Your majesty, I have a she-camel and he has a mare. Both were pregnant. One day, they gave birth in the middle of the night. When we got up, we found the she-camel suckling a foal and the mare suckling a baby camel. Have you ever heard of a camel bearing a foal?' The king said: 'It could be the result of a craving.' The farmer protested: 'That's impossible!' The king insisted: 'Quite possible!' The farmer exclaimed: 'That's crazy!' The king said: 'There is nothing crazy in God's Creation. Whatever each of you found, take it and that's an end to it. Case dismissed!'

As the two men were leaving, she called the plaintiff whom she felt had been wronged. 'You there! Listen. Go back to the king and tell him you had a quintal of barley which you had grown on the seashore. The fish came out of the water and ate it. If he says, "Do fish eat barley?" answer, "Do camels bear foals?" ' So the farmer hurried

back to the palace and asked to see the king urgently.
When he came before him the king said: 'Your case was
settled. Are you bringing another action?' The farmer
answered: 'No, your majesty, I've come to ask you something else. I had a quintal of barley which I had grown on
the seashore. The fish came out of the water and ate it.'
The king scoffed: 'That's the last thing I could believe!
Do fish eat barley?' The farmer replied: 'Do camels bear
foals?' The king thought to himself: 'This must be her
idea.' He said to the farmers: 'You take your camel, and
you take your mare.' And he hurried up to his wife, saying:
'By God, you are divorced. Take whatever you want, and
go.' She answered: 'Grant me three days to pack.' He
replied: 'Take a week if you want.' And with that, he left.

The queen immediately summoned a porter and gave
him a purse of gold and told him; 'Go to the carpenter
and ask him to make a case big enough for a man to hide
in. Cover it with velvet of the highest quality, and bring it
to me within three days.' The queen continued to serve
the king's dinner until the three days were up. On the
third night, she served him tea after his dinner, spiked
with a sleeping-potion. As soon as he drank it, the king
keeled over, unconscious. With the help of Dadah, she
picked him up and put him in the case. Then she called
the coachman to load it into the carriage.

The queen arrived at her father's *saniya*, with the king
hidden in her luggage. As she entered the tent, she
unlocked the case and laid the king on a divan, stretching
out next to him until the morning. The cool morning

breeze revived the king, who woke to the lowing of the cows and the chirping of the birds. 'Am I dreaming?' he thought. He turned and found his wife beside him. He enquired: 'Where am I?' She replied: 'You're with me, safe and sound.' He asked: 'What brought me here?' She replied: 'You told me to leave and take with me whatever I valued most. I thought, gold and silk are earthly possessions. What else do I have dearer than you? So I brought you with me.' He replied delightedly, 'Come back with me.' The carriage brought them back to the palace and from that day on, the queen sat in court with him.

V

Fate

Declare that there is no God but Allah, and He who has sinned should implore his pardon.

Once upon a time there was a chief of a tribe who was married to a barren woman. He had always yearned for a child to fill the house with joy; at last God willed that she should bear him a child. She went into labour and gave birth to a baby girl as beautiful as the moon. The chief of the tribe had a brother who had a son, who was then twenty. Tradition had it that he would marry his cousin, but the young man wasn't prepared to take a wife so much younger. He was a thief and decided to bide his time until he could sneak into his uncle's house to steal something. As he was doing so, he saw two men come in and make their way to the baby's cot. He followed them and hid to watch. They took the baby between them and sat on the

361

floor to write her destiny. One asked: 'What name shall
we give her?' The other answered: 'Beauty,' so he wrote it
on her forehead. Then he asked: 'What shall her lifespan
be?' The other answered: 'Such and such.' Then: 'Who is
to be her destined husband?' The other answered: 'That
thief hiding in the corner is to be her legitimate husband,
and she will take a lover besides.' They wrote it all on her
forehead and put her back in her cot and left the room.

The young man was taken aback by what he heard and
saw and decided to cut her in two rather than disgrace
himself by taking an adulterous wife. *A new day is born and
he who praises the Prophet will blessed.* To his surprise, there
was no news of her death; on the contrary, she was found
safe and sound and more beautiful than ever.

The girl was brought up spoilt, being an only child, and
her cousin couldn't get his predicted fate out of his mind.
So he hastened to take a wife and have children to escape
his fate. After some years he decided to go to the city to
look for work. The girl came of age to marry and many
suitors presented themselves to ask for her hand. But her
father refused to give her to an outsider. The cousin was
summoned by his father and ordered to marry the girl.
In those days, a father's word was law. At first he refused, but
finally gave in and came back to marry her; but he decided
to watch her carefully. He never trusted her but watched
her every move.

She was young and beautiful. *Praise to God the creator,*
wherever she went she attracted attention and many young
men courted her although everyone knew she was mar-

ried. In order to rid herself of their attentions, she told them she had a lover who was the King of Egypt who came once a month to visit her. Her admirers didn't believe her, and one of them decided to go and find out for himself if it was true.

So he travelled on horseback, filling one land and emptying the other and no land can be filled except by Almighty God, until he came to Egypt. He happened to arrive on the Eid, when the fast of Ramadan is broken. Everyone was going to present their respects to the king on this occasion, so he decided to join them. After he had done so, he asked to see the king privately. His request was granted, so when he came before him he asked: 'I hope your honour doesn't mind my asking you this question. In our village there is a girl of exceptional beauty who is married to someone twenty years older. Each and every young man of the village tries to win her love but she says your honour is her lover.' The king smiled to himself and warned him angrily: 'Don't any of you dare to trouble her any more.' With these words the man was dismissed.

The king turned the idea over in his mind again and again, and said to himself: 'Why should a bedouin girl choose me, of all people?' He had a brother who lived in that village, so he decided to pay him a visit and find out whether the girl really loved him. When he came to the village, he found a shepherd and asked him if he knew where Mr So-and-So lived. The shepherd answered: 'I happen to work for them.' The king gave him a purse of gold and asked him to take him to the house in secret. The shepherd suggested he could hide him among the cattle.

That night, the husband's first wife went into labour so the husband went to congratulate her, together with his young bride. While he stayed on, the young bride made her way back to her own house alone. *Being in the country, the hut had no electricity.* On entering, she found a man sleeping in her bed. She enquired: 'Who are you?' He answered: 'Shhhh.' She lit an oil lamp and asked 'What made you come here?' He answered: 'Aren't I your lover, the King of Egypt? You asked for me and here I am.' She was taken aback, but passed the night with him; that was her fate, God willed it. Now, as her husband didn't trust her, he came back in the middle of the night to check on her and discovered them together. He immediately brought a camel-chain and shackled them. In the morning he went to call her folk and make a scene. She woke up in fright to find her feet tied to those of her lover, and decided to act immediately. Rising carefully to their feet together, they managed to hobble to the door of the hut, where she found her stepson. He had always had a soft spot for her, and she had no difficulty in persuading him to release her lover from the chain and take his place, on the grounds that if anything happened to him, the whole country would be thrown into chaos. When her husband returned, accompanied by a throng of people, they seized the sides of the tent and tore it open. She opened her eyes and her stepson exclaimed 'Whatever's wrong, father?' All the elders turned to the husband abusively: 'Have you gone mad? You suspicious bastard! He's like her own son.' The stepson explained: 'The night became chilly so I slipped in beside Dadah for warmth.' At this, the husband became the butt of insults from the crowd and kept silent, but was not convinced.

Time passed. The husband wanted to set his mind at rest and find out the truth. So he chose a beautiful slave girl and bought seven black slaves and travelled with them to Egypt to present them to the king. When the husband saw him, he recognized him immediately. Seven days later, he invited the king to accompany him on a hunting party. Each took his own weapons and they set off. When they arrived at a deserted clearing, the husband pointed his gun at the king and asked: 'Wasn't it you I found with Beauty that night?' The king replied: 'Indeed it was. Had you harmed her in any way I would have killed you and married her.' The husband answered: 'You could neither kill me nor marry her. I have not yet reached the end of my misfortunes. I just wanted to find out the truth.' And he related the whole story to the king. The king in turn explained that he too was destined to seduce her. The husband continued: 'It was ordained that she should remain with me and bear me two children.' The king reproached him: 'Why then did you investigate, and rebel against what God has willed?'

So he travelled back to his village and took back his wife. A few years later she bore him two children *and they lived safely and procreated until death did them part.* (And thus the eyes saw what God had written on the forehead.)

VI

The Prophet Suleyman and the Griffin

Declare that there is no God but Allah, and He who has sinned should implore his pardon.

Once upon a time, when birds could talk, the prophet Suleyman was discussing fate with a griffin. She said: 'Al-hadhar yighlib al-qadar' ['Caution can thwart fate']. The prophet Suleyman insisted that God's will must always triumph. She strongly denied it. The prophet Suleyman told her: 'So-and-so's wife is going to give birth to a daughter who, when grown-up, will marry the prince, bear a child by him and nobody will know. Can you prevent that?' The bird answered: 'I will look after her and prevent it from happening.' He told her: 'The baby is due today.' She answered: 'I will kidnap her today.' When the baby girl was born, the bird came unseen and stole her away. She travelled with her for miles under the sea until they reached a faraway island and settled there. *It was the girl's fate to live on that island.* There was no one else there. She fed her from her beak year after year until the girl turned fifteen.

In a faraway land the king's son fell ill and all the physicians in the land were summoned, but none could find a cure for his condition. A sage advised the king to send his son away on a voyage for a change of scene. A ship was laid on for him, with everything he could possibly need: provisions, entertainment and companions. They set sail and everyone tried to entertain the prince, but to no avail. A storm arose in which the ship was tossed on the waves and driven on to the shore of a faraway land. The prince suggested he would explore the island, unaccompanied. Nobody dared object. As he was exploring, he heard a girl's voice coming from underground. He asked: 'Who are you?' She answered: 'I am the bird's daughter, and I have never seen anyone on this island before.' He asked: 'How can you be the daughter of a bird and be able to talk?' She answered: 'I don't know. I only realized when I grew up that my mother was a bird. She would fly away during the day and come back to me at night.' He said: 'But you're a human being!' She gave him a copious meal and invited him to stay with her and they lived happily together for weeks. When the bird came back, she would hide him. Oblivious, the bird never noticed. A veil of distraction descended on her. The prince grew fond of the girl and recovered from his melancholy. He didn't want to leave.

Since the prophet Suleyman was omniscient, he knew that the girl was now carrying a child, *such is God's decree,* and would soon give birth. He summoned the bird and asked her: 'Is your daughter grown-up yet or not?' The bird replied: 'Yes, she is. Didn't you predict that by now she would be bearing a child? Well, she isn't. What about God's will then?' He answered: 'I want to see her right now.' She said: 'How can I do that? It's too windy for her.' He said: 'Cover her, then; but bring her.' The bird flew back to the island and told her daughter that the prophet Suleyman wanted to see her. She agreed to go, on condition that she would be carried in a palanquin. She managed to hide her lover in it without the bird noticing. The bird flew away with the palanquin suspended from her strong beak, and came before the prophet Suleyman. He called: 'Daughter of So-and-so, come out. Son of So-and-so, come out too.' The girl waddled out, followed by the prince. The bird gaped. The prophet asked her: 'Now, tell me how all this could happen, in spite of your caution? The truth is Allah willed it in order to fulfil what he had ordained upon his creature.' The bird shrieked and flew off, and never came back to earth again. *What is written shall be!*